How to Draw
AND SKETCH COOL STUFF
For Kids

Author Tony R. Smith

ITEMS NEEDED TO START DRAWING

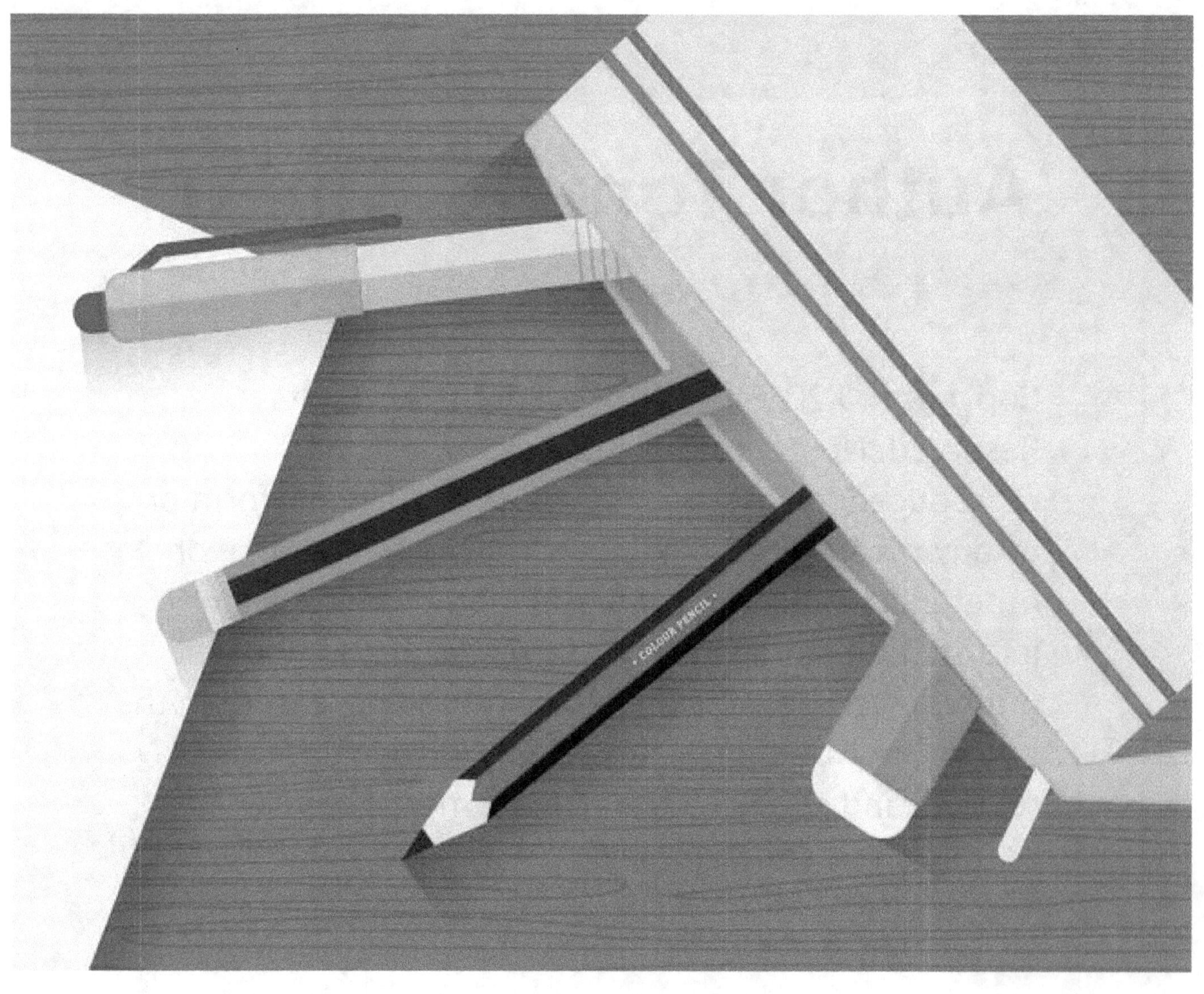

Example #1 Practice

Example of (Smudge Shading). Smudge Shading will give your drawing a complete look.

Example of (Tonal Shading). Tonal Shading will give your drawing a smooth contrast finish.

Example of (Light Smudge Shading). Light Smudge Shading will give your drawing a complete look.

Example of (Hatching Shading). Hatching Shading will help blend your drawing together.

Shading Elements in Steps

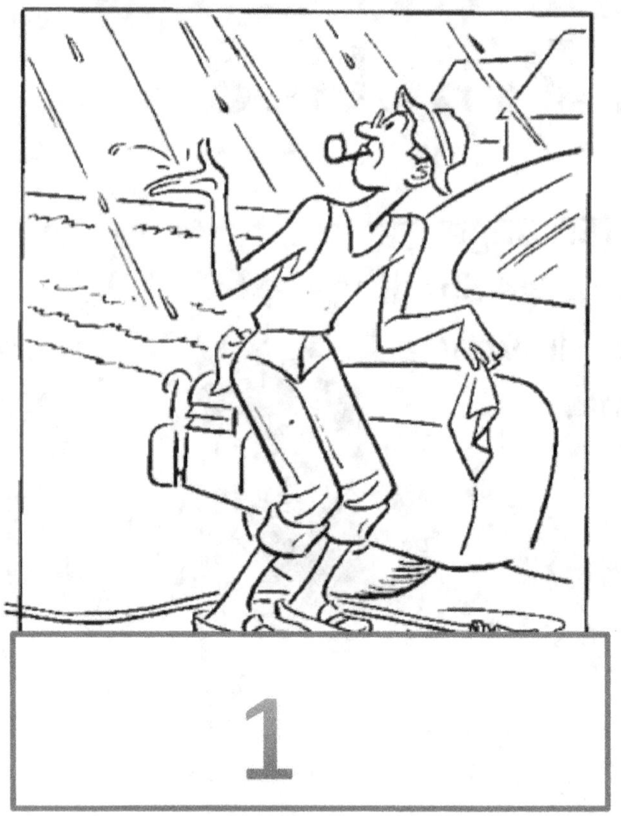

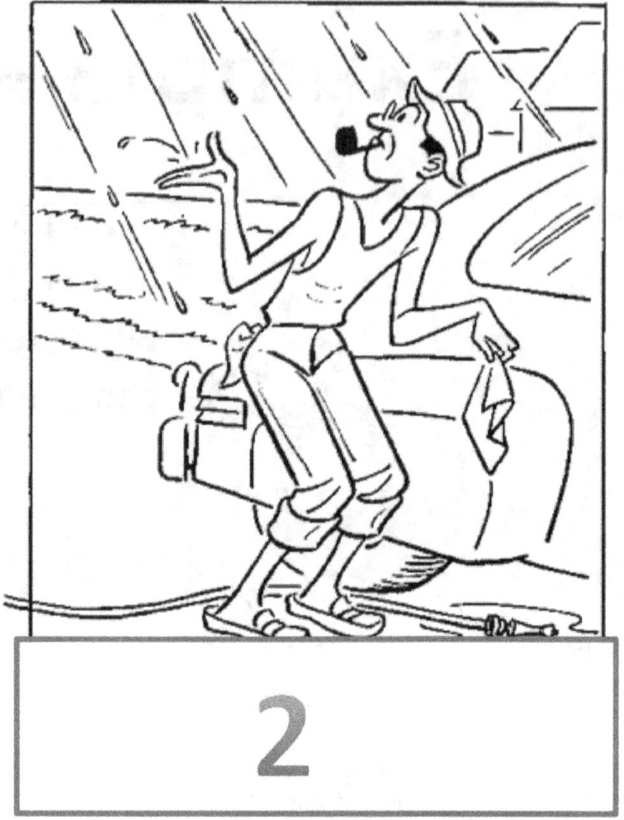

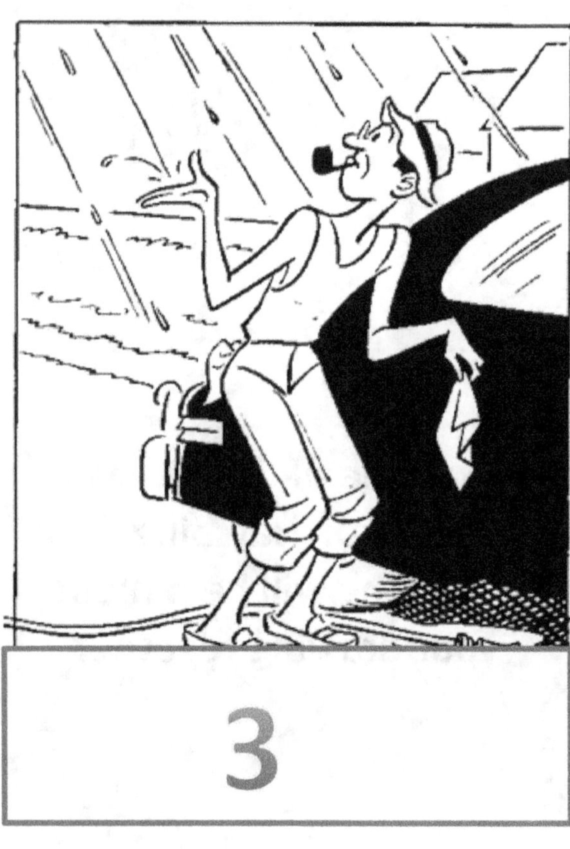

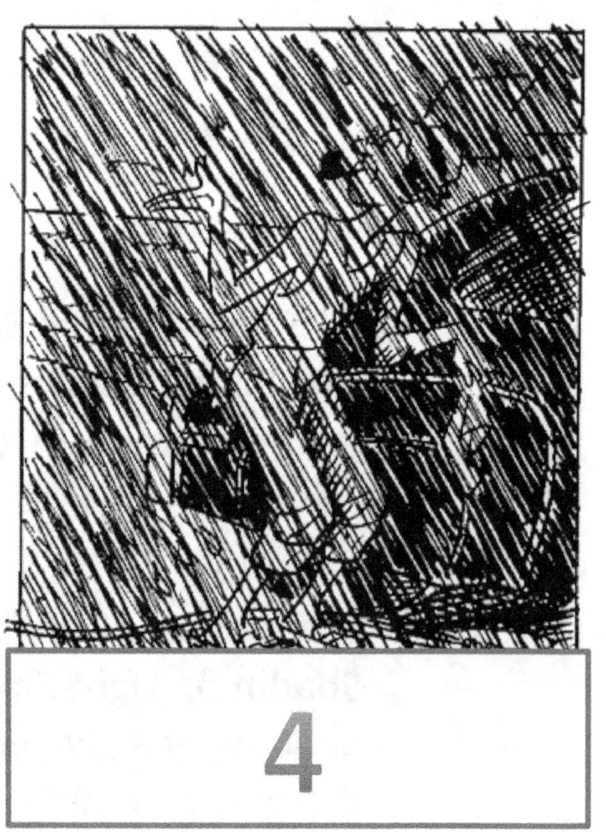

Big Face Circle Method

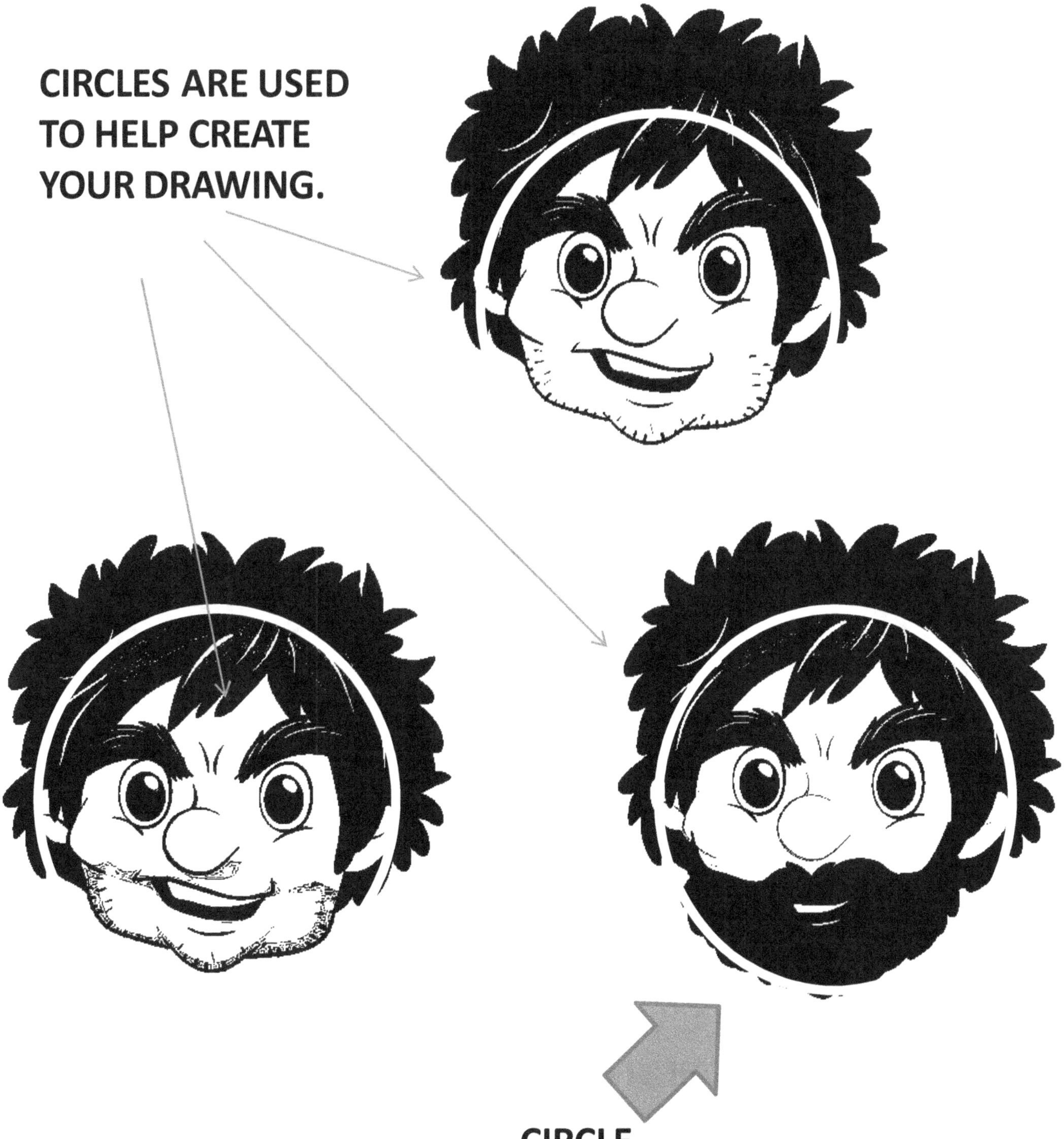

CIRCLES ARE USED
TO HELP CREATE
YOUR DRAWING.

Box Drawing

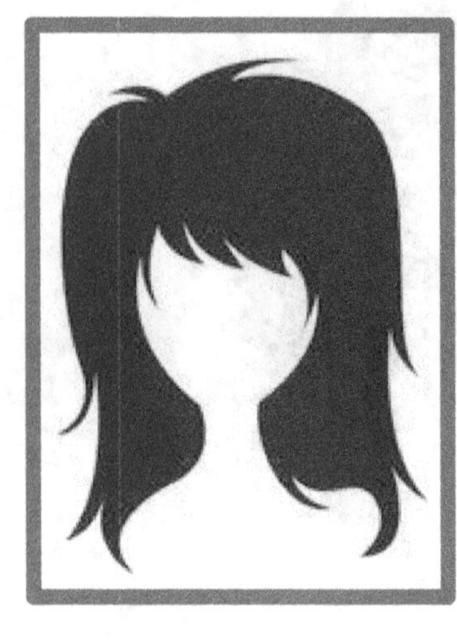 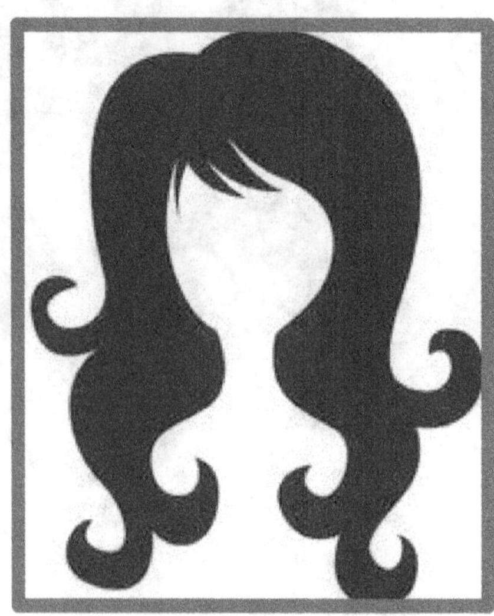 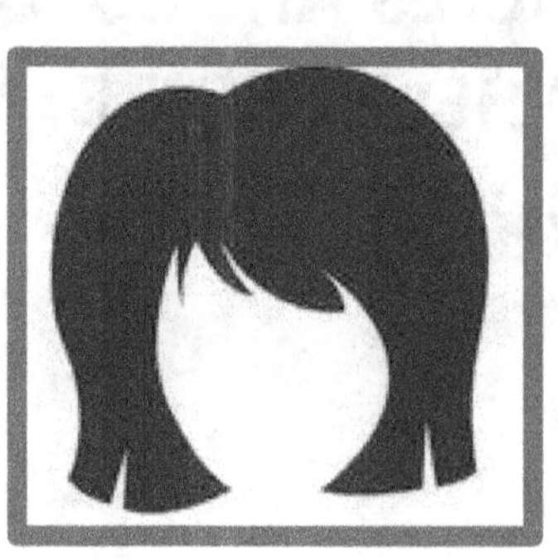

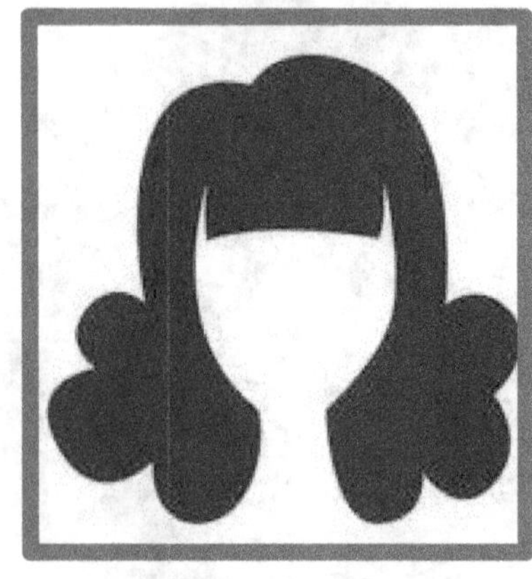 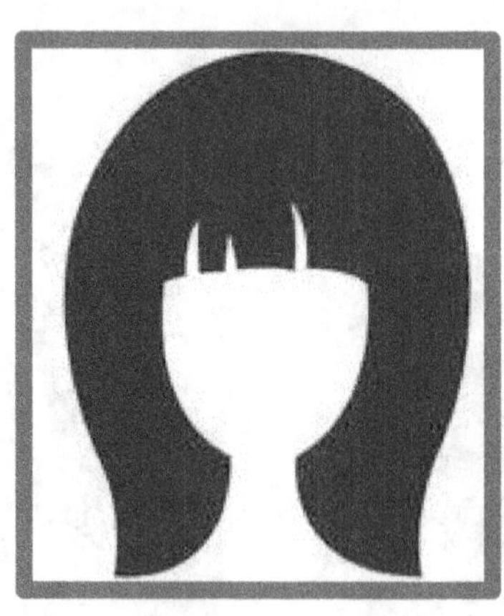 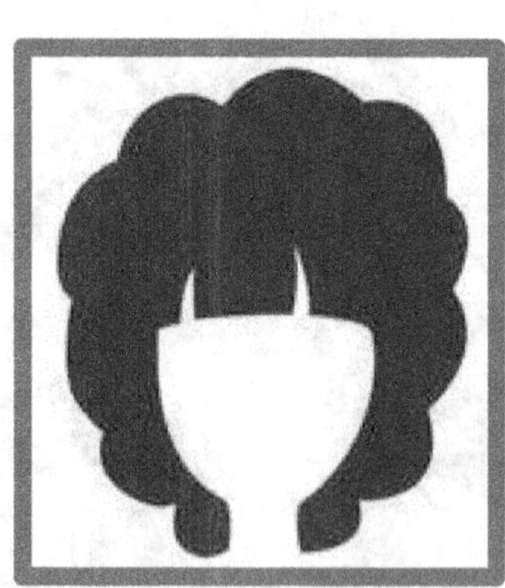

BOX DRAWINGS ARE USED TO CREATE DRAWING WITH SMALL DETAILS FOR A TIGHT FIT.

Cylinders and Circles

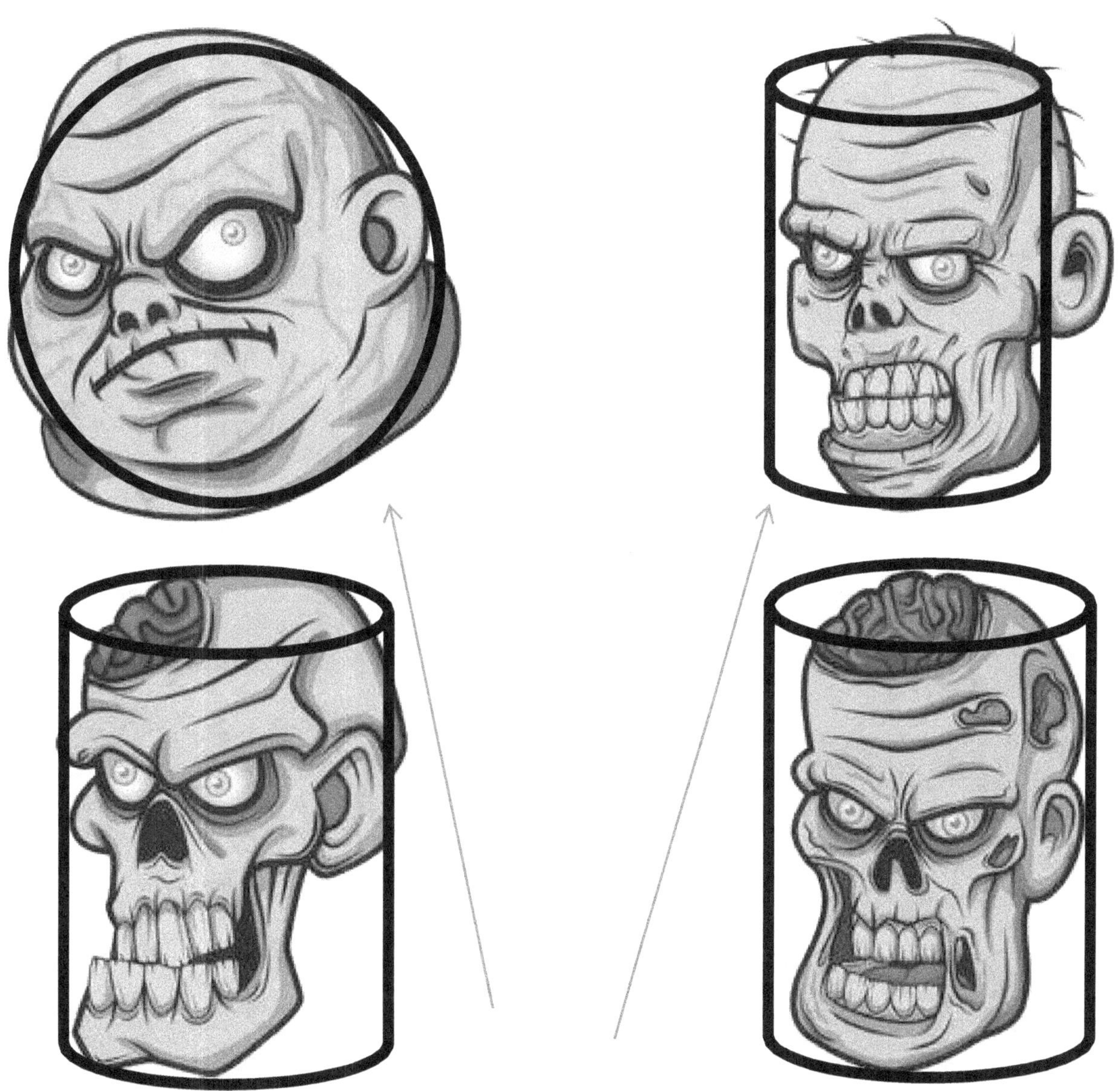

CYLINDERS AND CIRCLE
METHOD CAN BE USED
TO CREATE ODD HEAD SHAPES
LIKE MONSTERS OR ALIENS.

Plain Circle Method

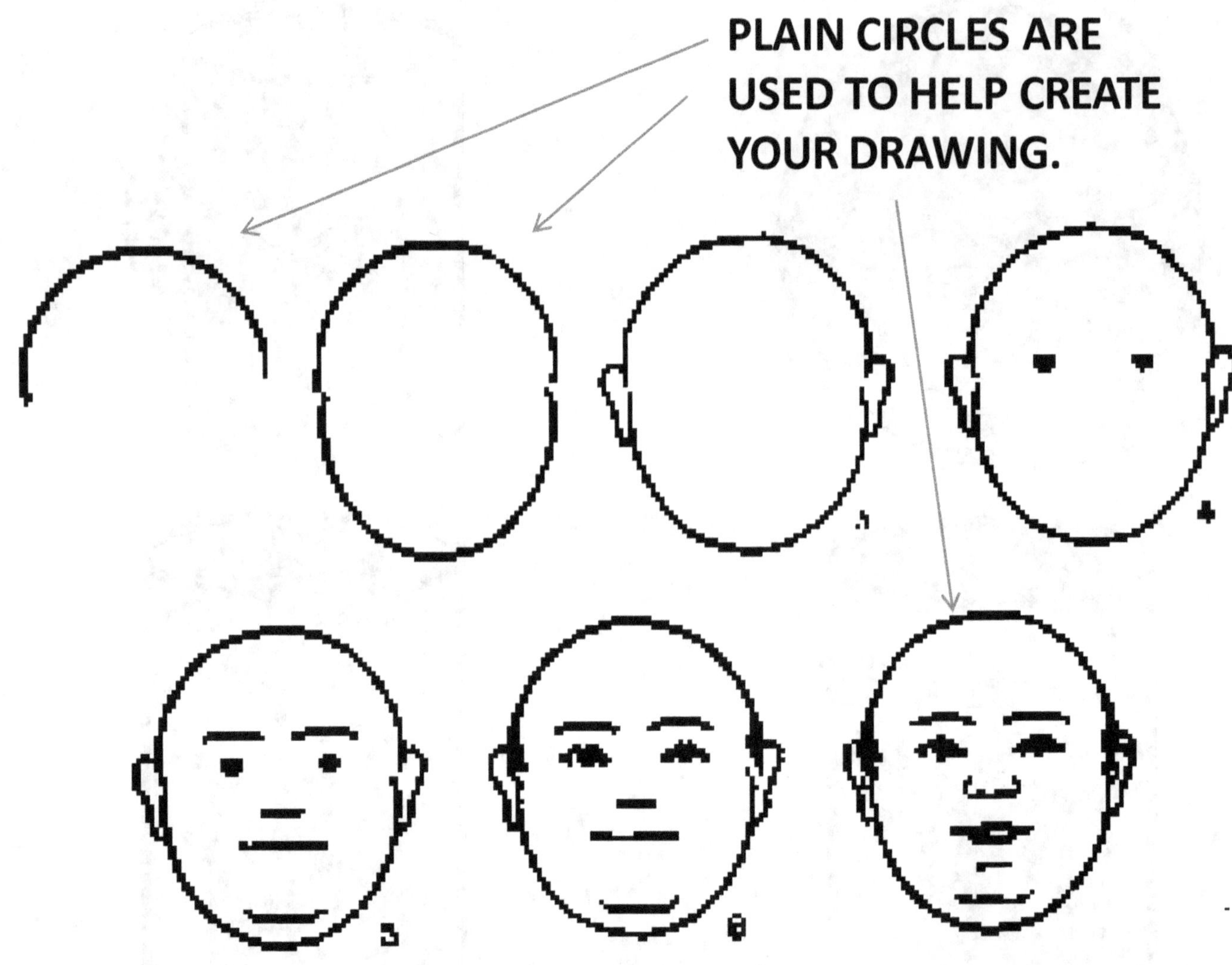

Oval Circle Method

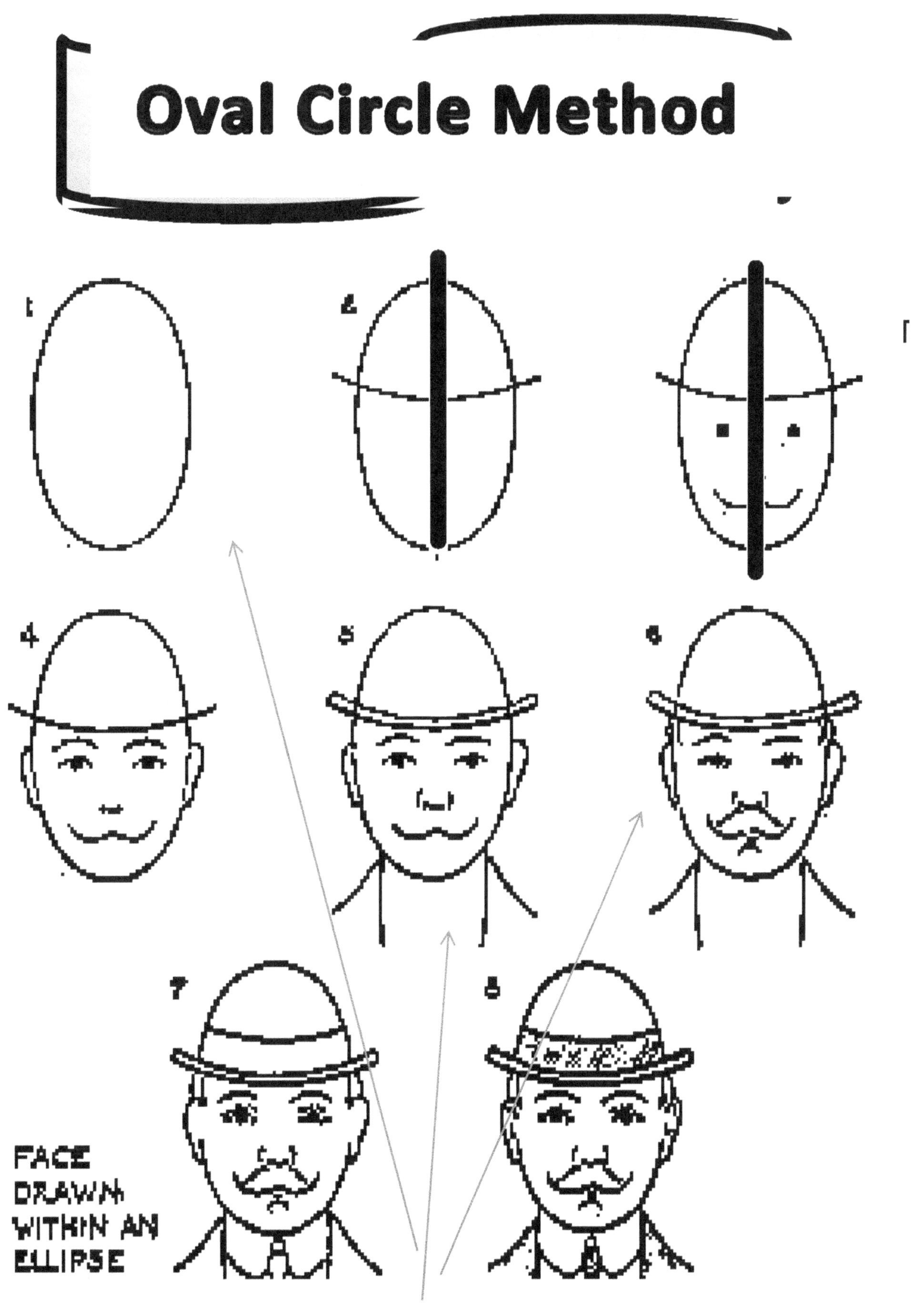

OVAL CIRCLES ARE USED TO HELP
CREATE YOUR DRAWING IN 8 STEPS.

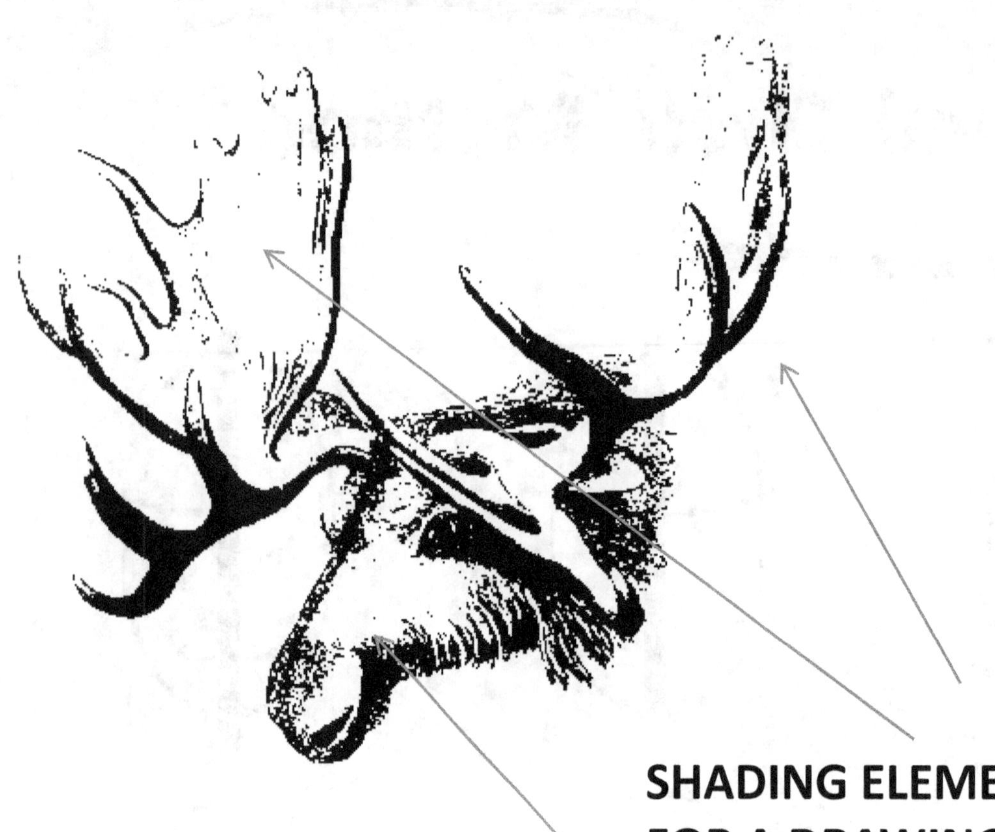

SHADING ELEMENTS: FOR A DRAWING TO BE COMPLETE YOU MUST FILL IN ALL HOLES IN YOUR DRAWING,

SHADING ELEMENTS: ONCE YOUR HOLES IN YOUR DRAWING ARE FILLED YOU WILL HAVE A COMPLETE DRAWING,

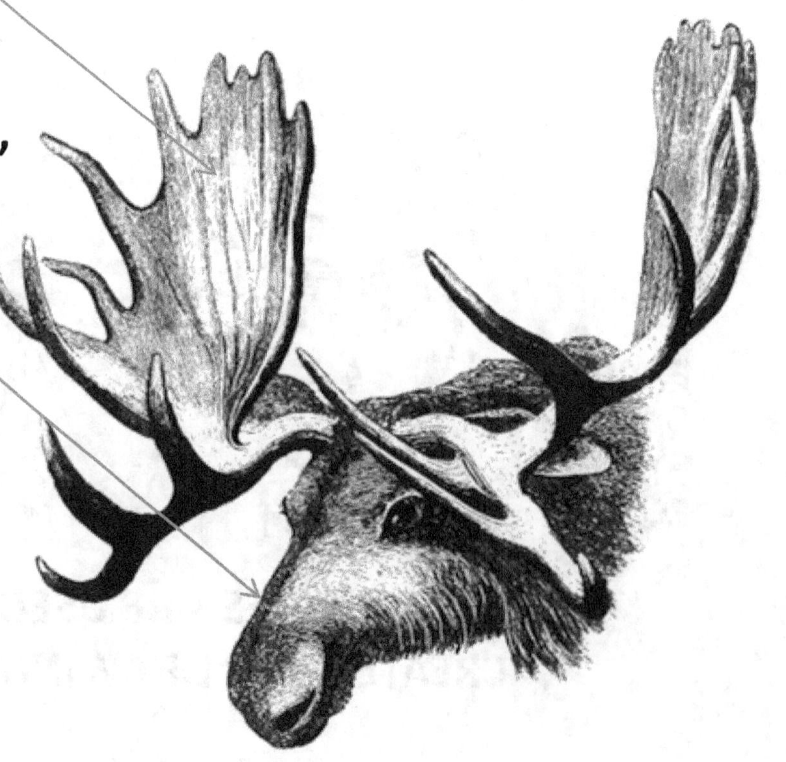

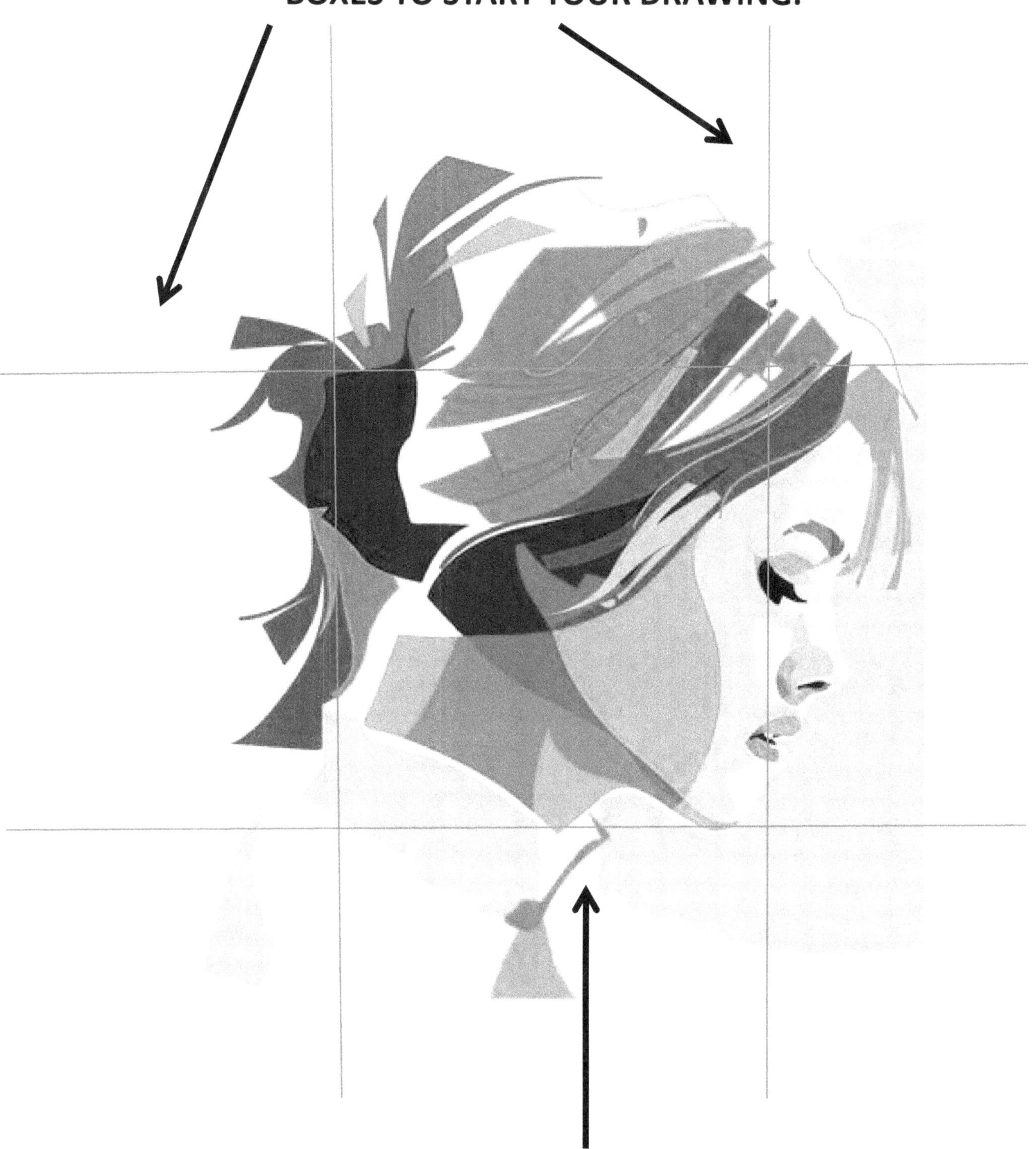

YOUR MIDDLE BOX SHOULD
COVER THE MIDDLE OF YOUR
IMAGE.

USE YOUR FIRST THREE BOXES
FOR YOUR DRAWING.

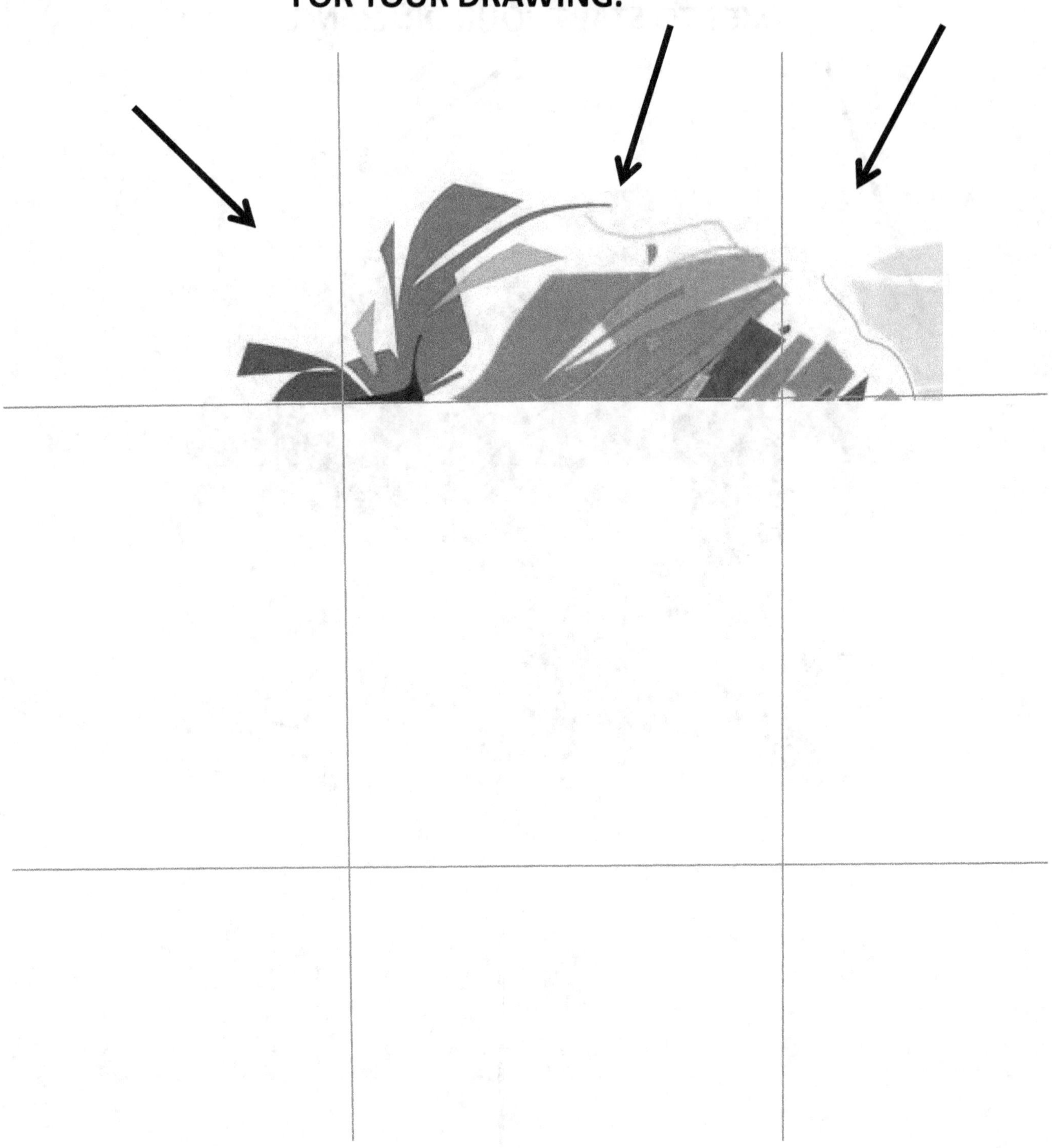

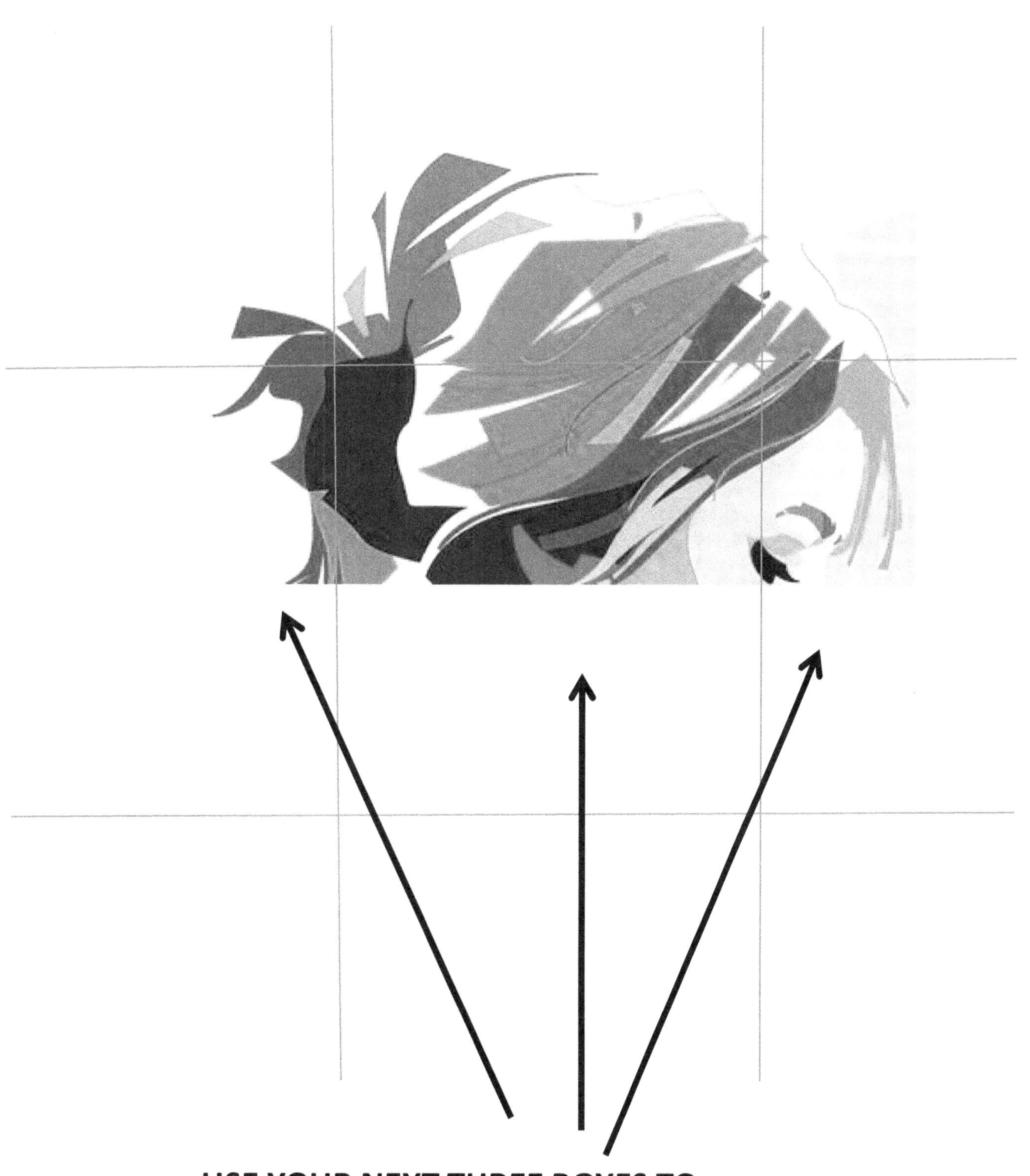

USE YOUR NEXT THREE BOXES TO
CONTINE YOUR DRAWING.

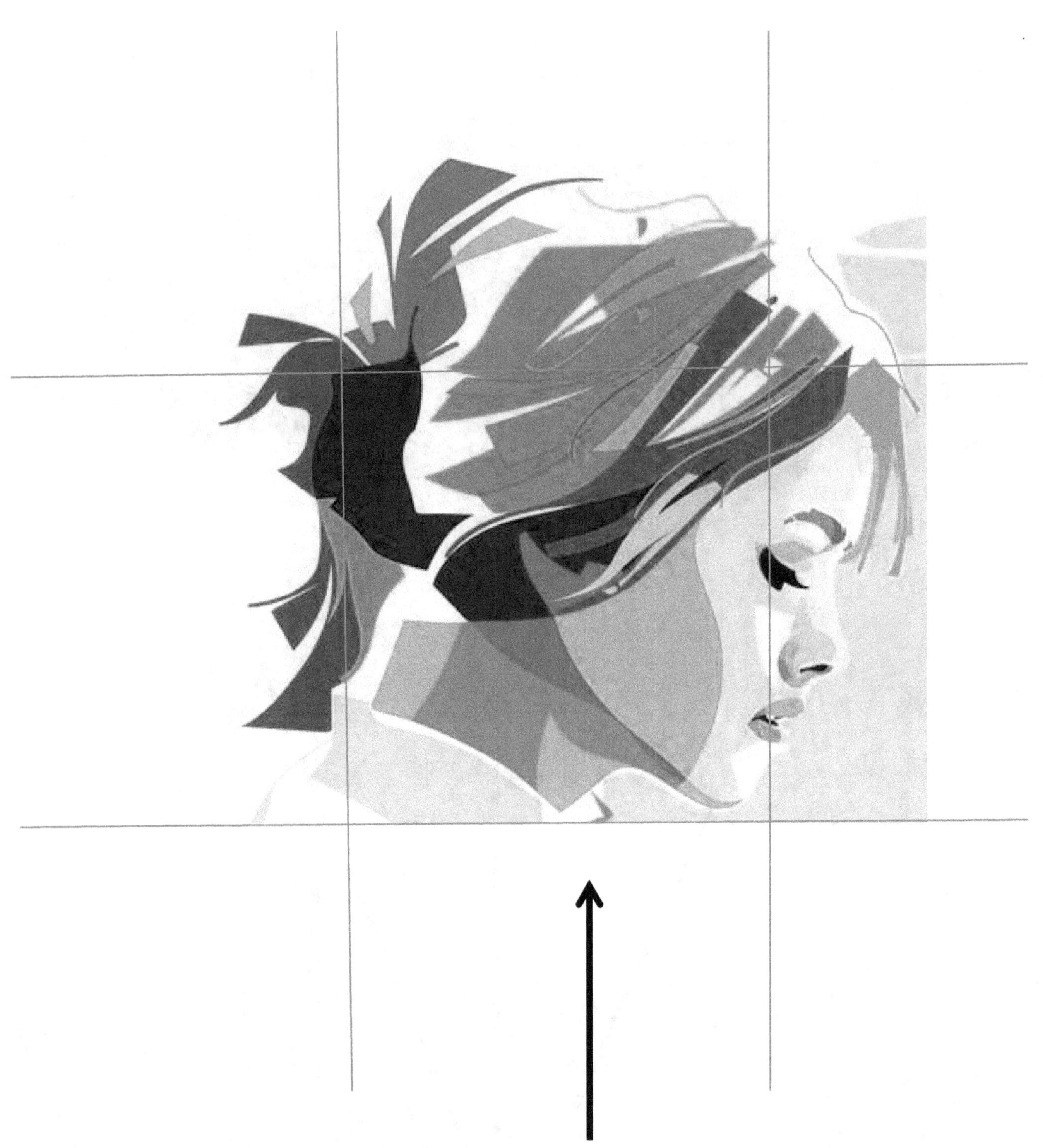

**COMPLETE THE DRAWING INSIDE
ALL SIX BOXES.**

ITEMS

DRAW/SKETCH

CITY

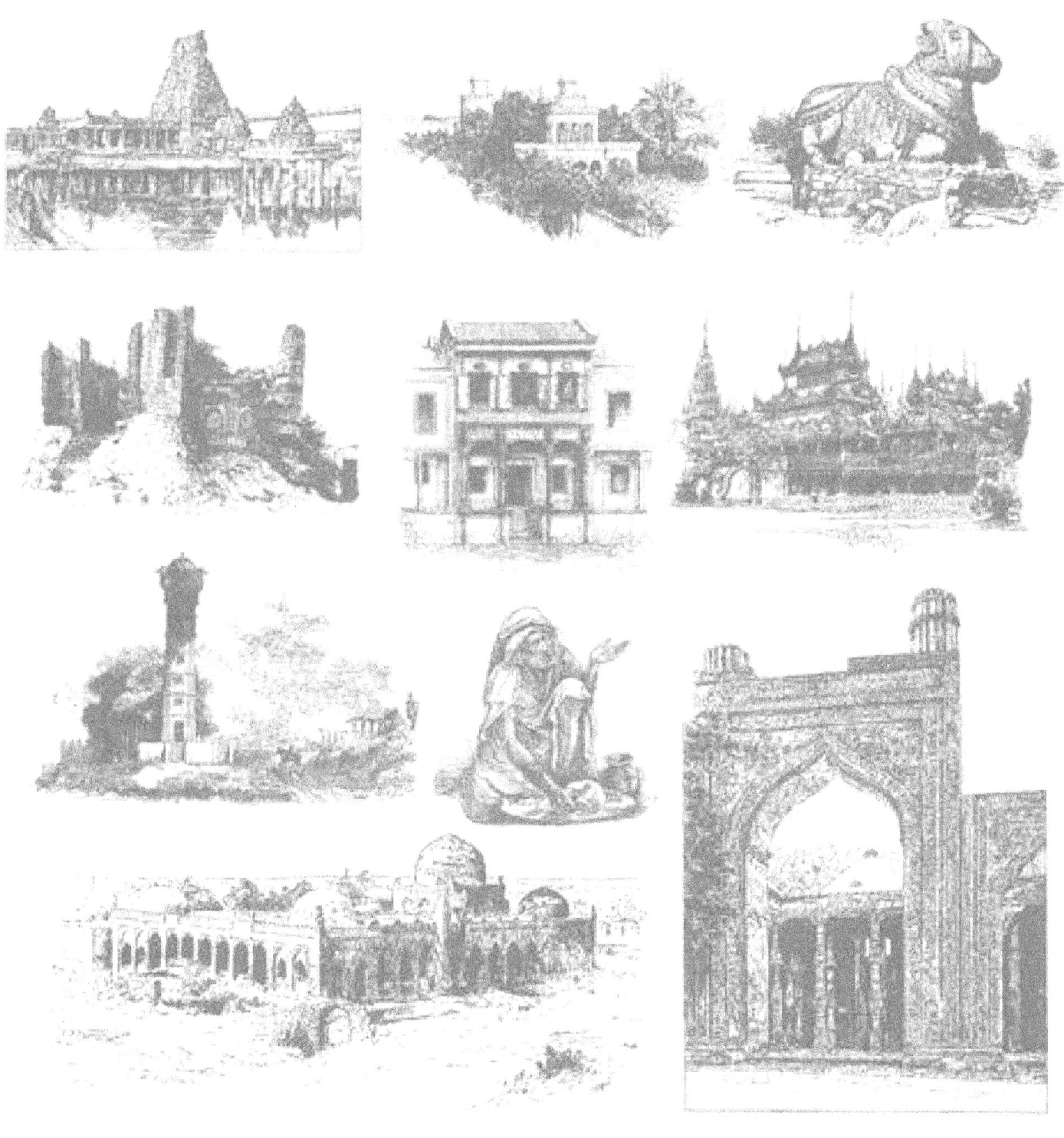

DRAW/SKETCH

ANIMALS

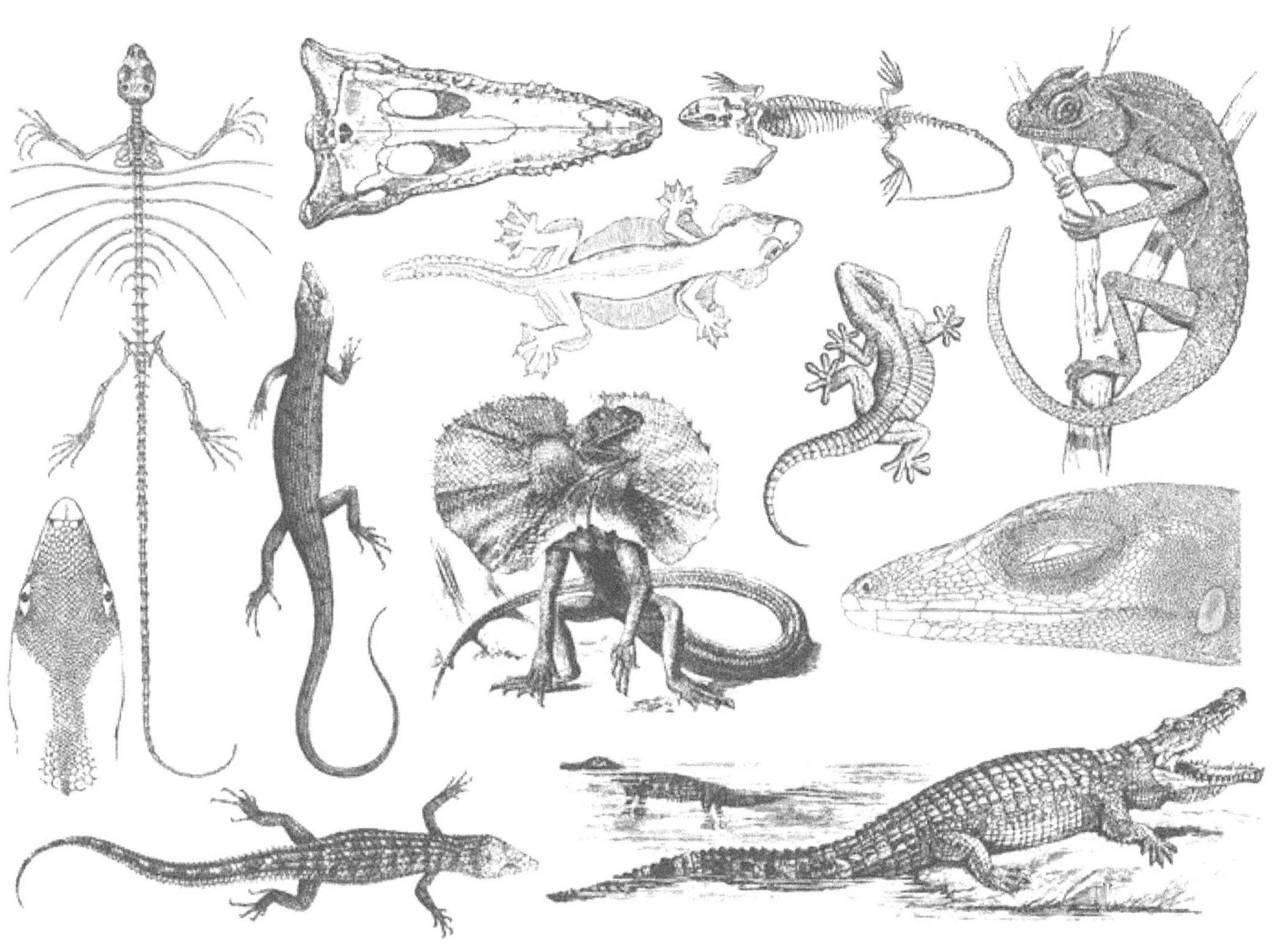

DRAW/SKETCH

PEOPLE

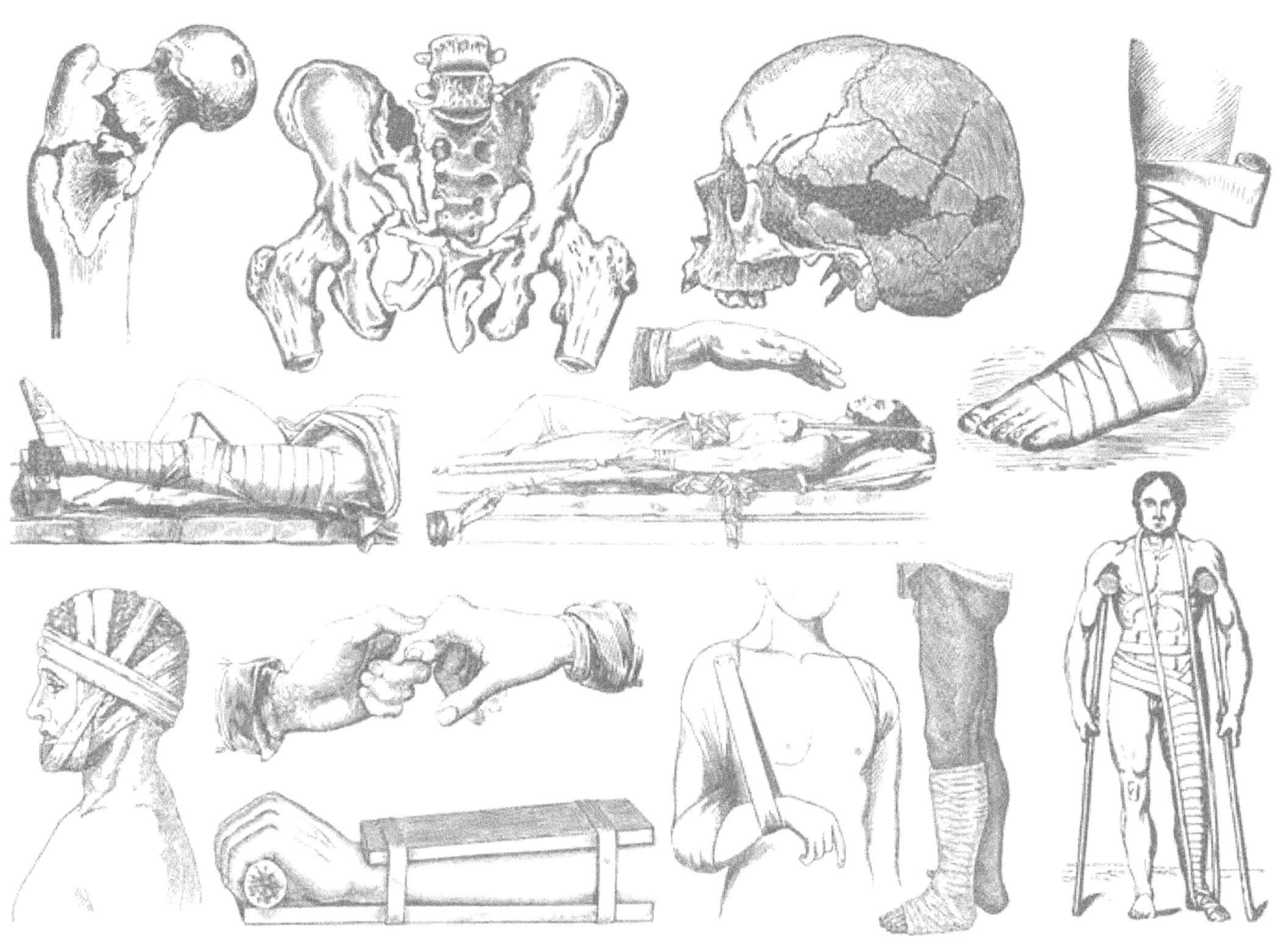

DRAW/SKETCH

TRANSPORTATION

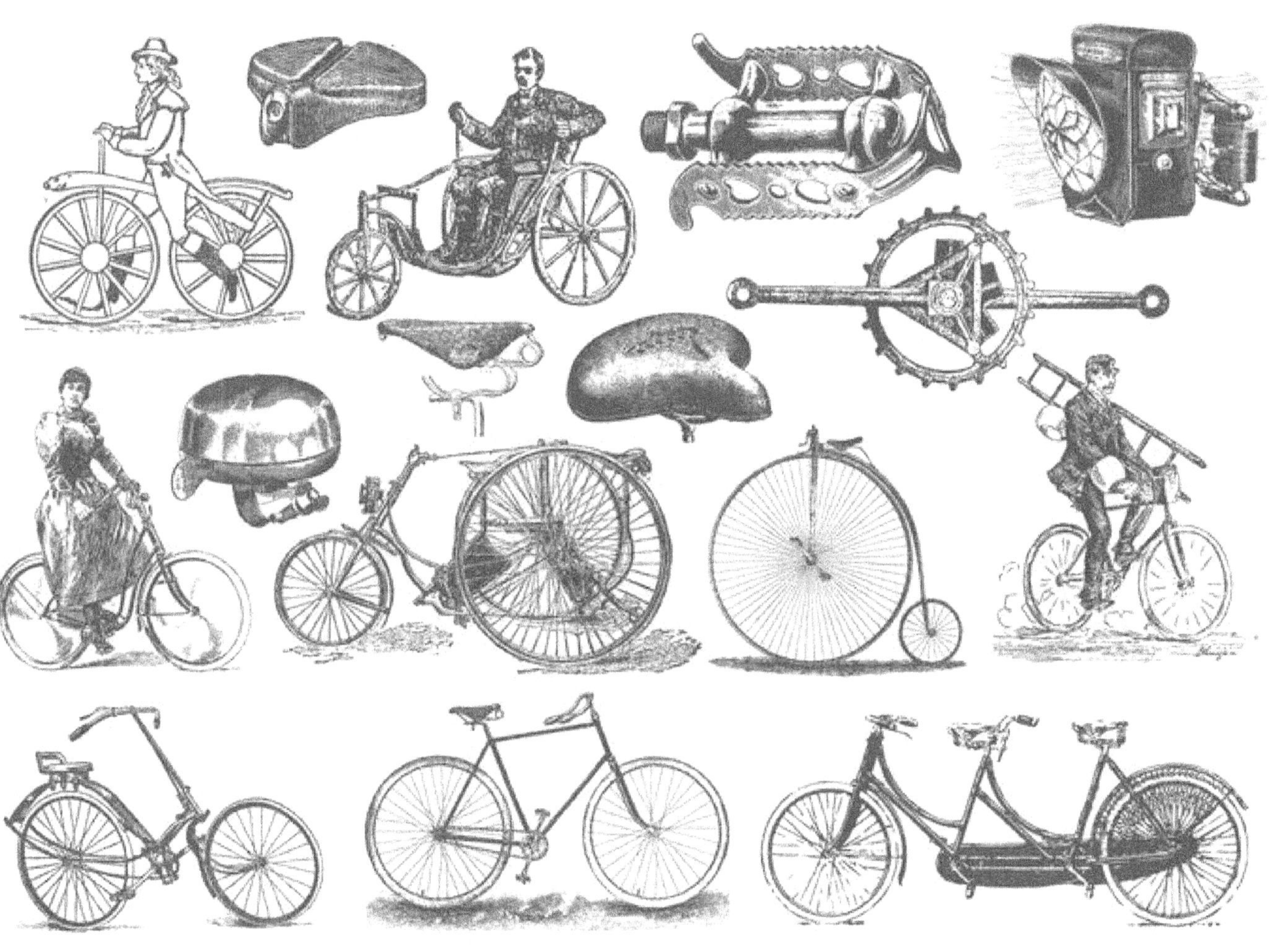

DRAW/SKETCH

ANIMALS

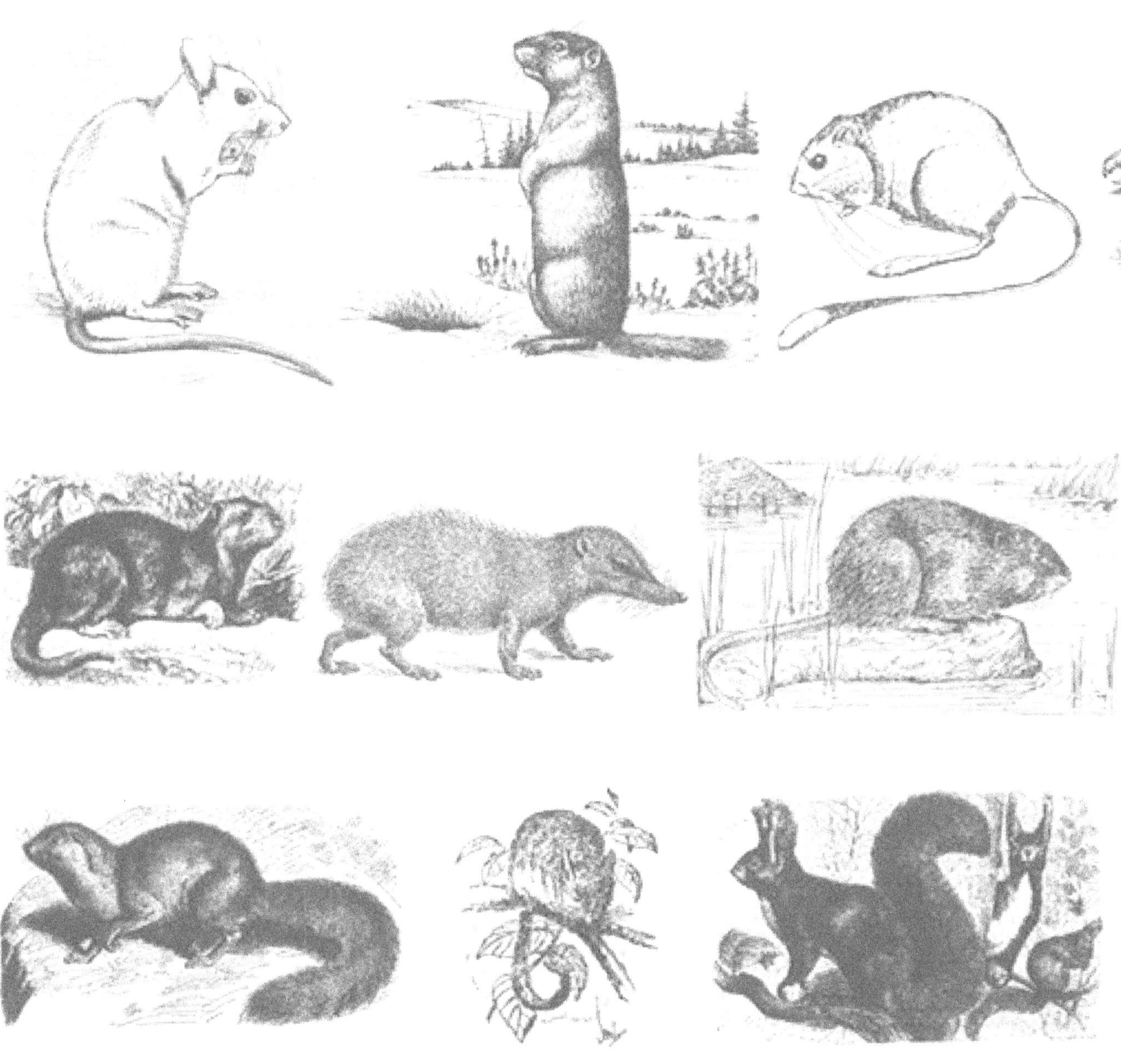

DRAW/SKETCH

PEOPLE

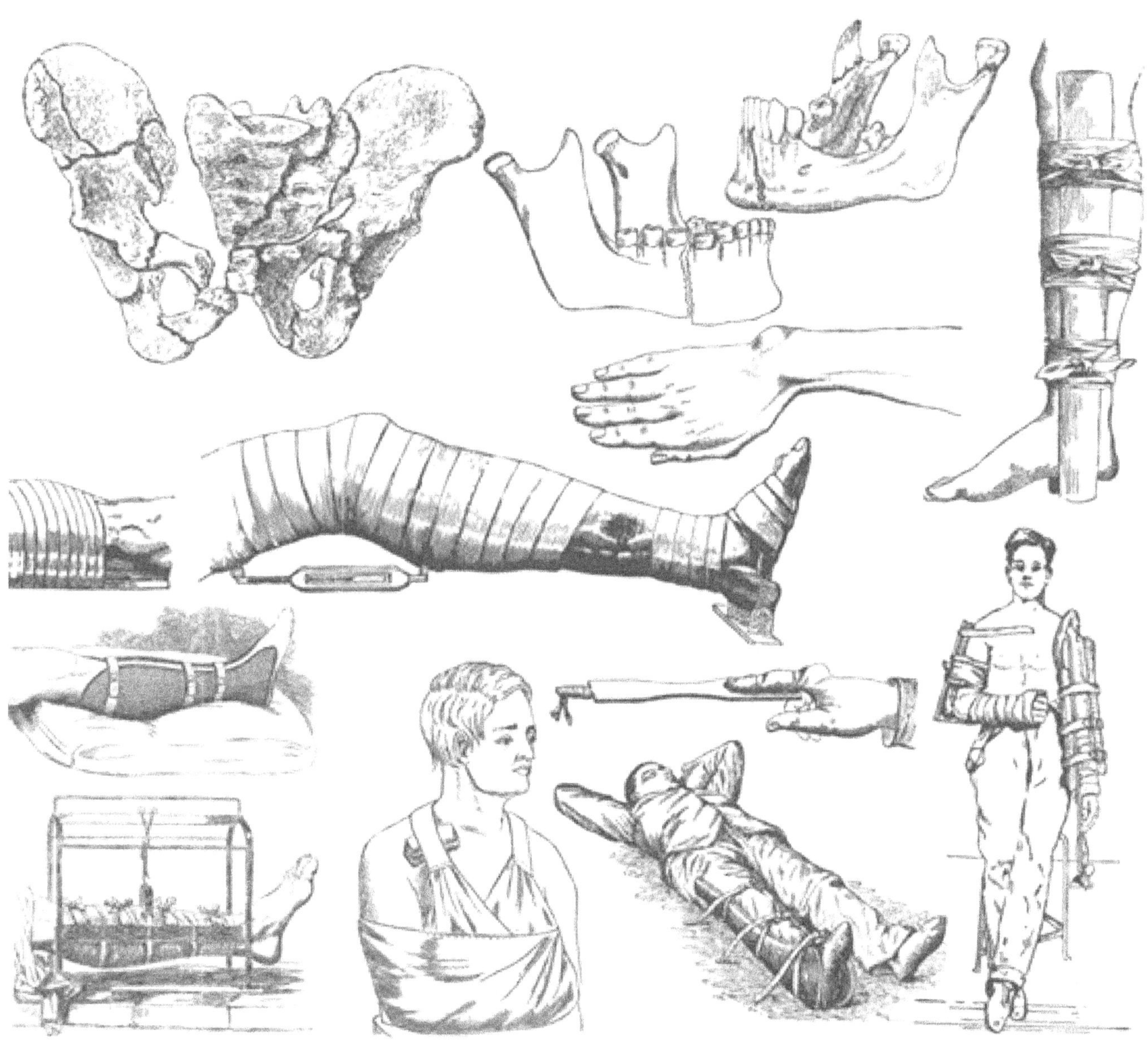

DRAW/SKETCH

ANIMALS

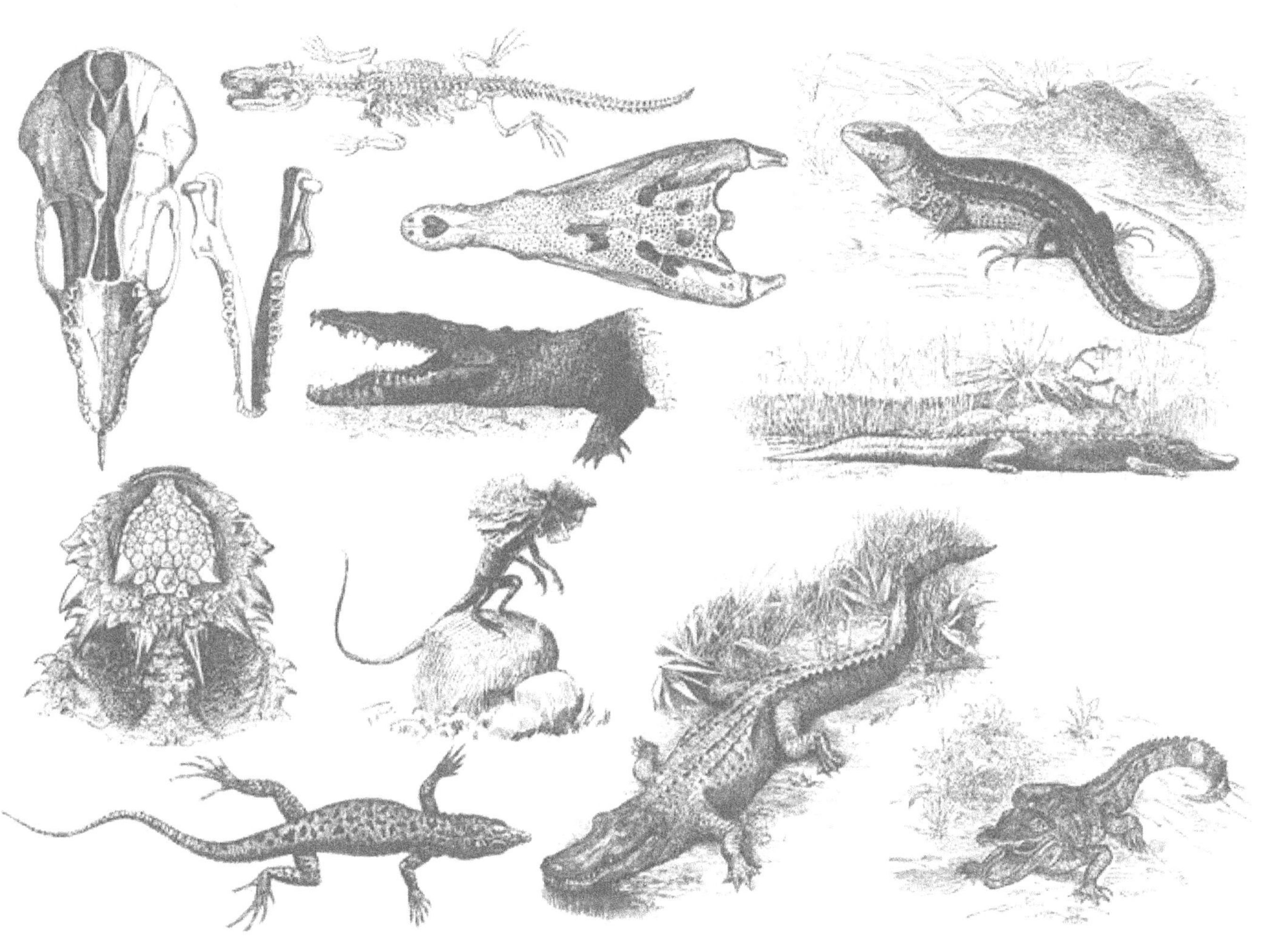

DRAW/SKETCH

ANIMALS

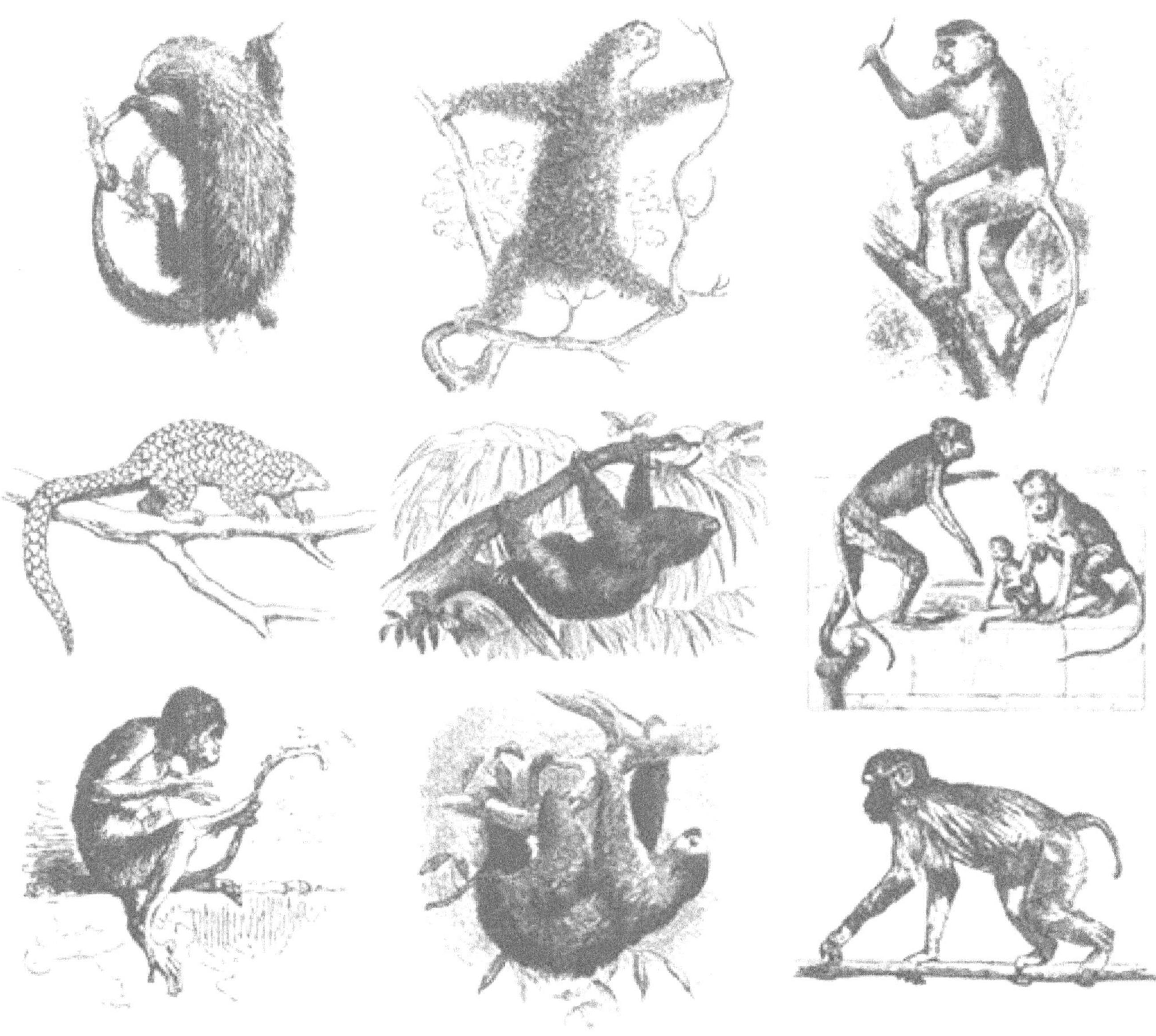

DRAW/SKETCH

ANIMALS

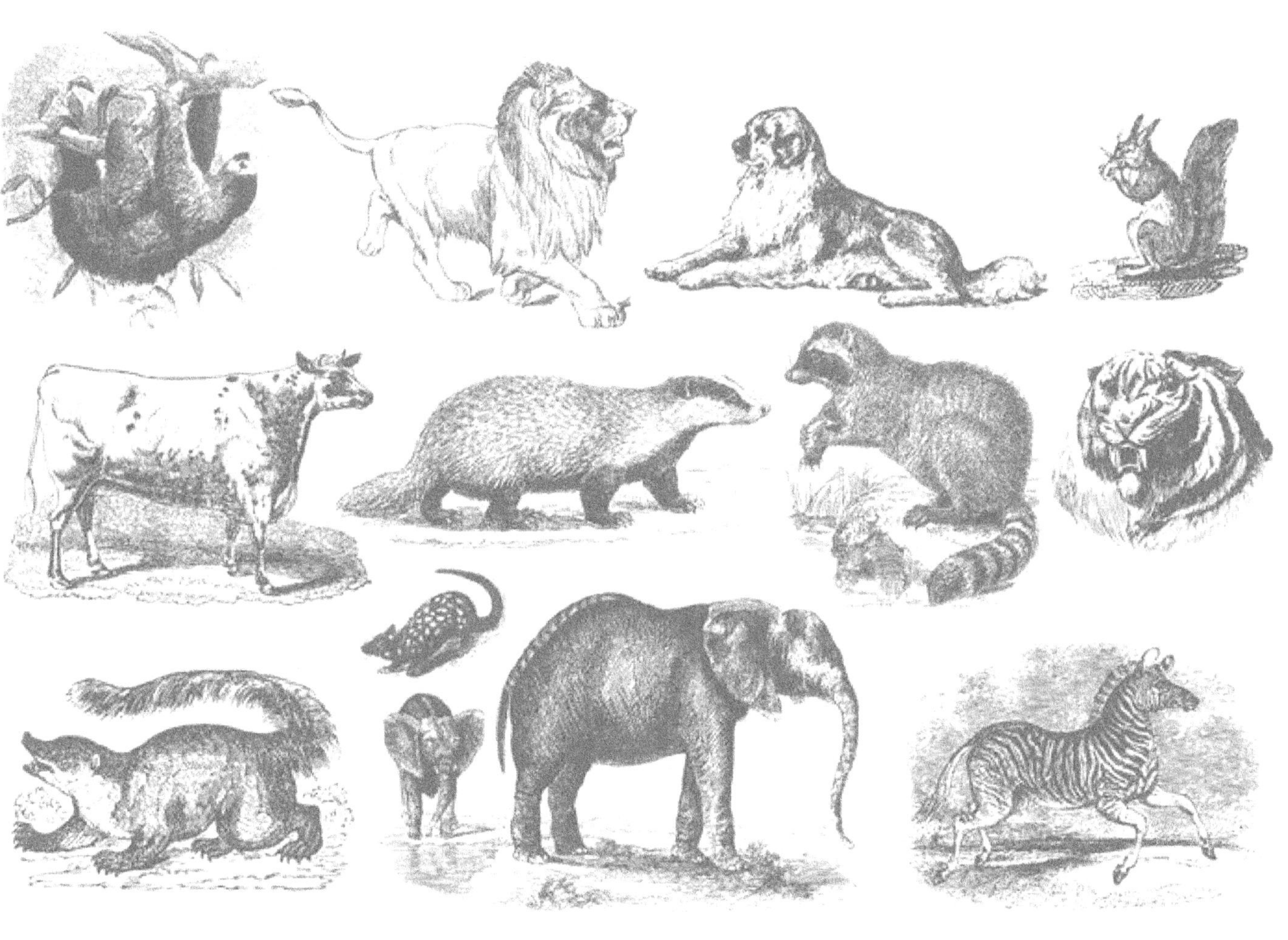

DRAW/SKETCH

PEOPLE

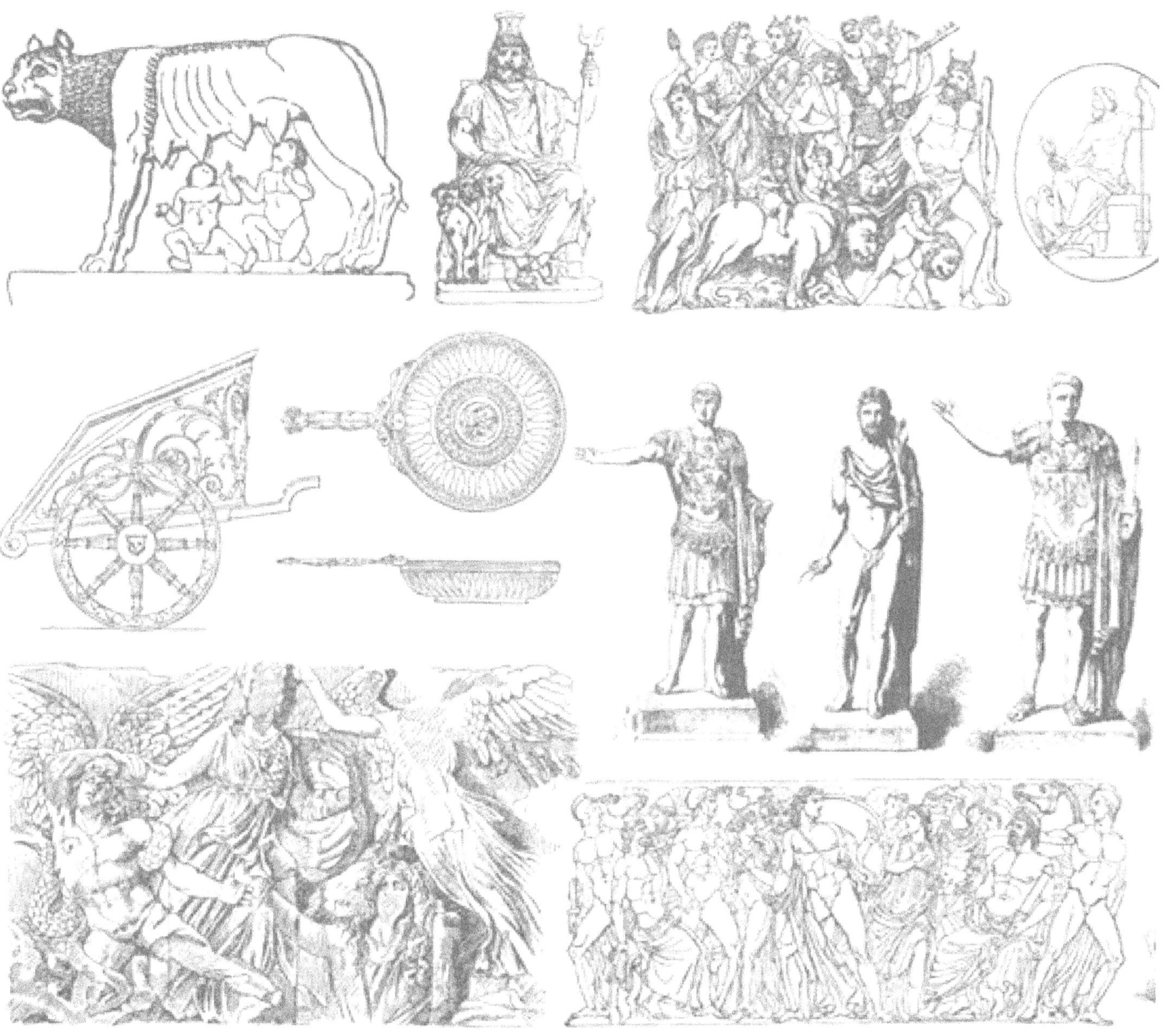

DRAW/SKETCH

PEOPLE

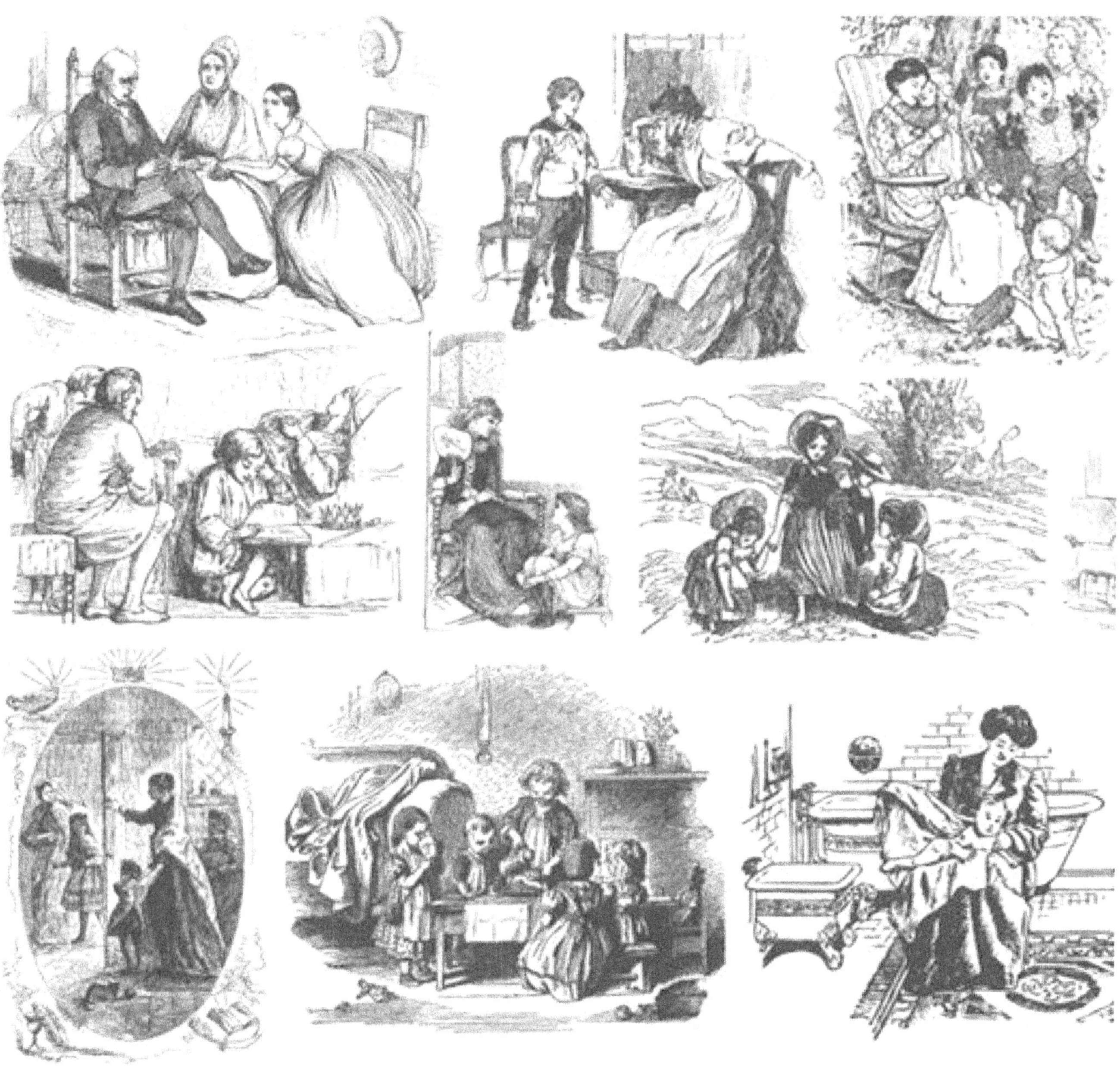

DRAW/SKETCH

ITEMS

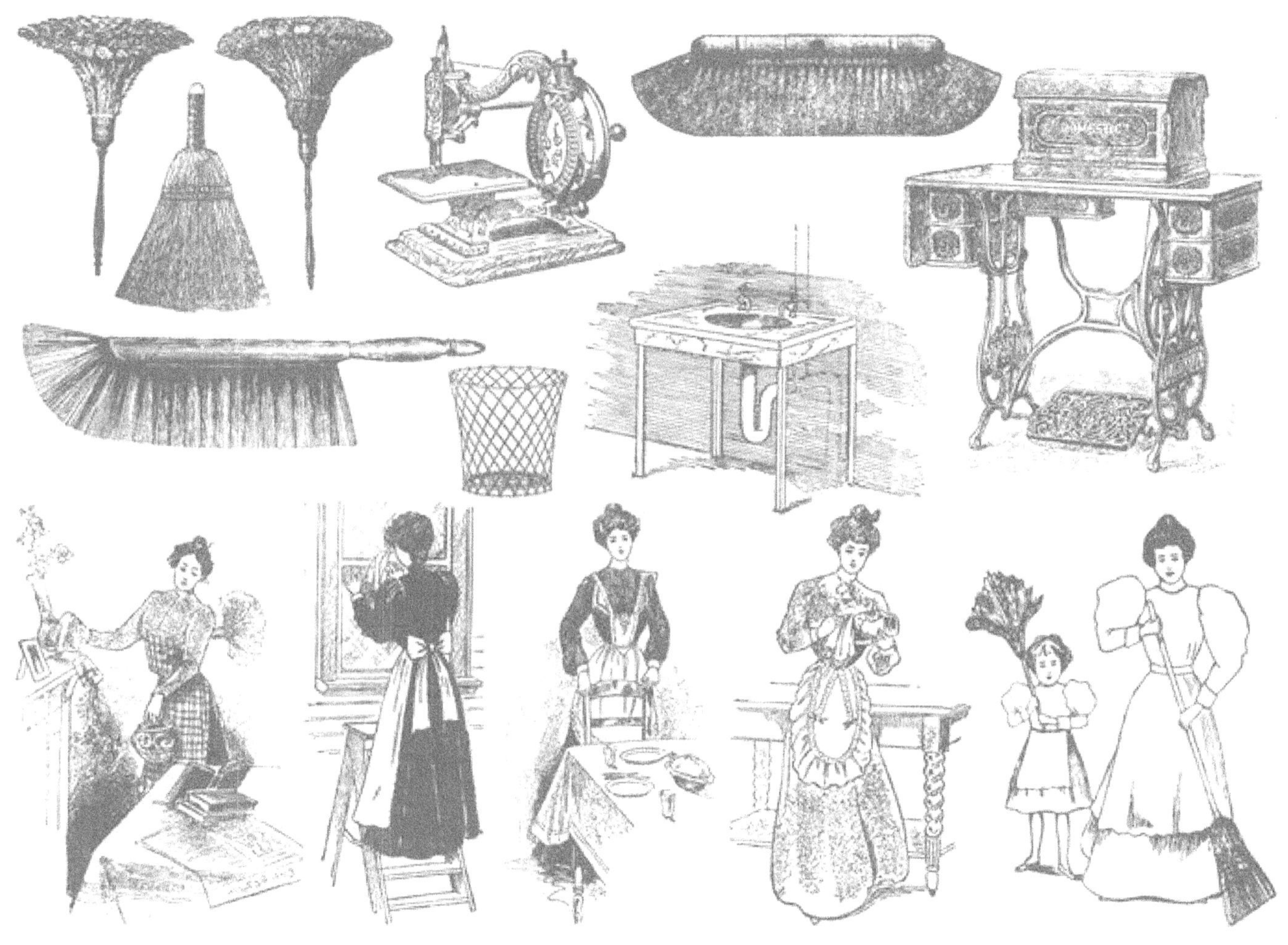

DRAW/SKETCH

PEOPLE

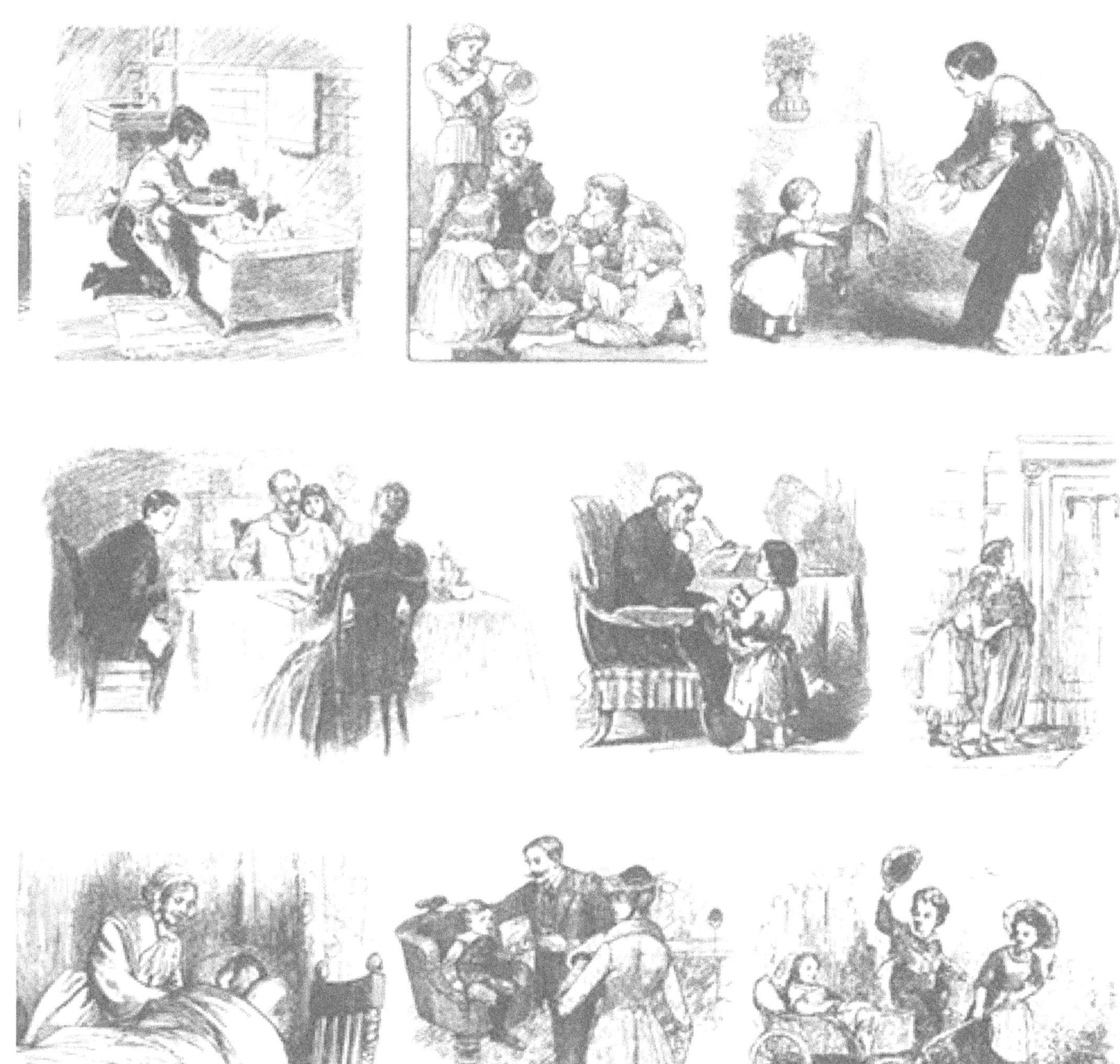

DRAW/SKETCH

ANIMALS

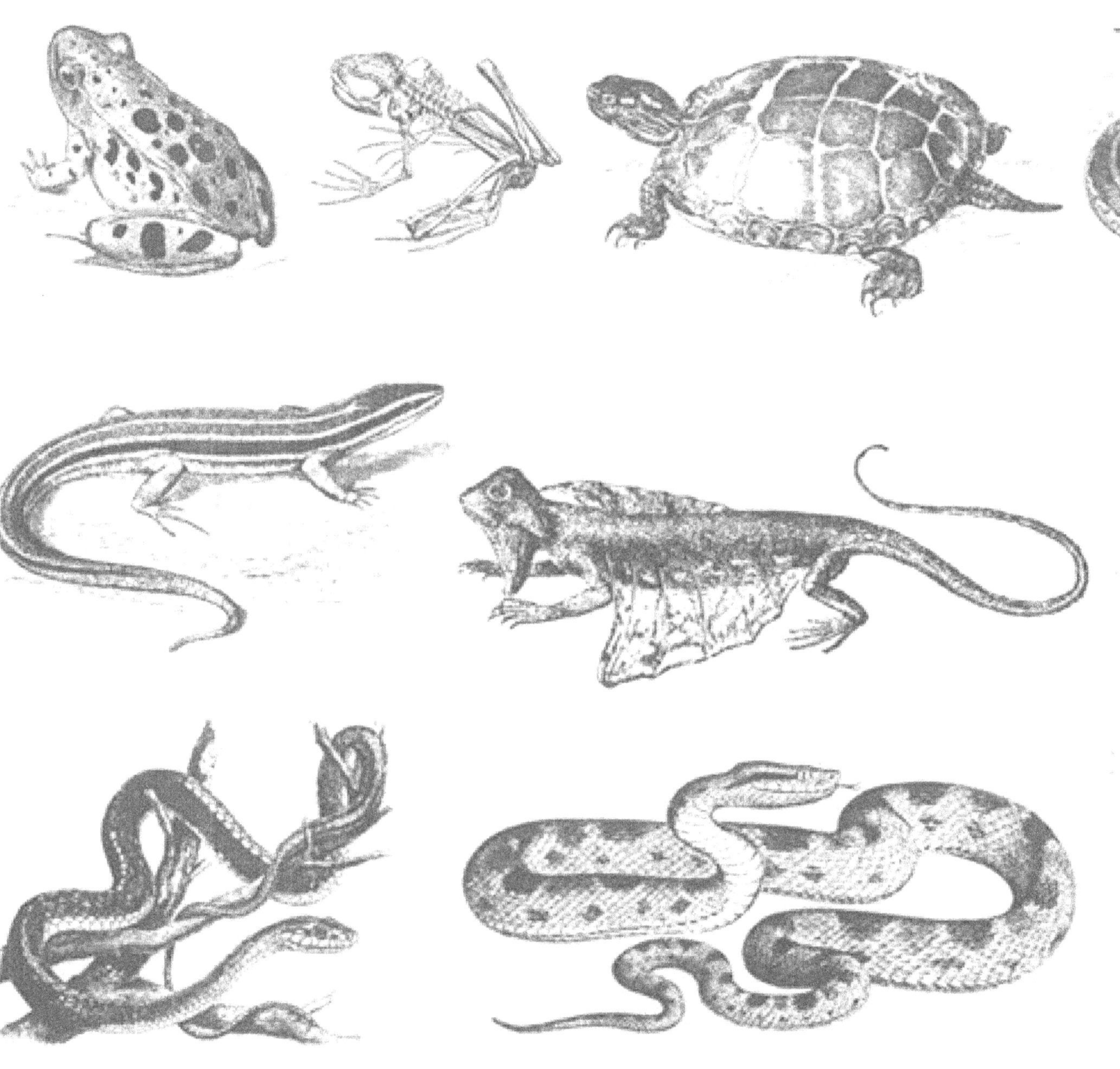

DRAW/SKETCH

FLOWERS

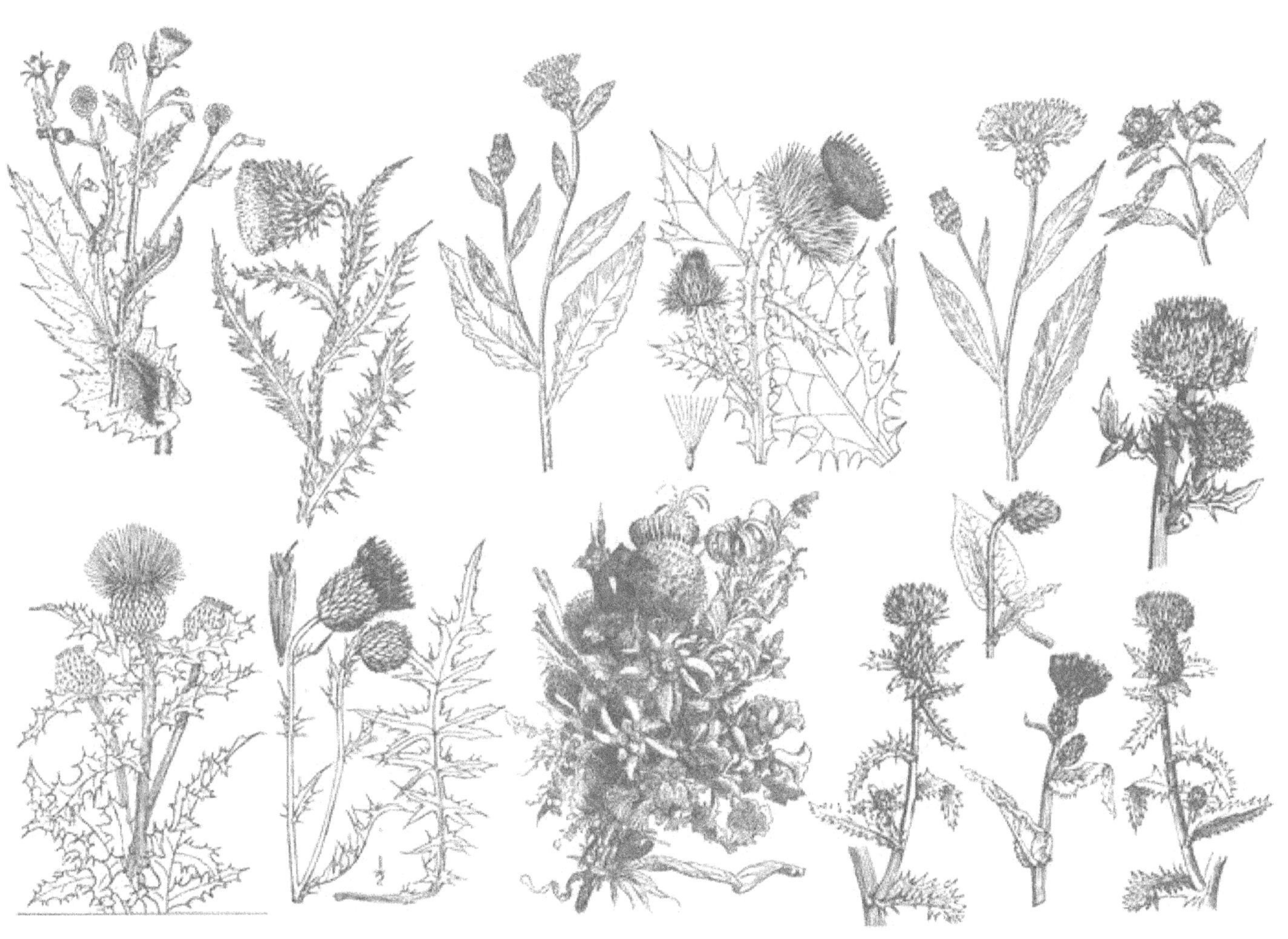

DRAW/SKETCH

ANIMALS

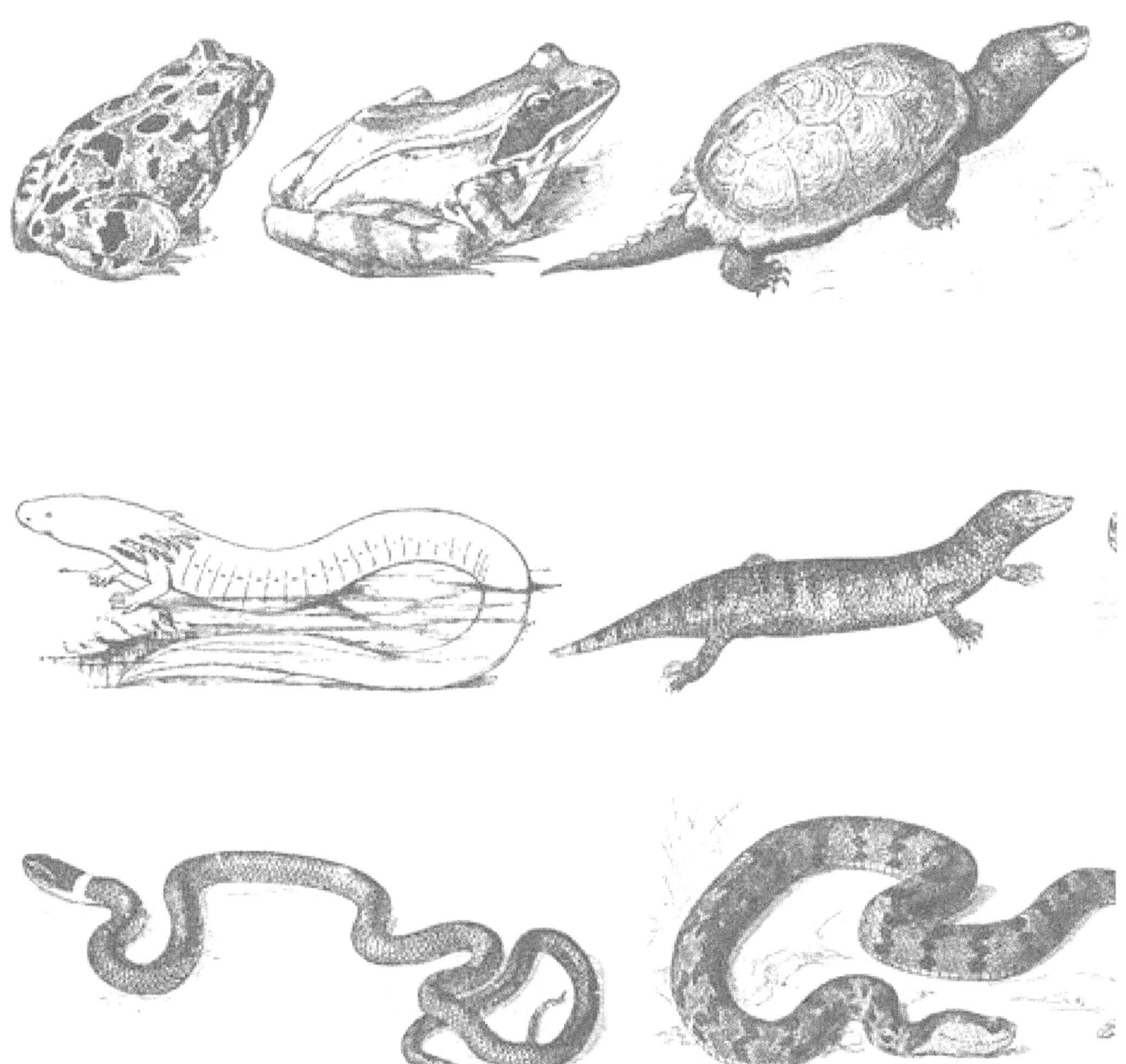

DRAW/SKETCH

TEETH

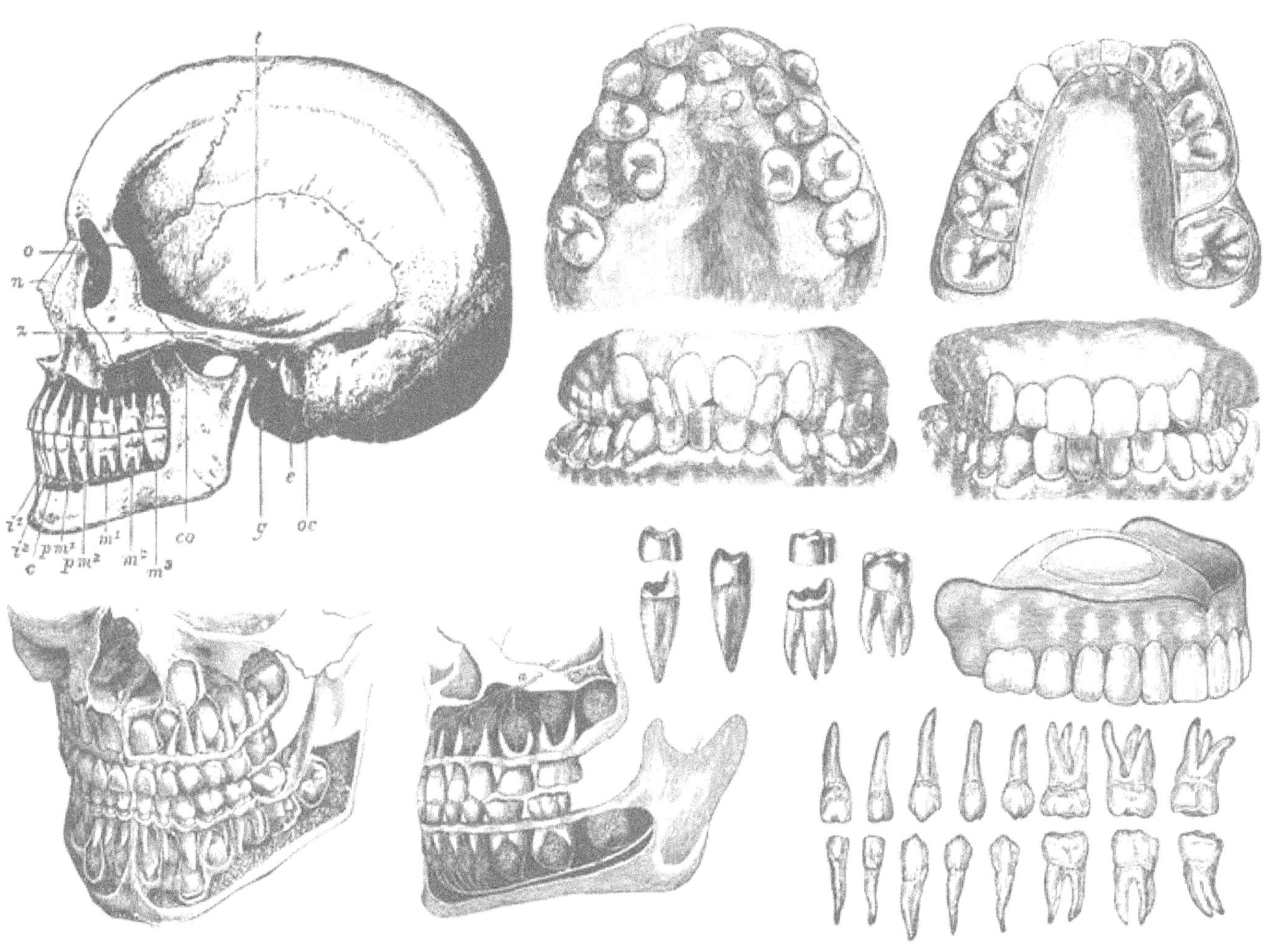

DRAW/SKETCH

ANIMALS

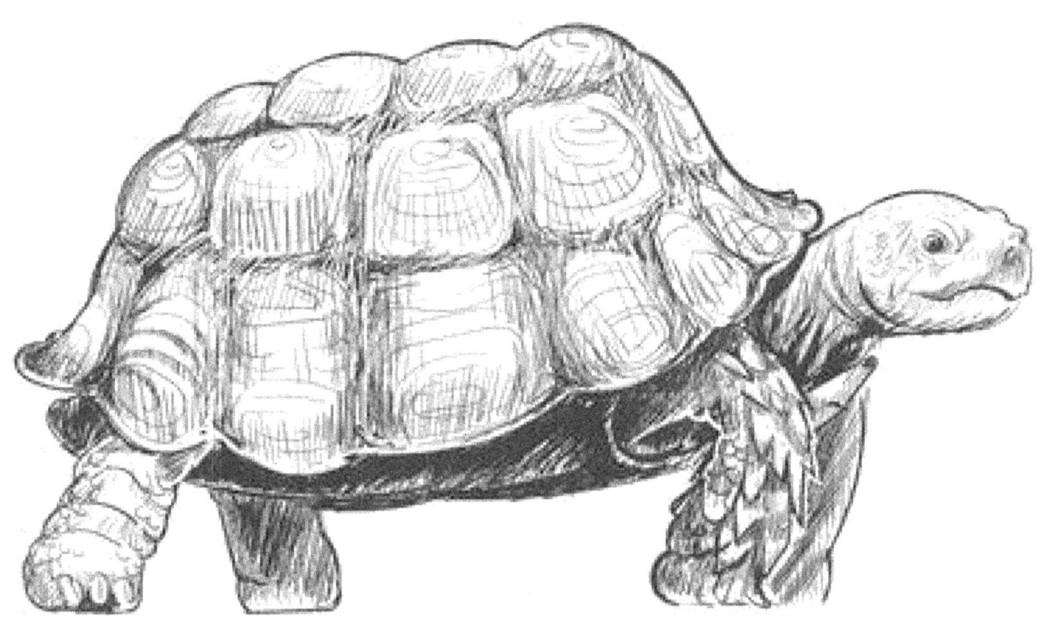

DRAW/SKETCH

ANIMALS

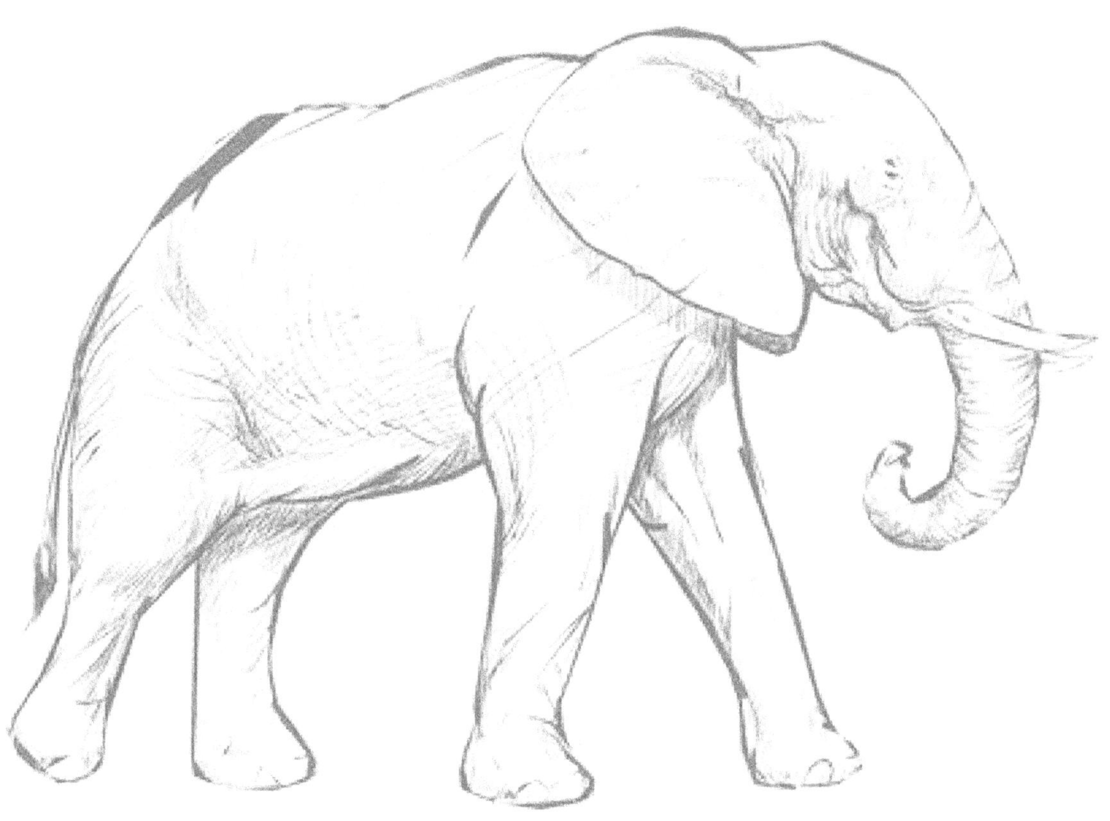

DRAW/SKETCH

ANIMALS

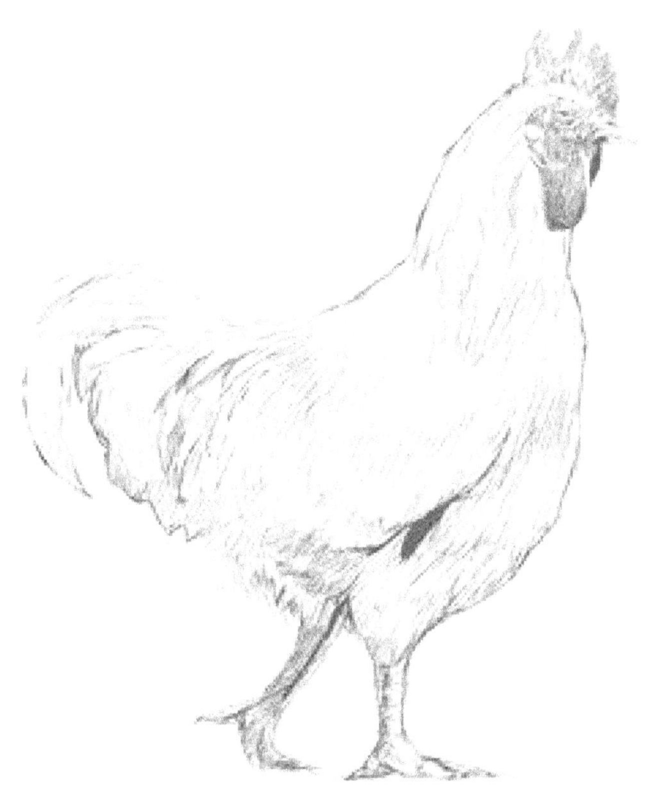

DRAW/SKETCH

ANIMALS

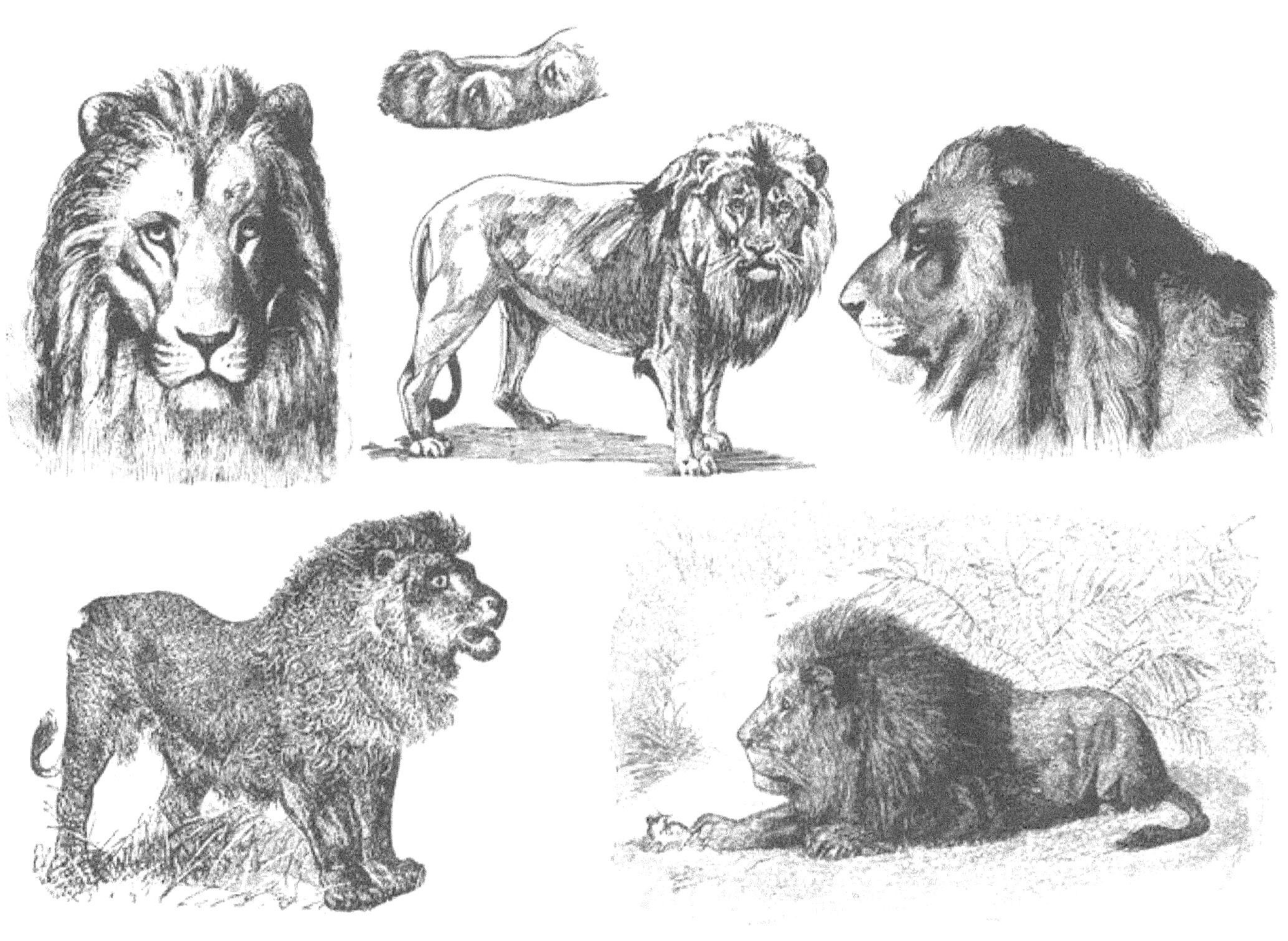

DRAW/SKETCH

ANIMALS

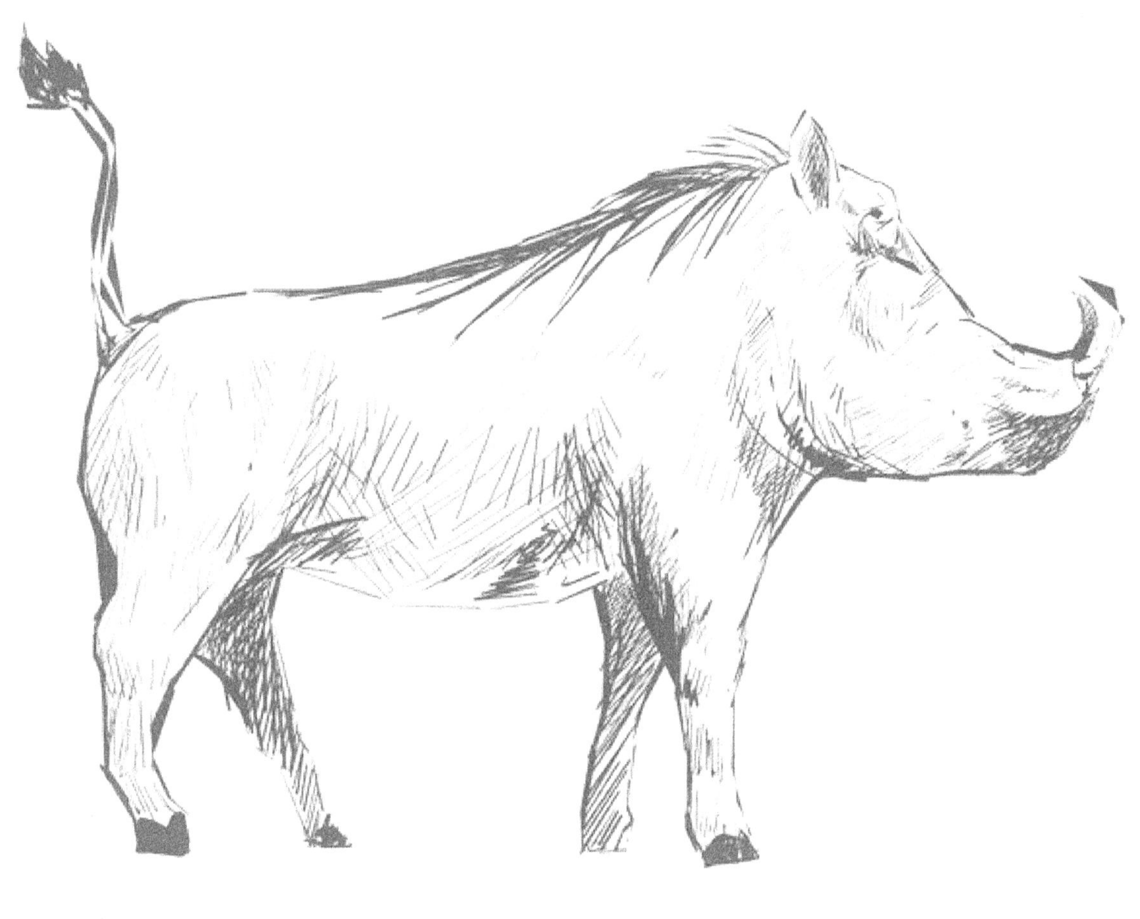

DRAW/SKETCH

ANIMALS

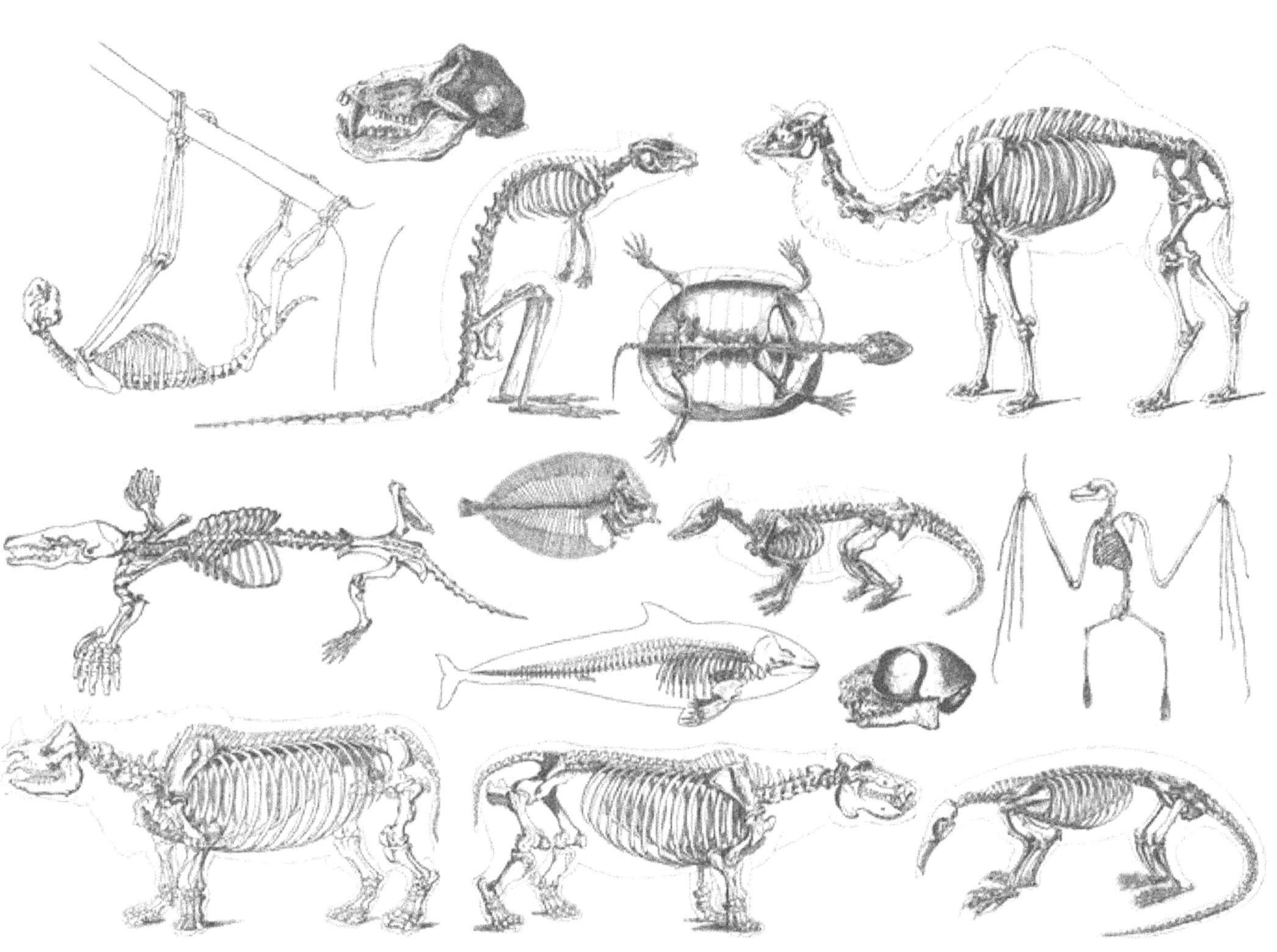

DRAW/SKETCH

ANIMALS

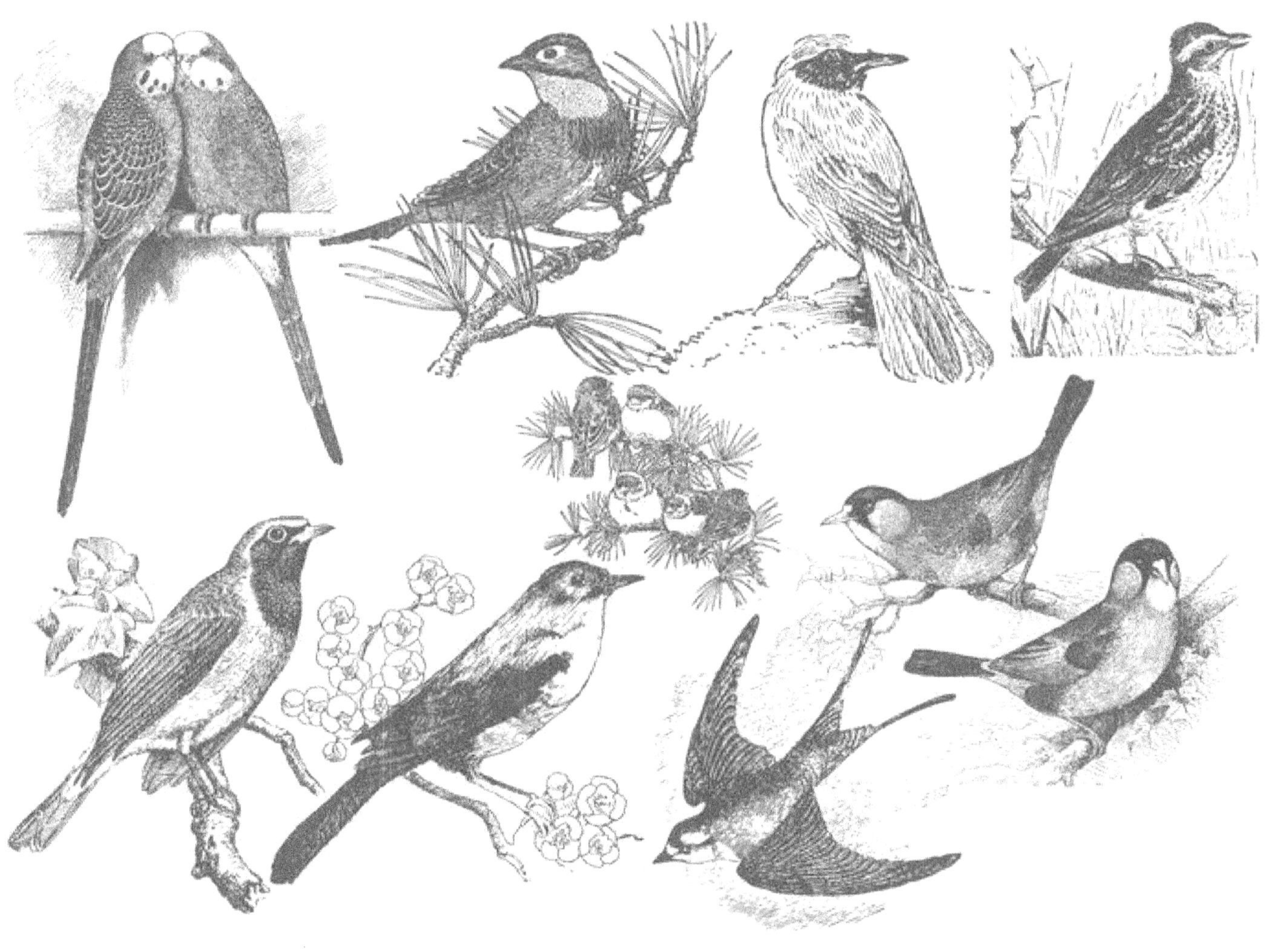

DRAW/SKETCH

ANIMALS

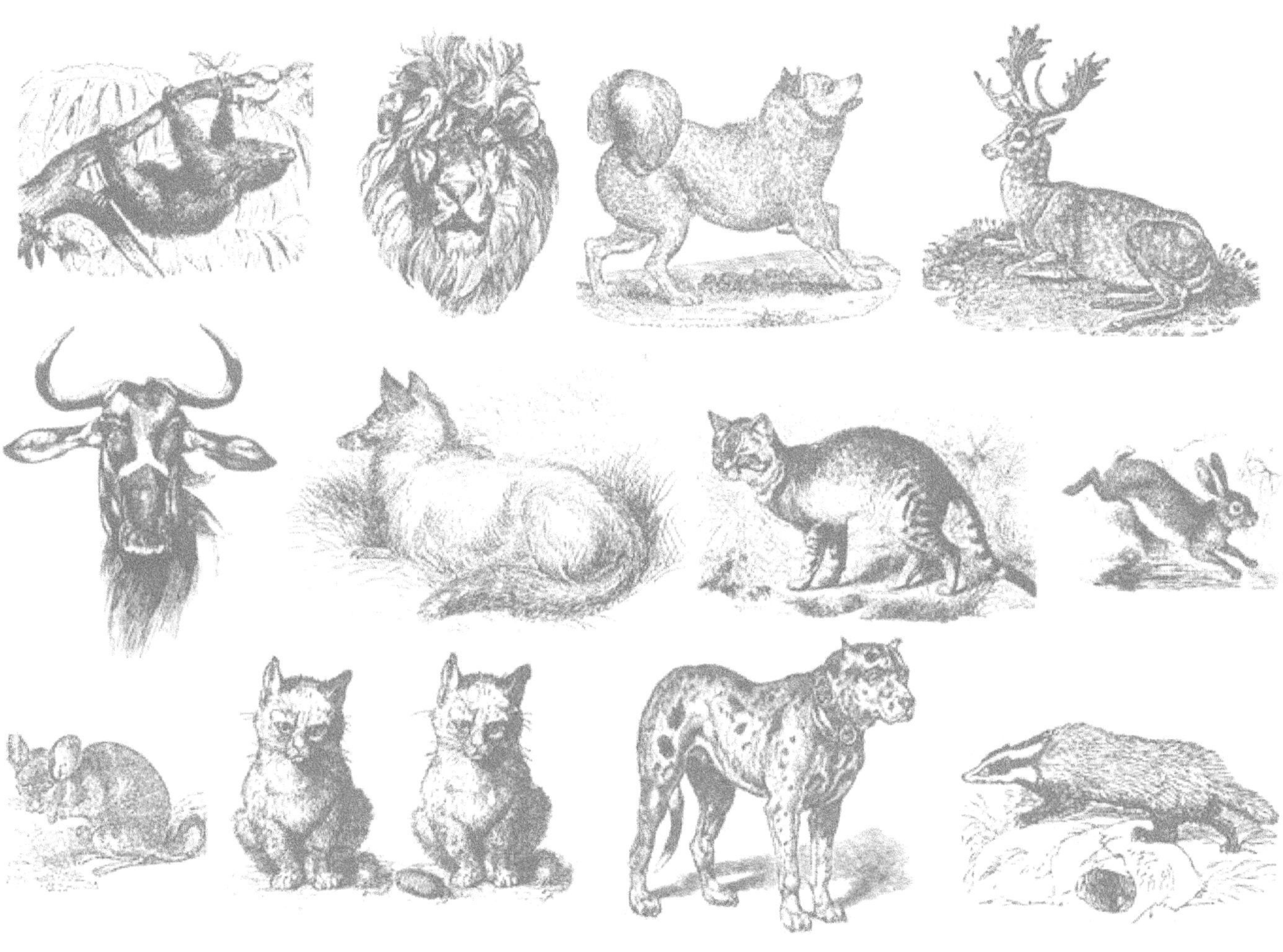

DRAW/SKETCH

PEOPLE

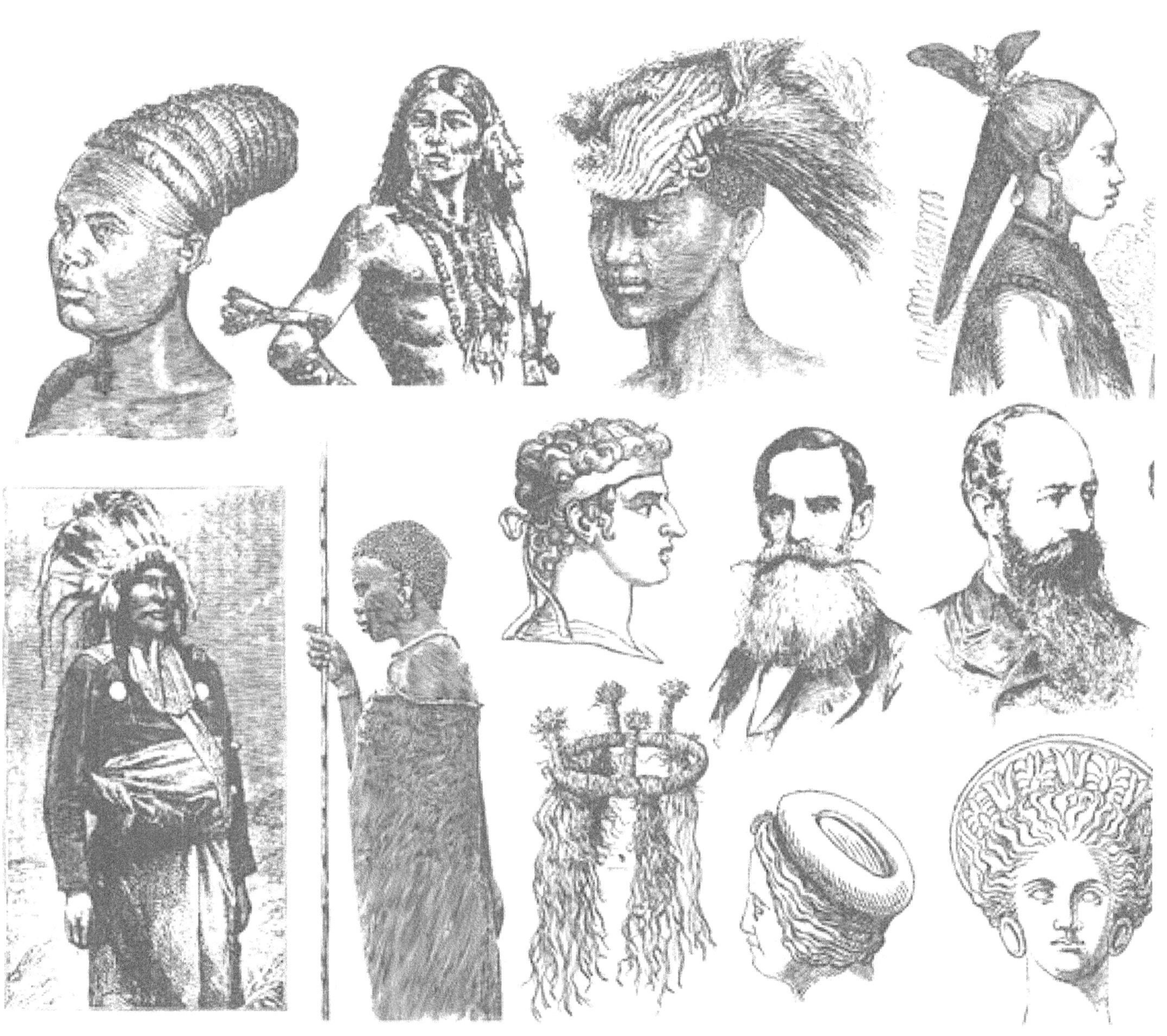

DRAW/SKETCH

PEOPLE

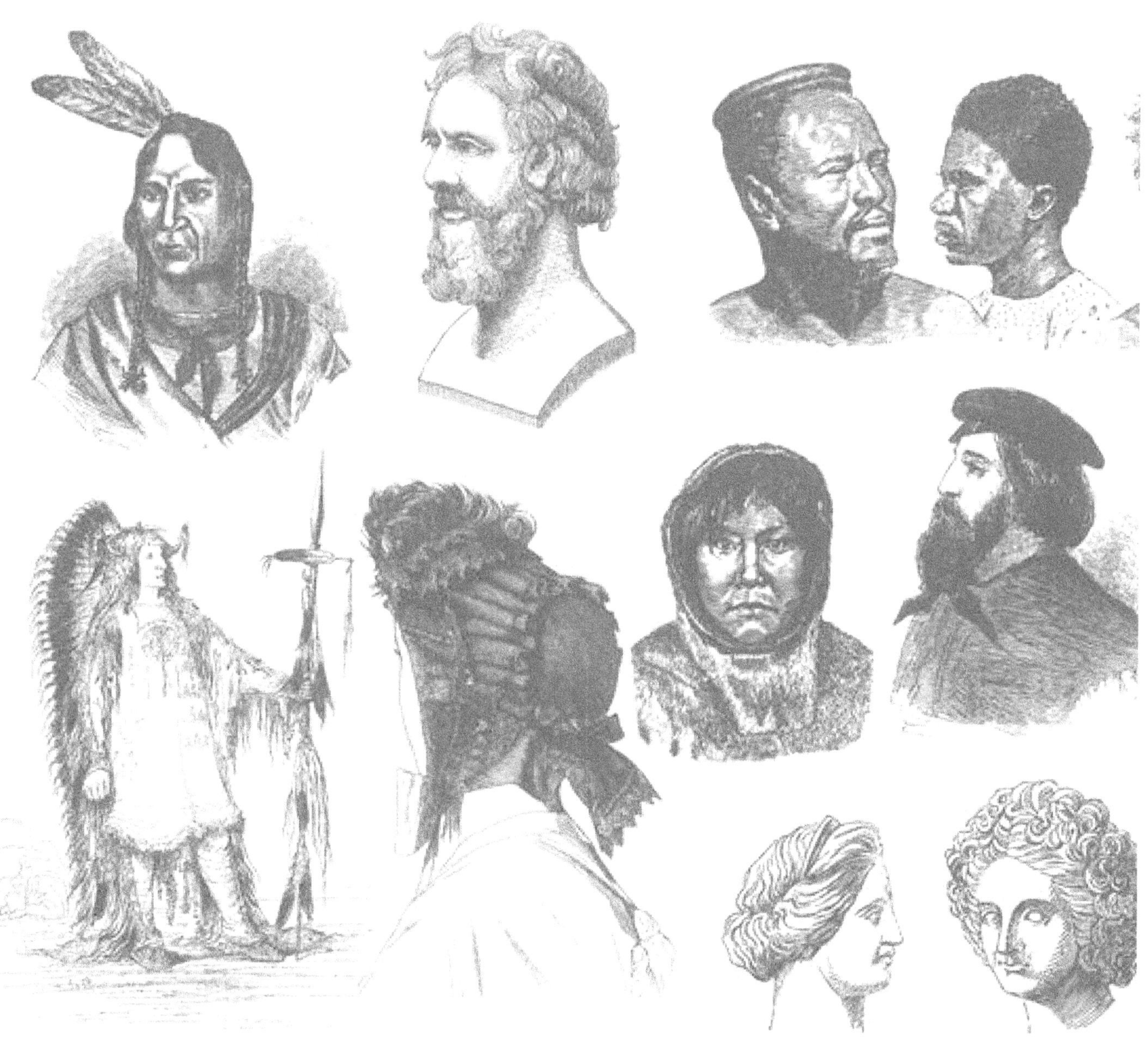

DRAW/SKETCH

PEOPLE

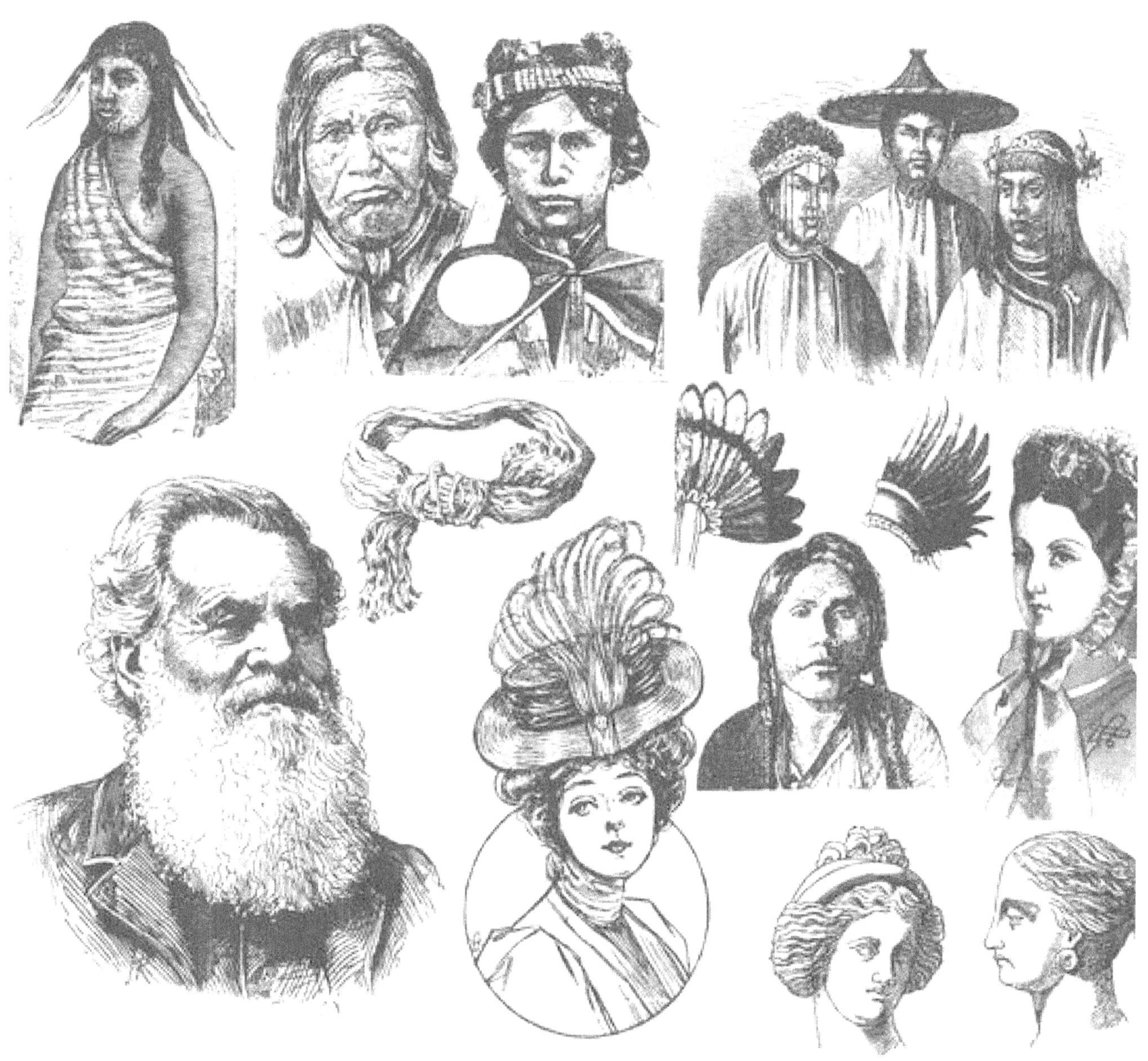

DRAW/SKETCH

PEOPLE

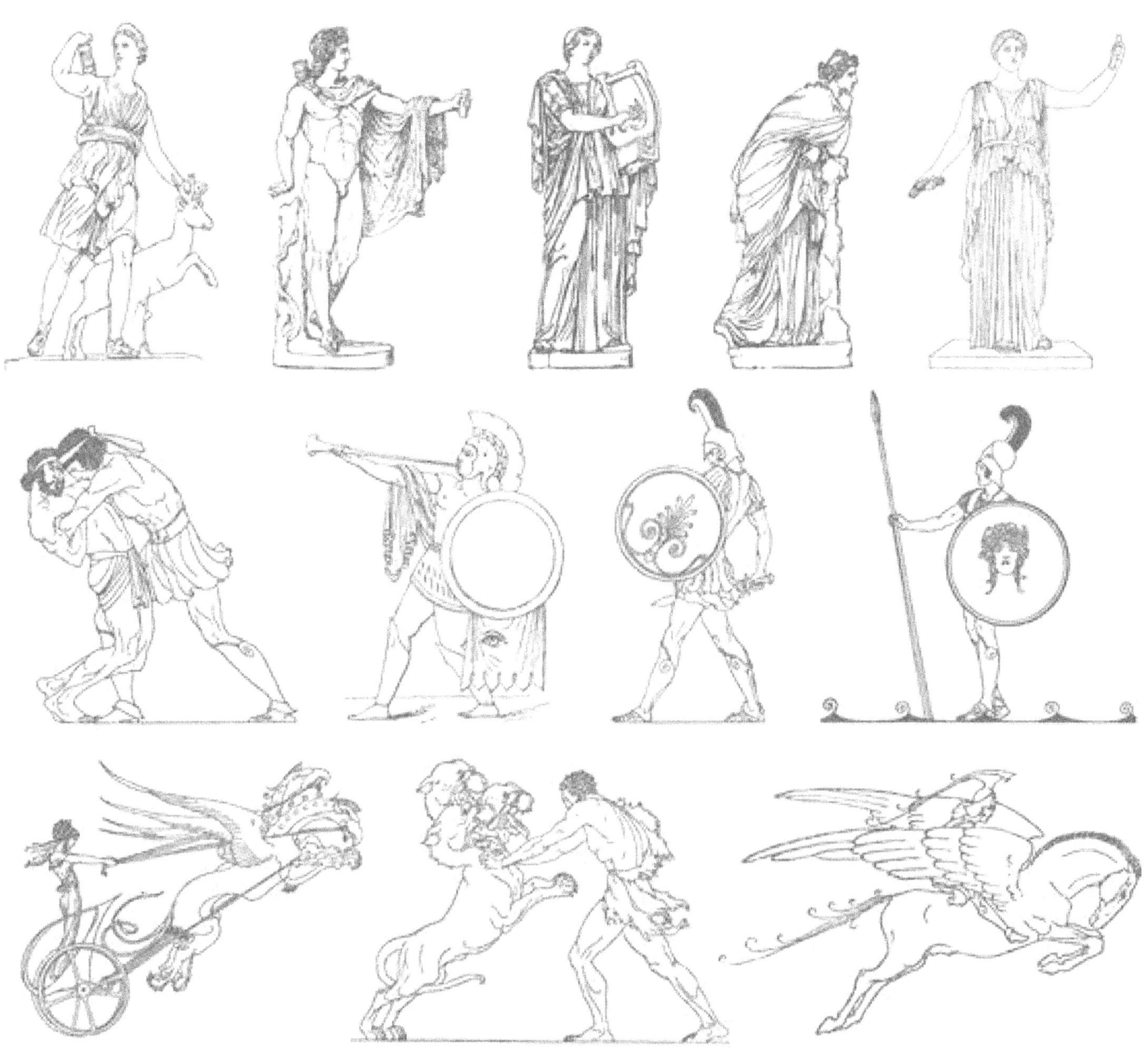

DRAW/SKETCH

PEOPLE

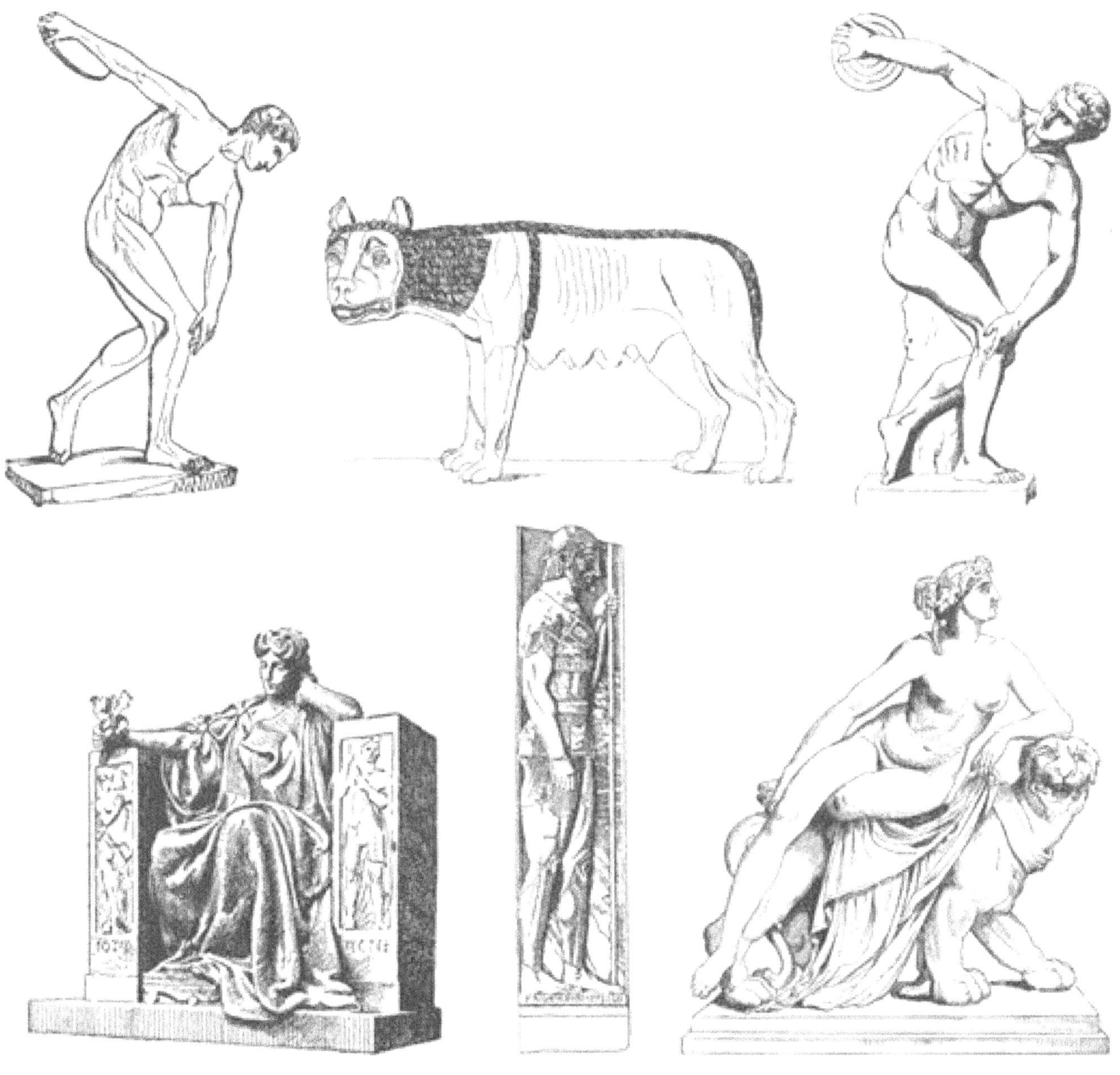

DRAW/SKETCH

PEOPLE

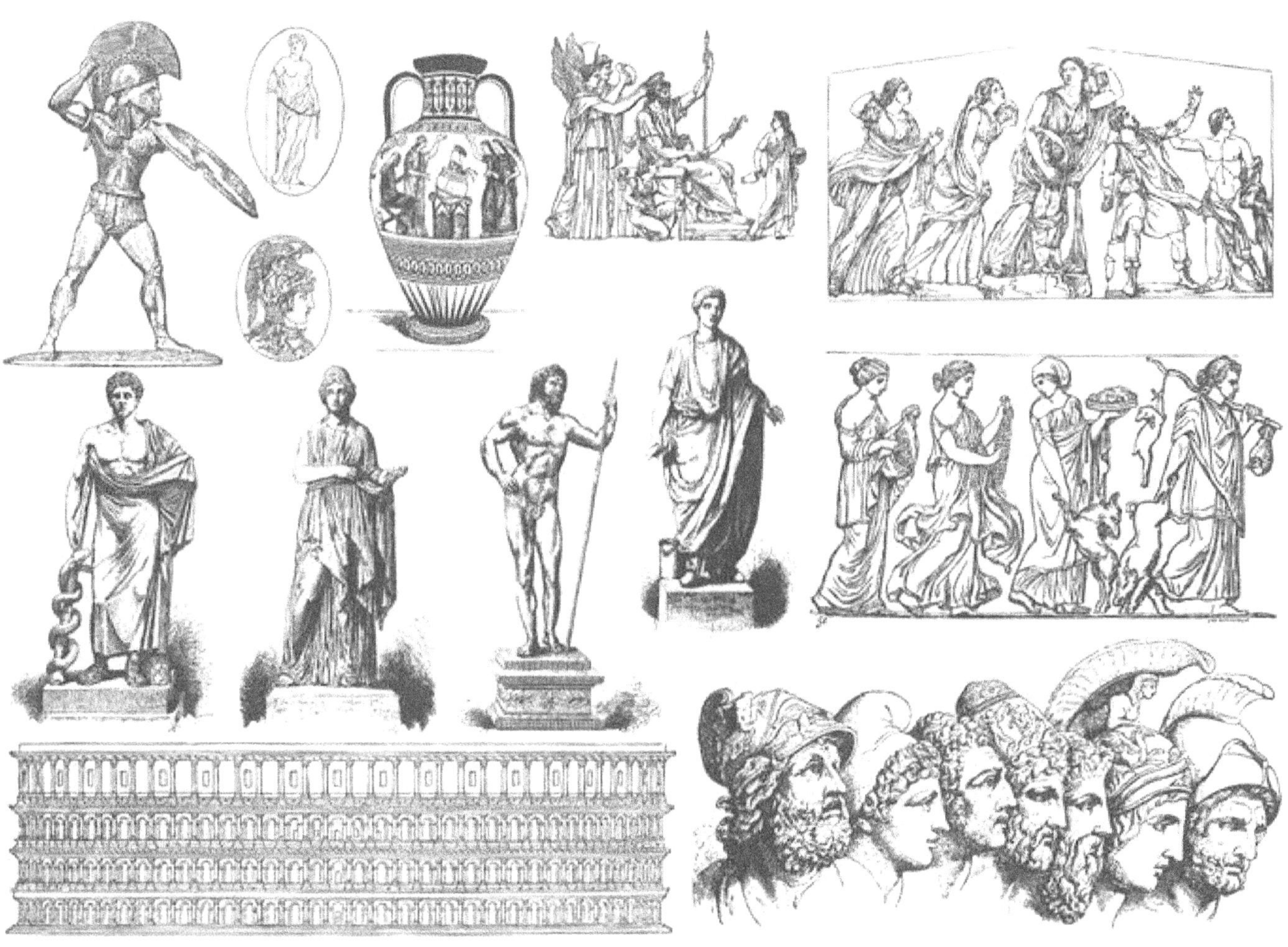

DRAW/SKETCH

MYSTIC

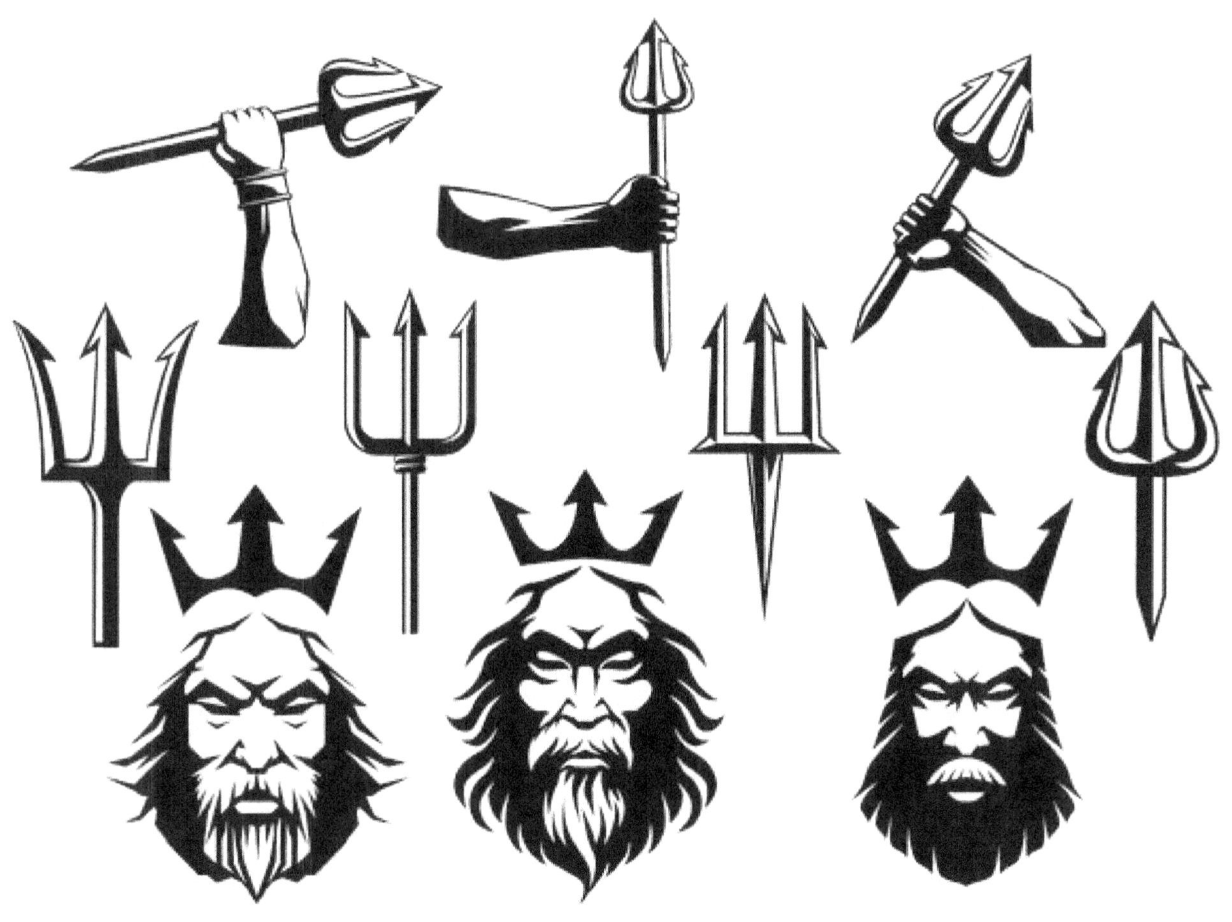

DRAW/SKETCH

ITEMS

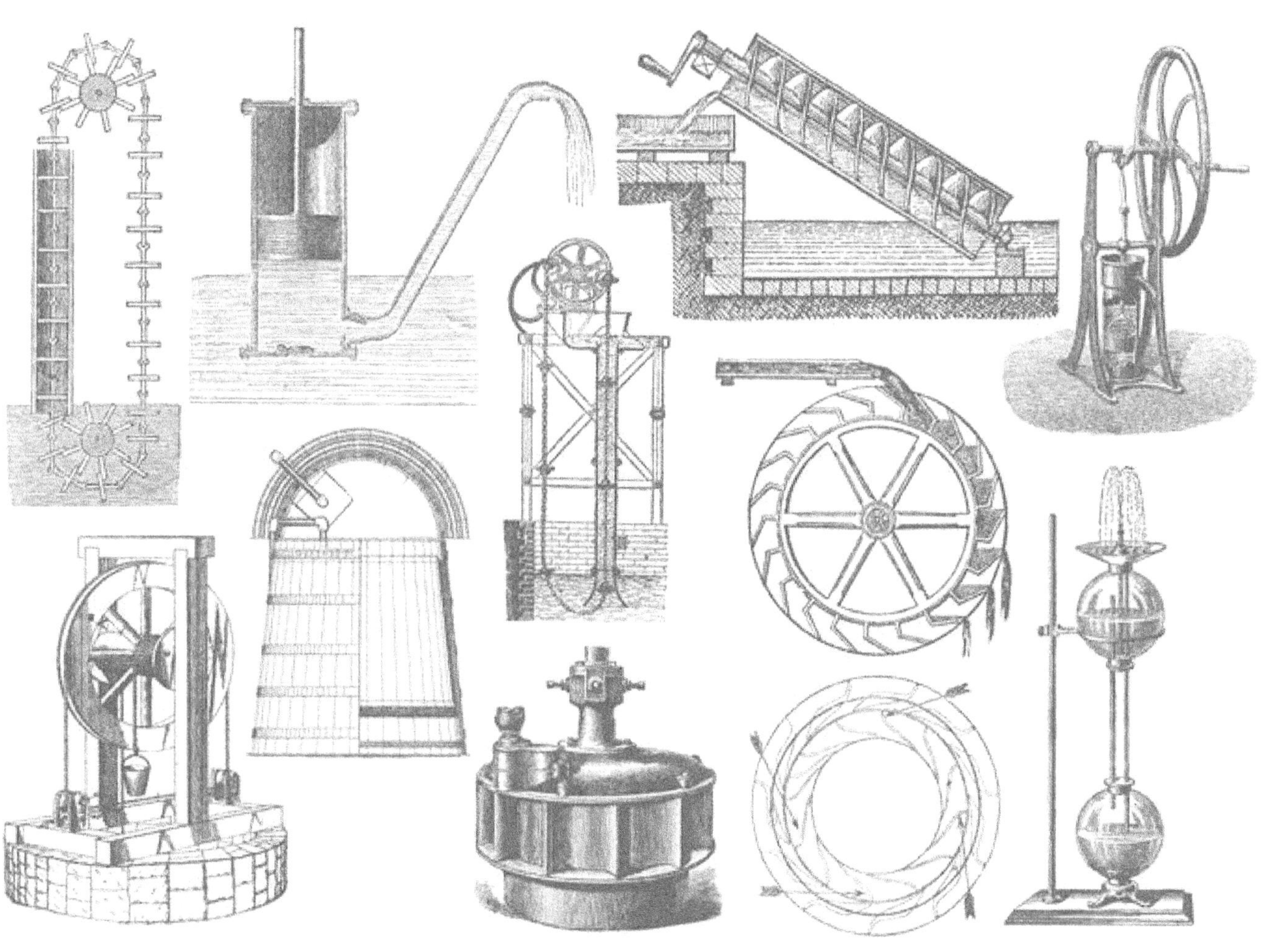

DRAW/SKETCH

CHAIRS

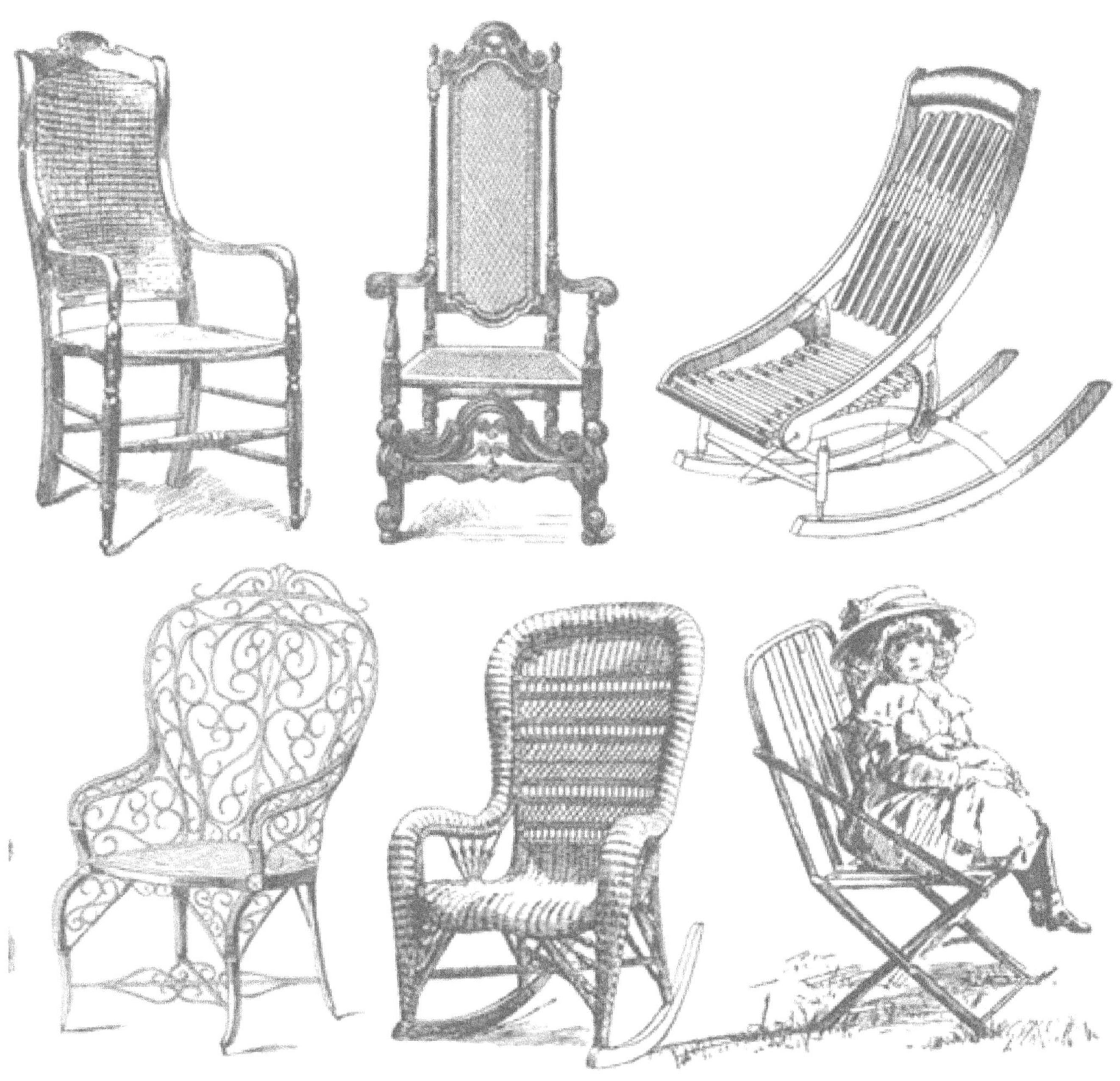

DRAW/SKETCH

CLOCKS

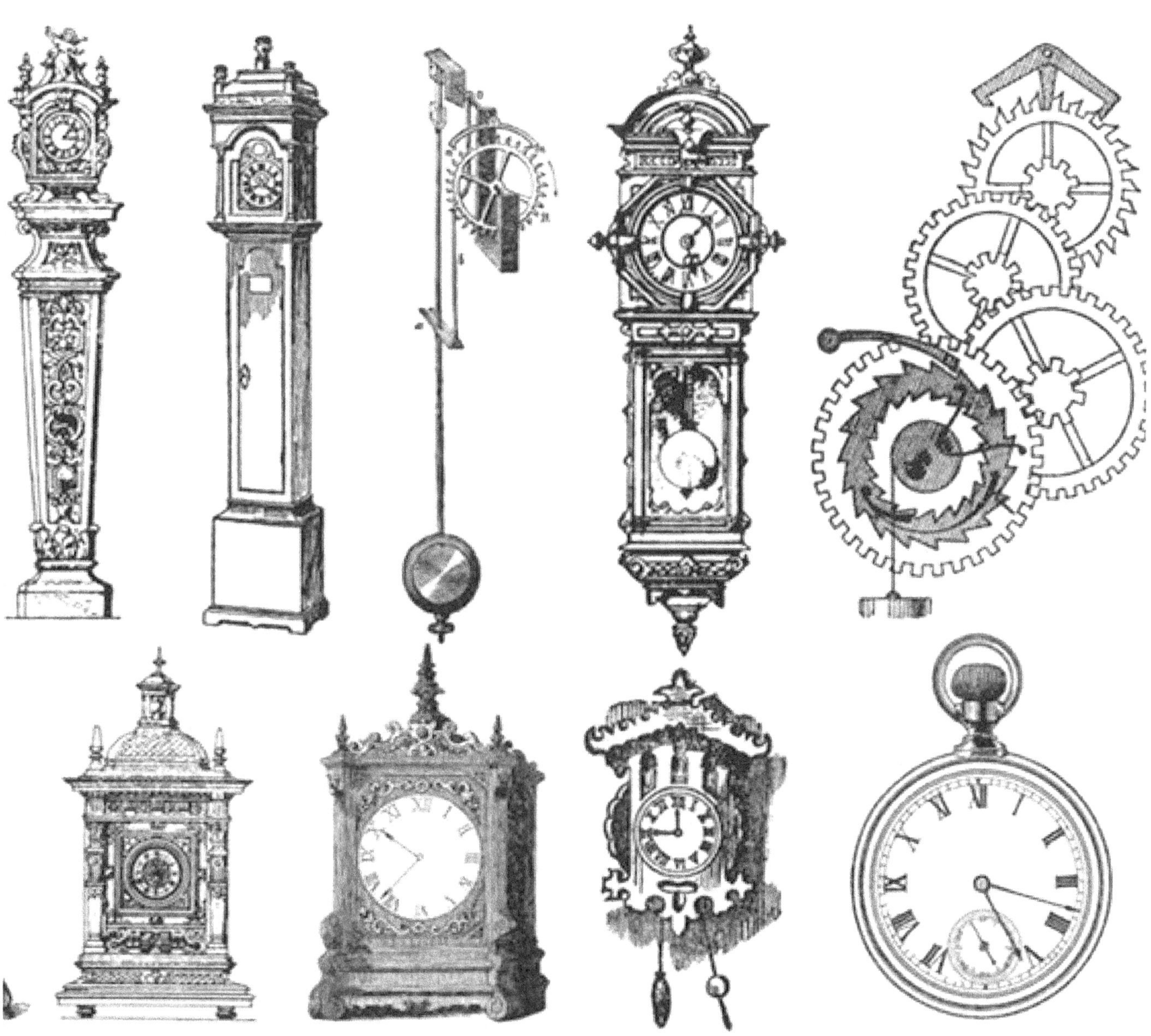

DRAW/SKETCH

ANIMALS

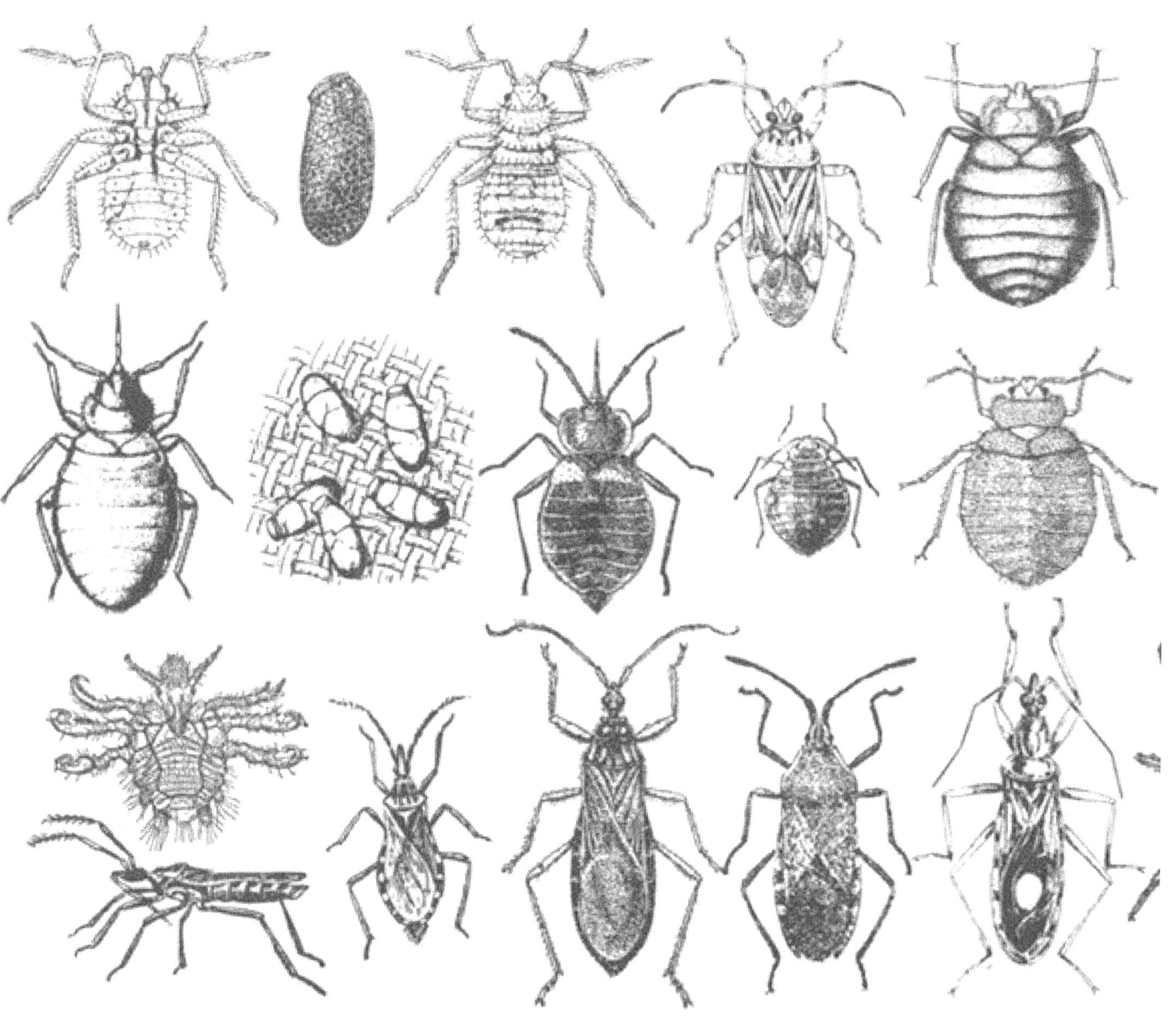

DRAW/SKETCH

FOOD

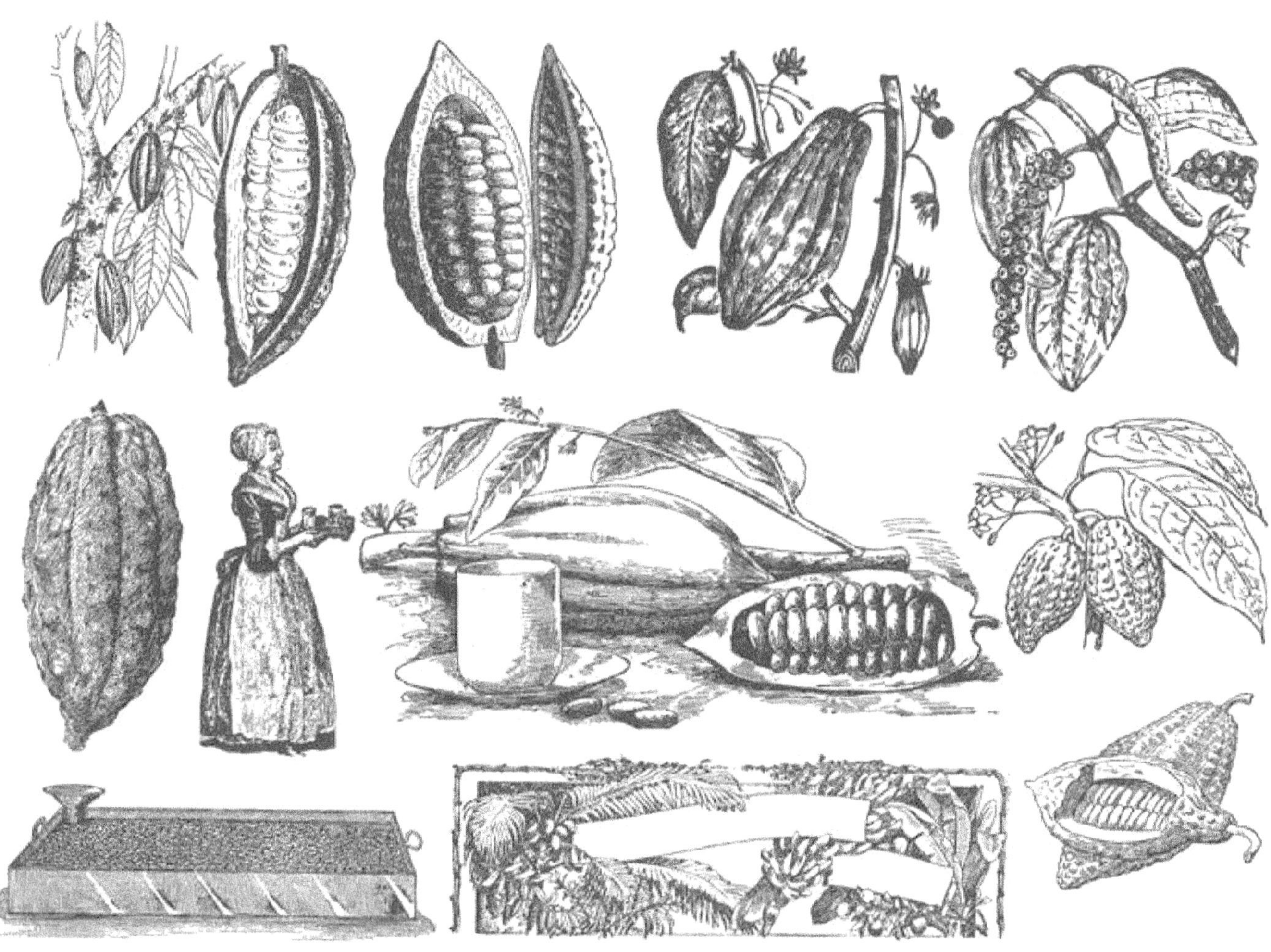

DRAW/SKETCH

FOOD

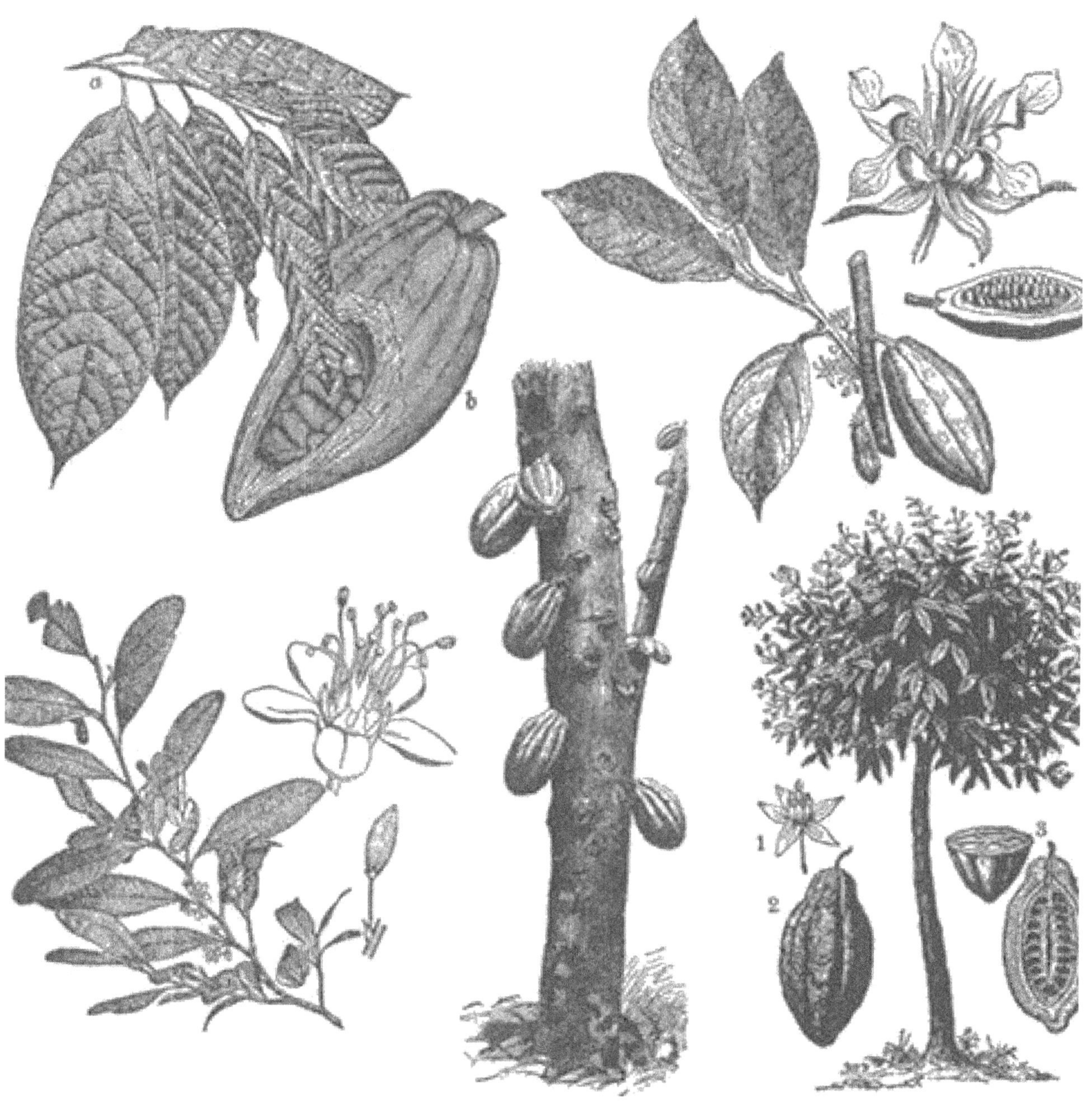

DRAW/SKETCH

FOOD

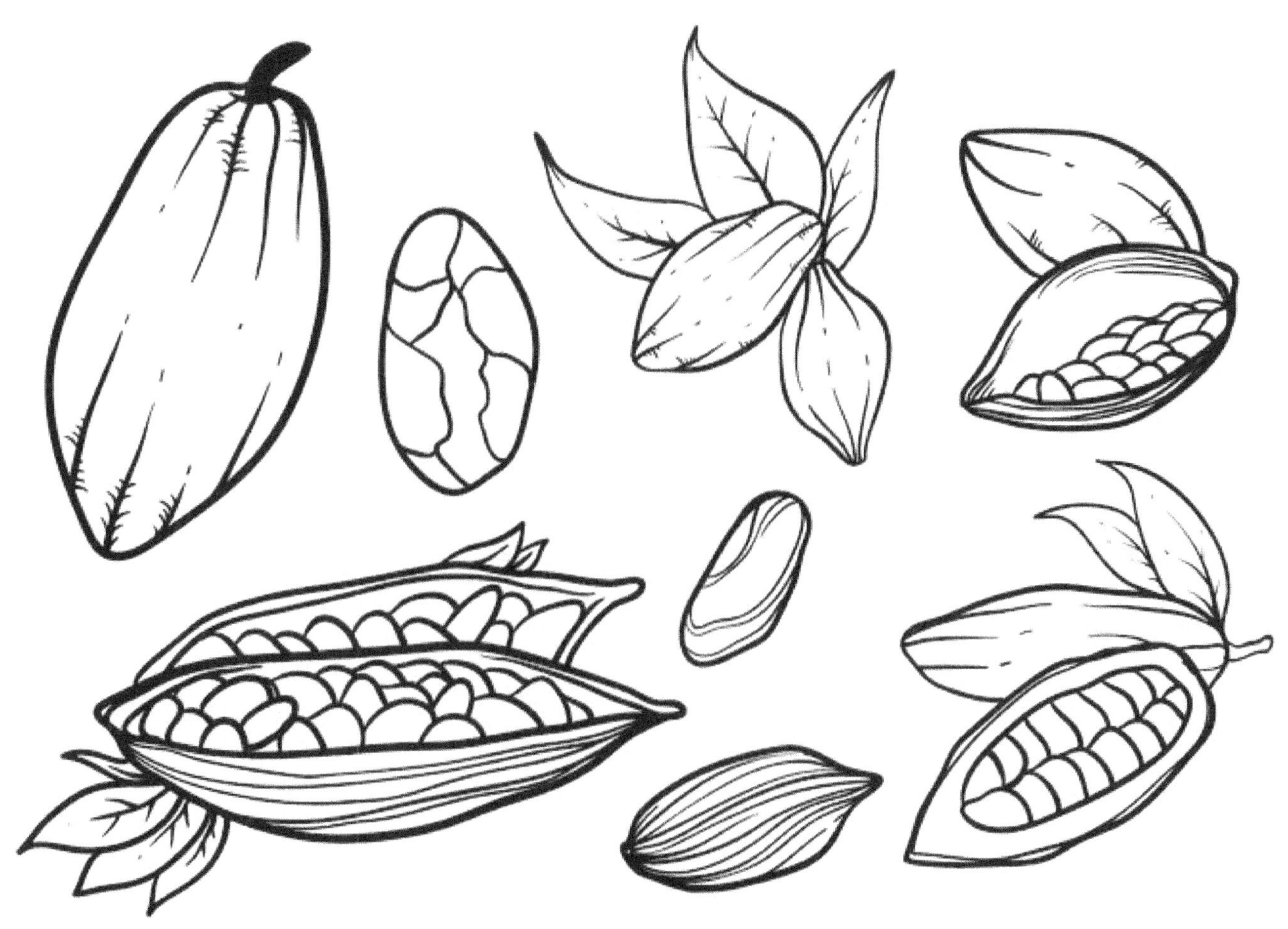

DRAW/SKETCH

ANIMALS

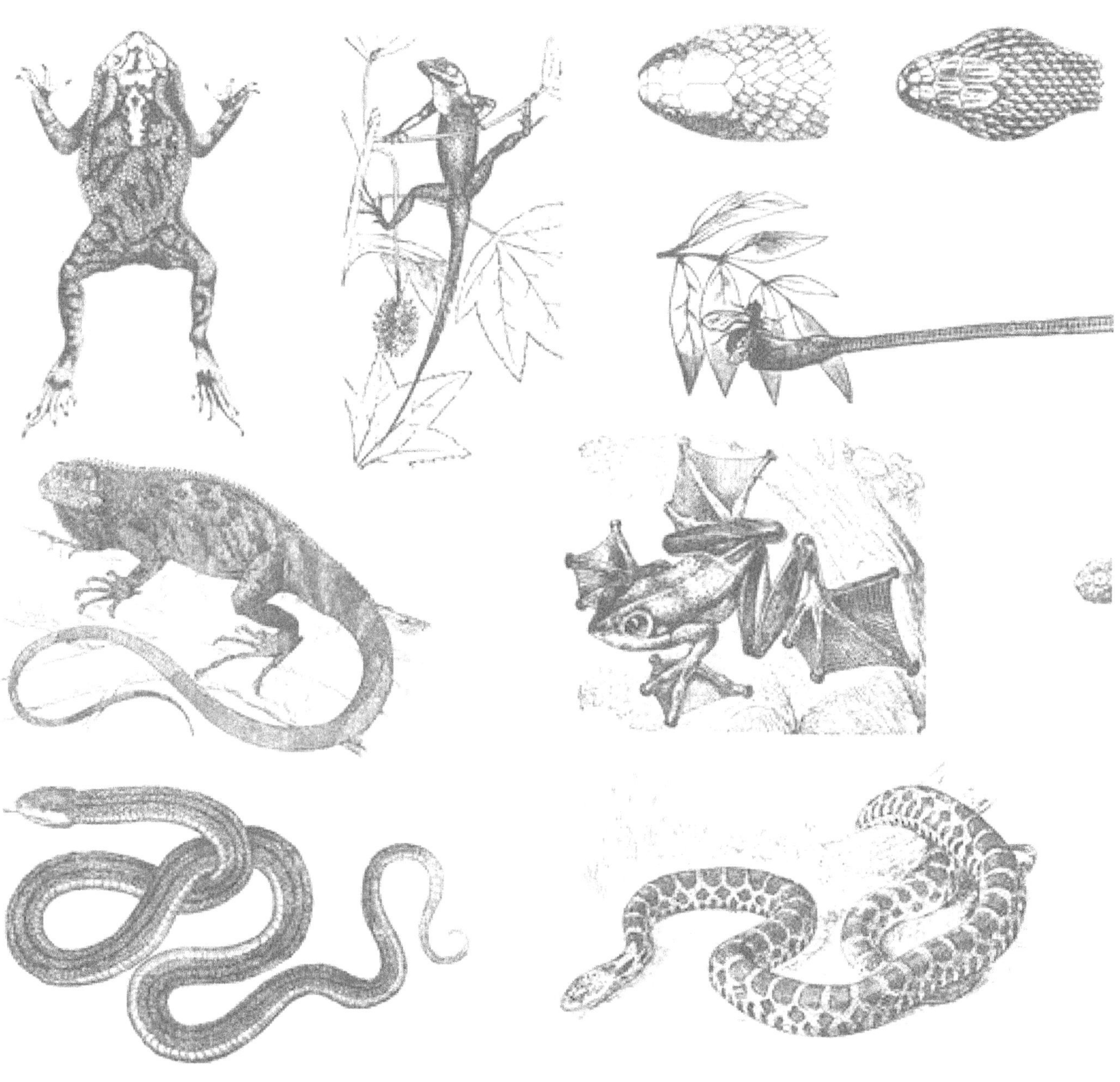

DRAW/SKETCH

ANIMALS

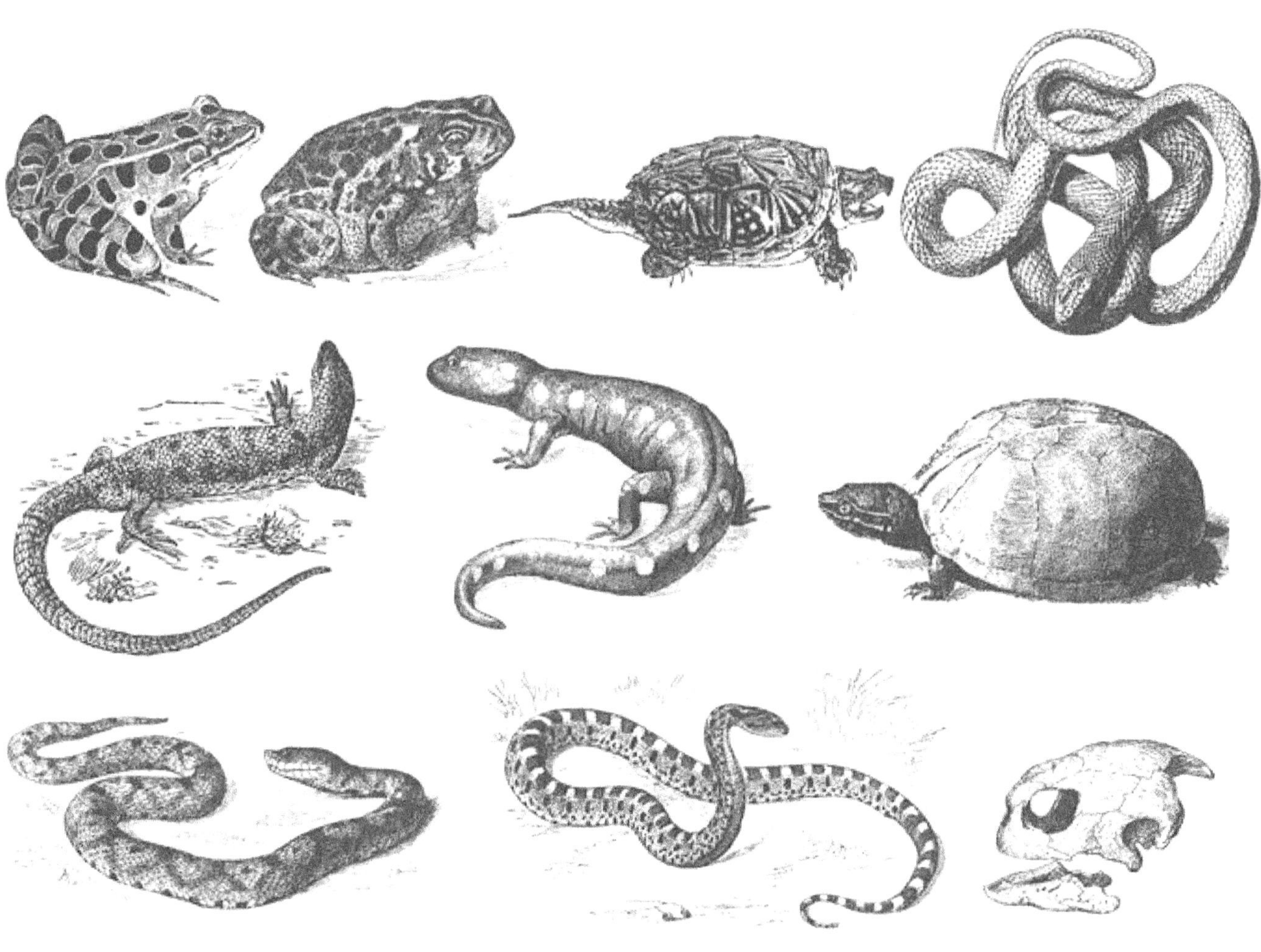

DRAW/SKETCH

ANIMALS

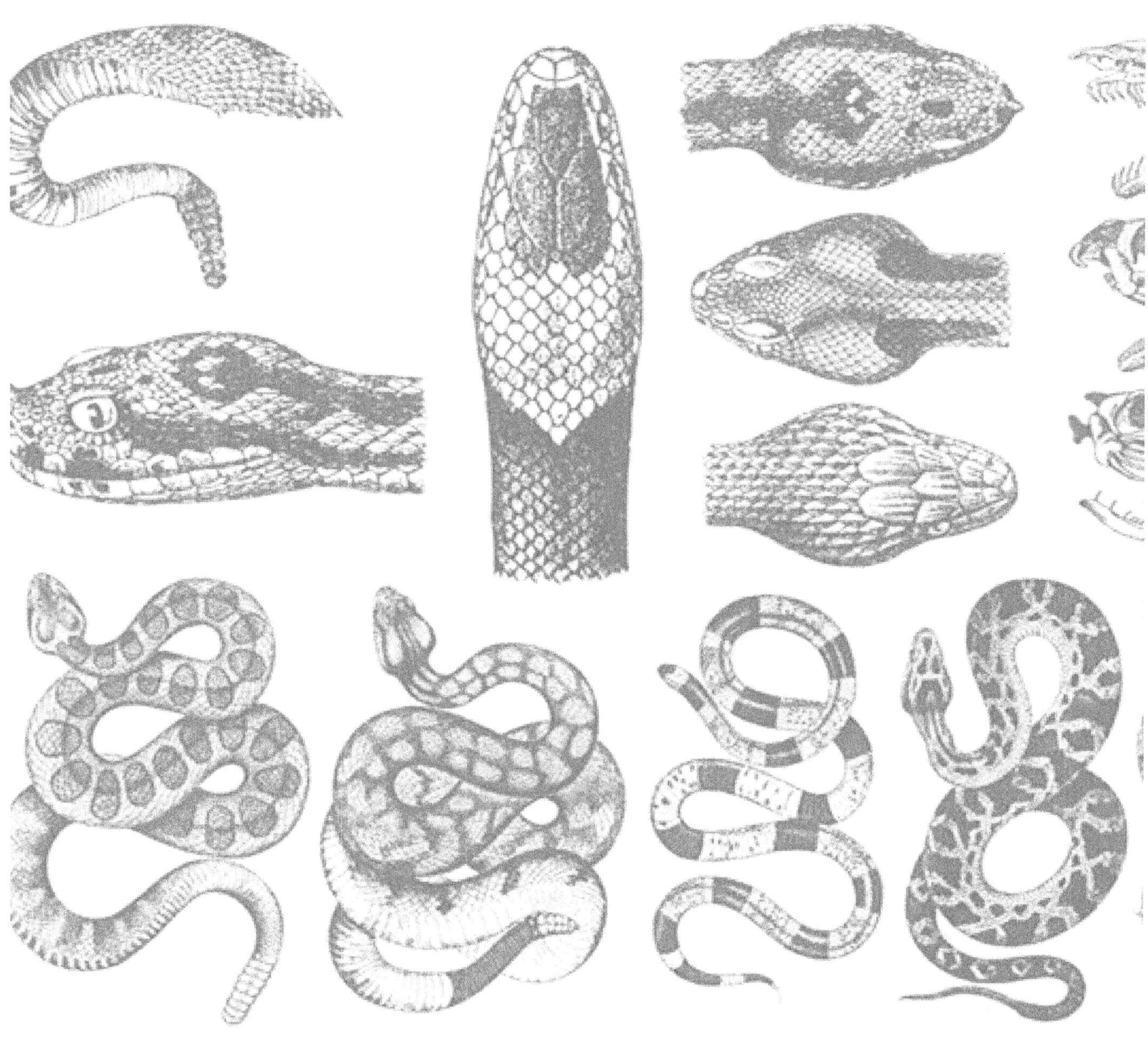

DRAW/SKETCH

ANIMALS

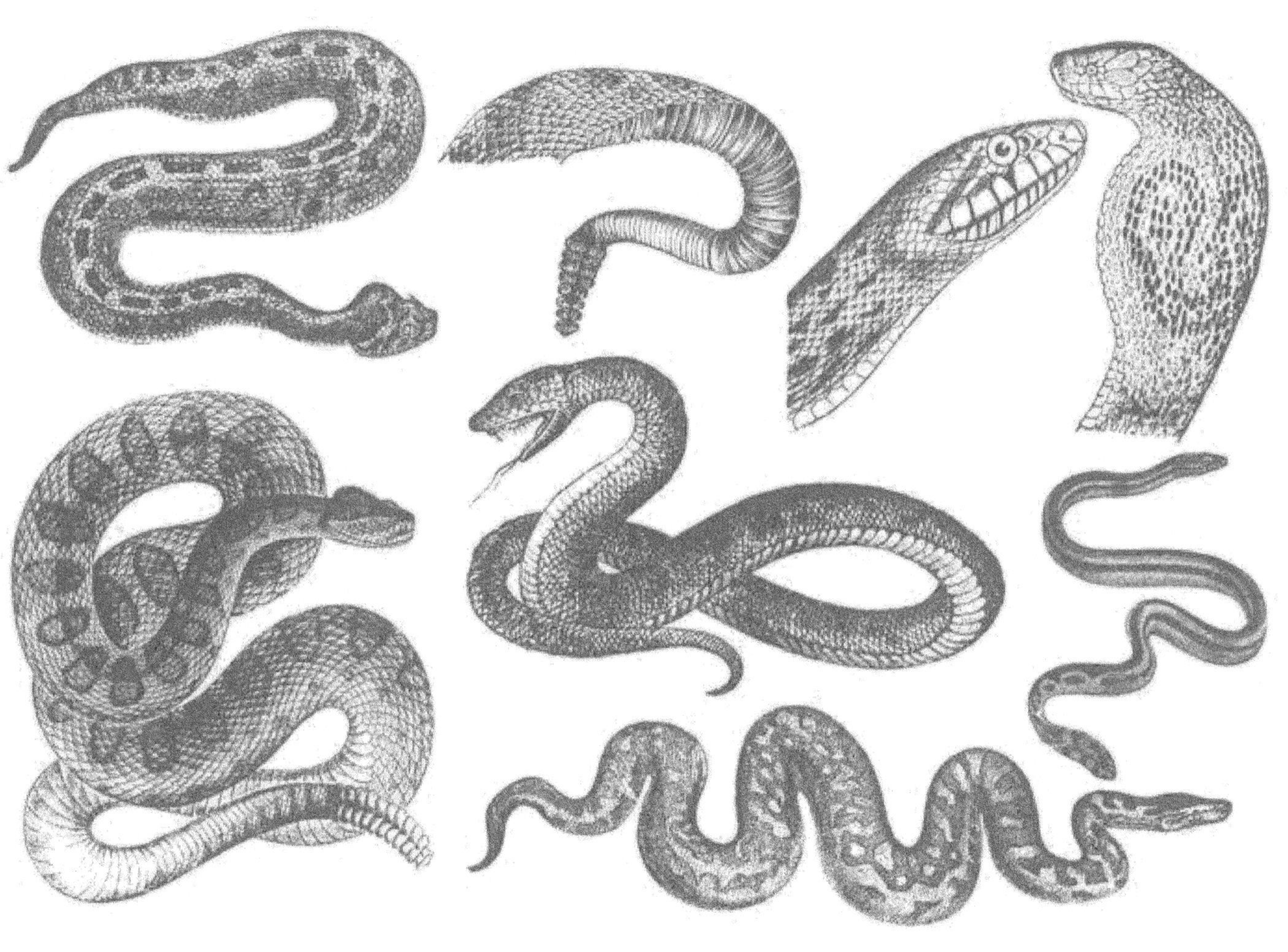

DRAW/SKETCH

ANIMALS

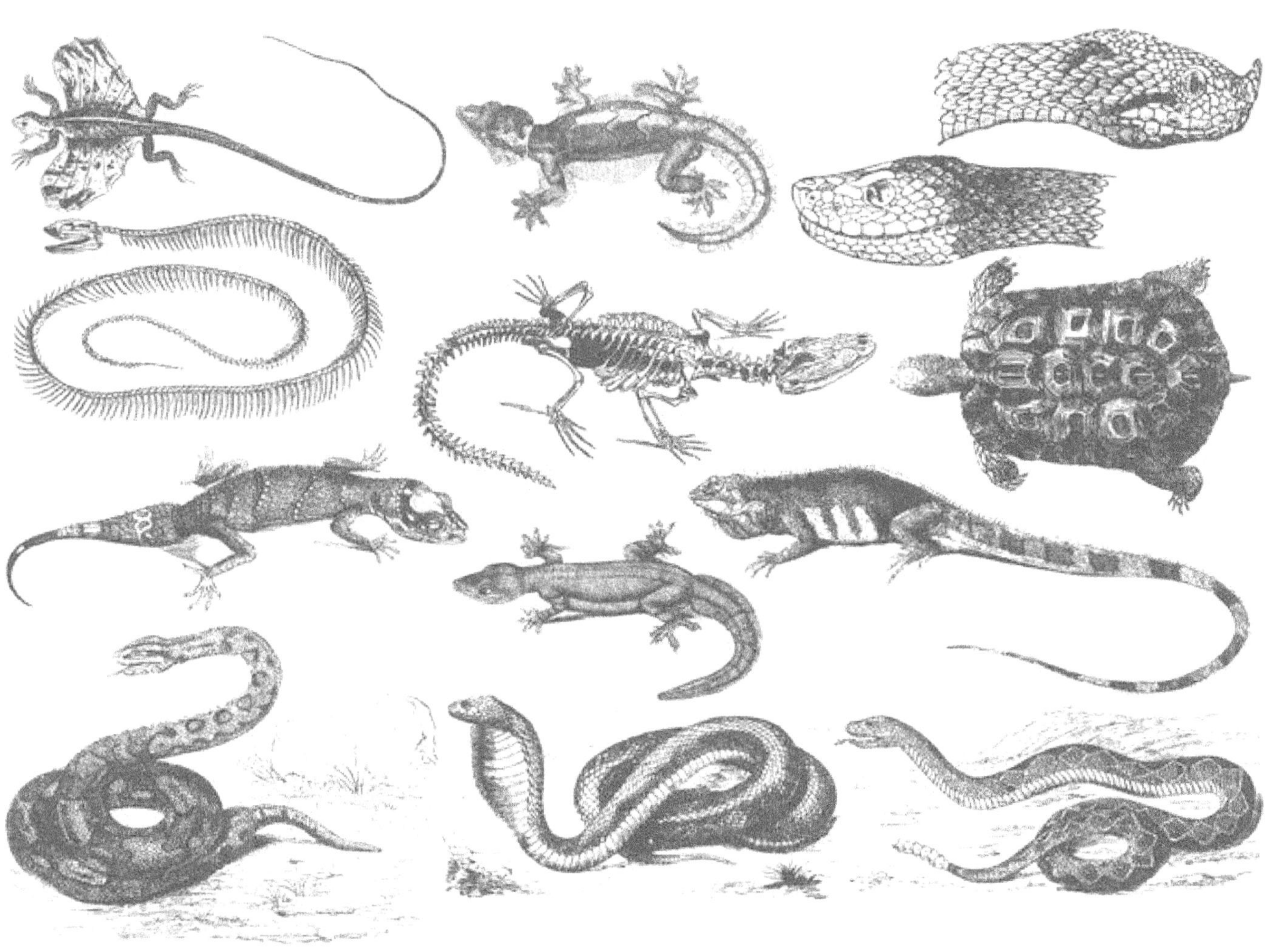

DRAW/SKETCH

ANIMALS

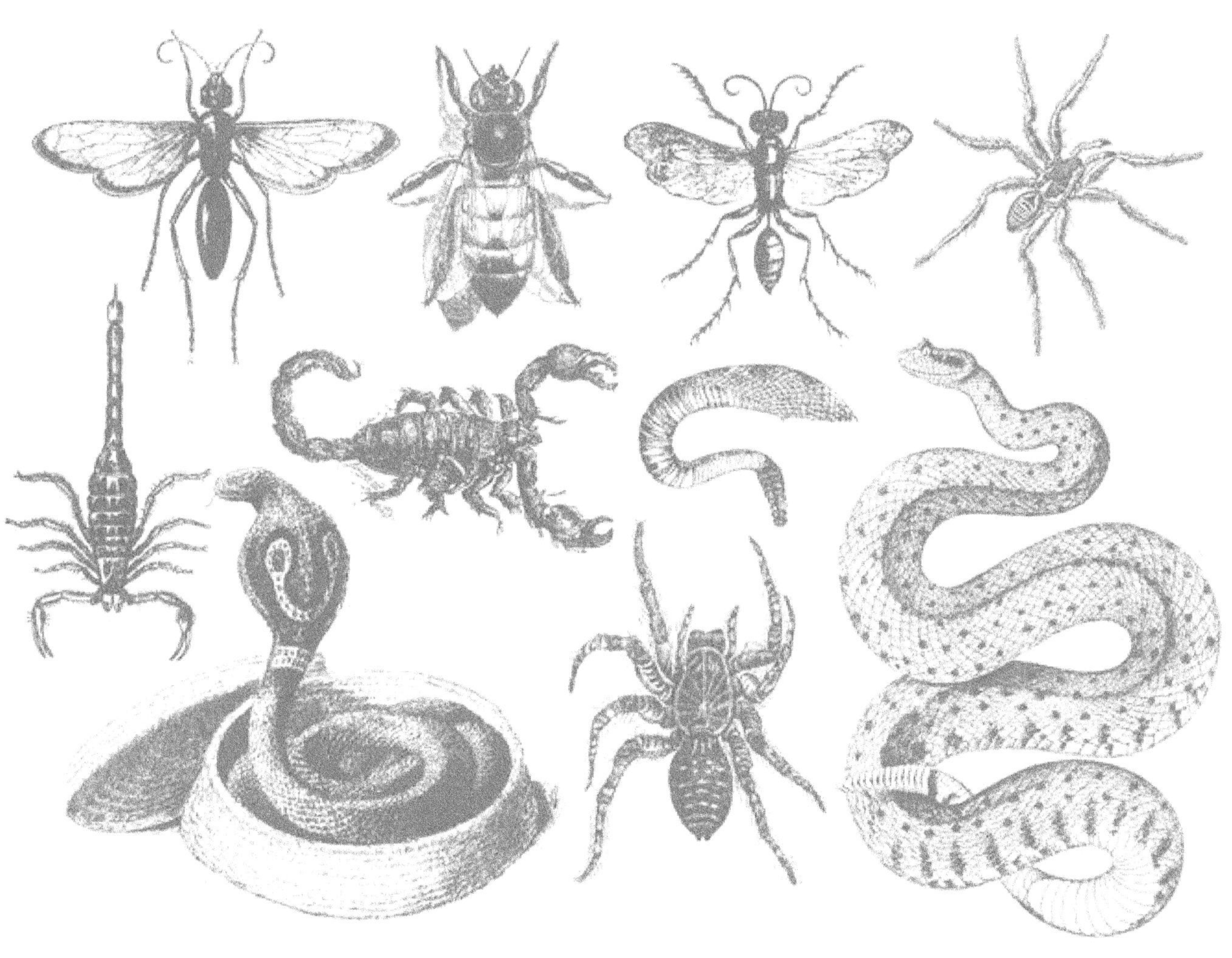

DRAW/SKETCH

ANIMALS

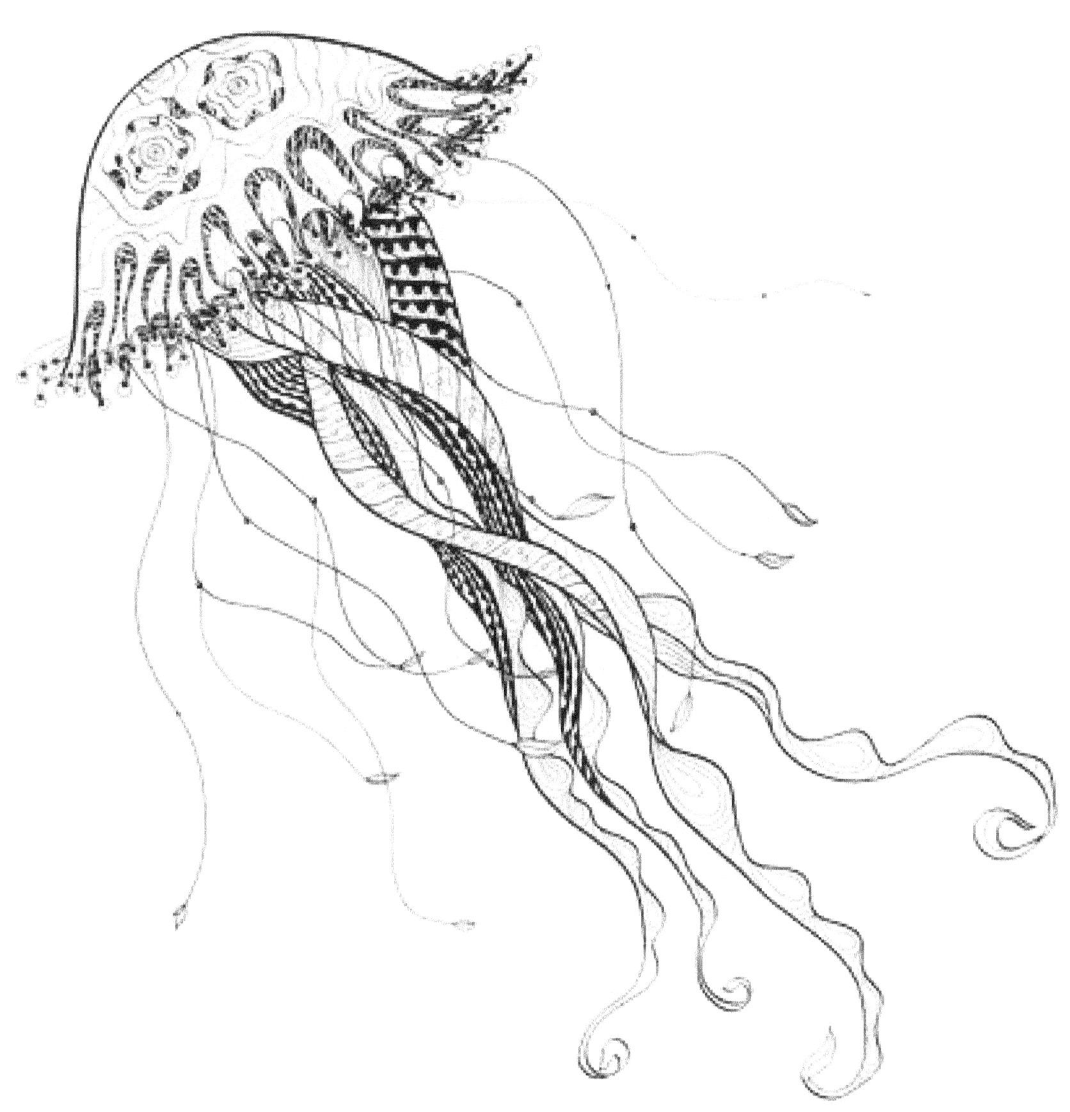

DRAW/SKETCH

ANIMALS

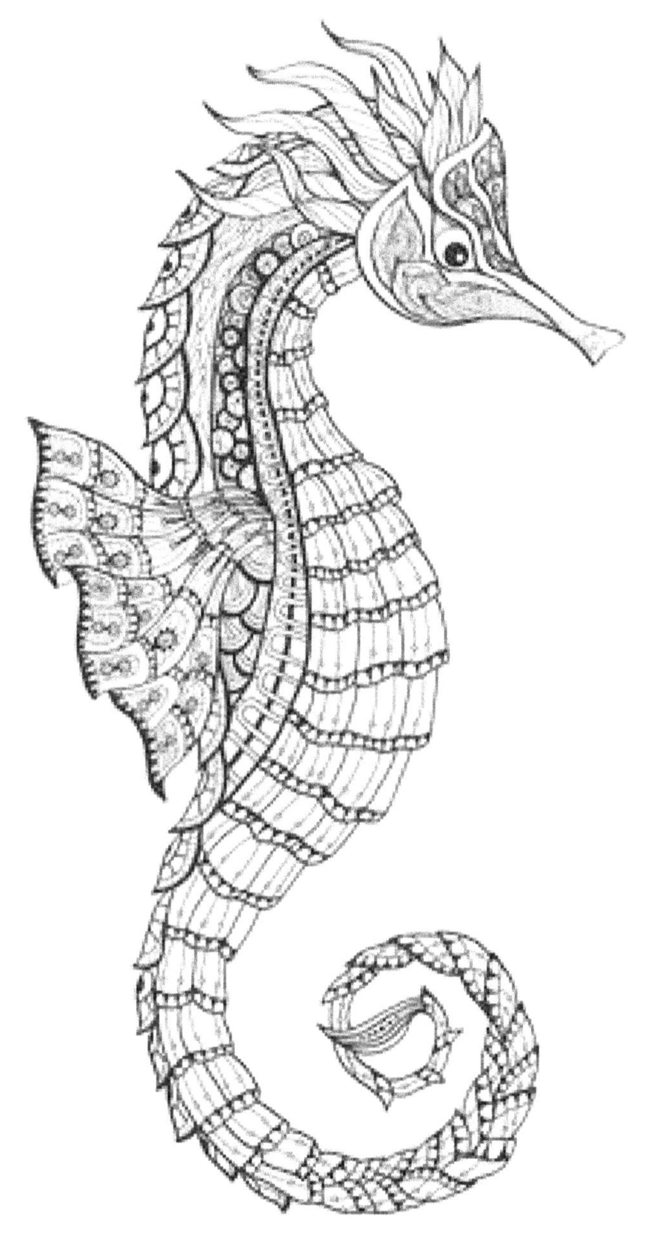

DRAW/SKETCH

ANIMALS

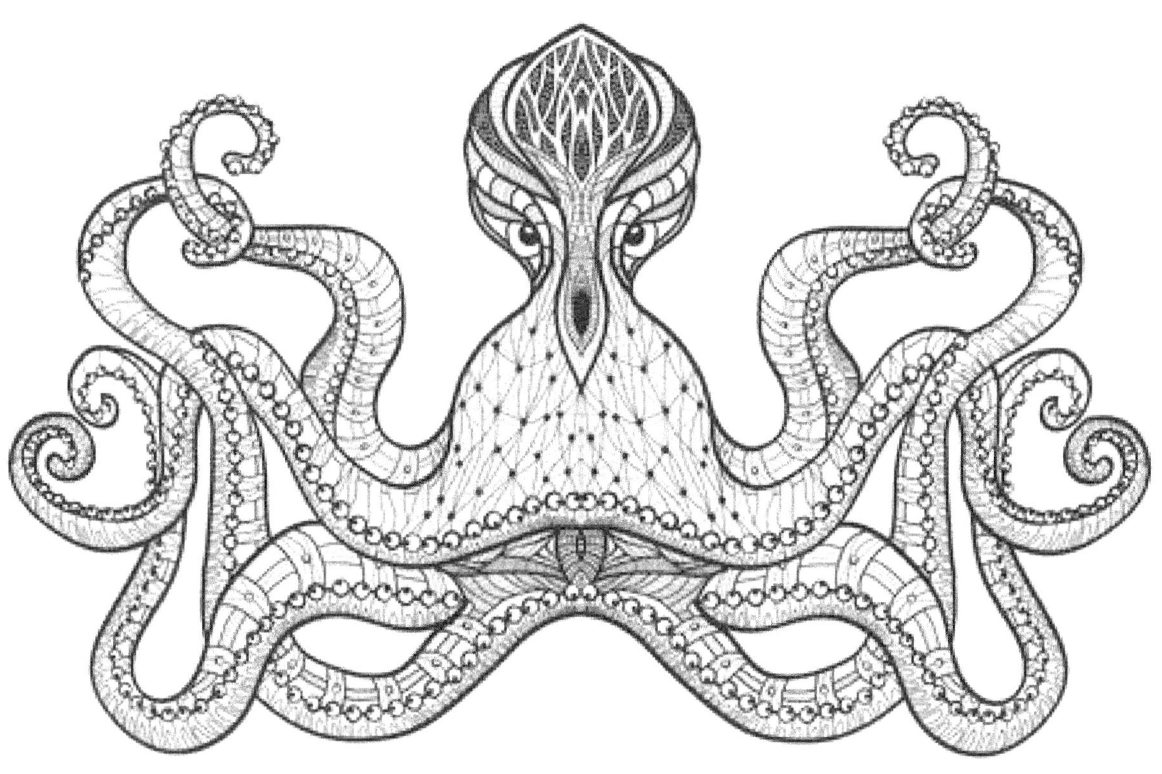

DRAW/SKETCH

ANIMALS

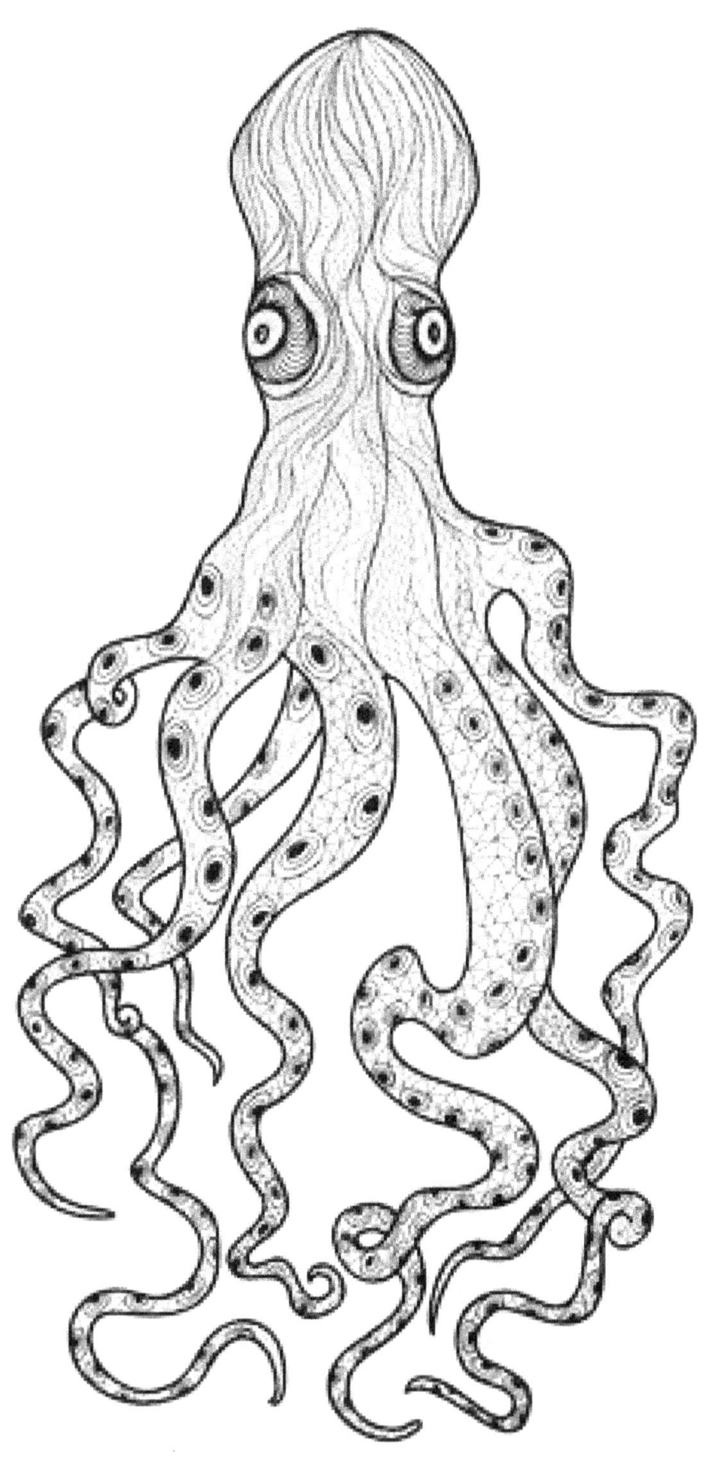

DRAW/SKETCH

SEA SHELL

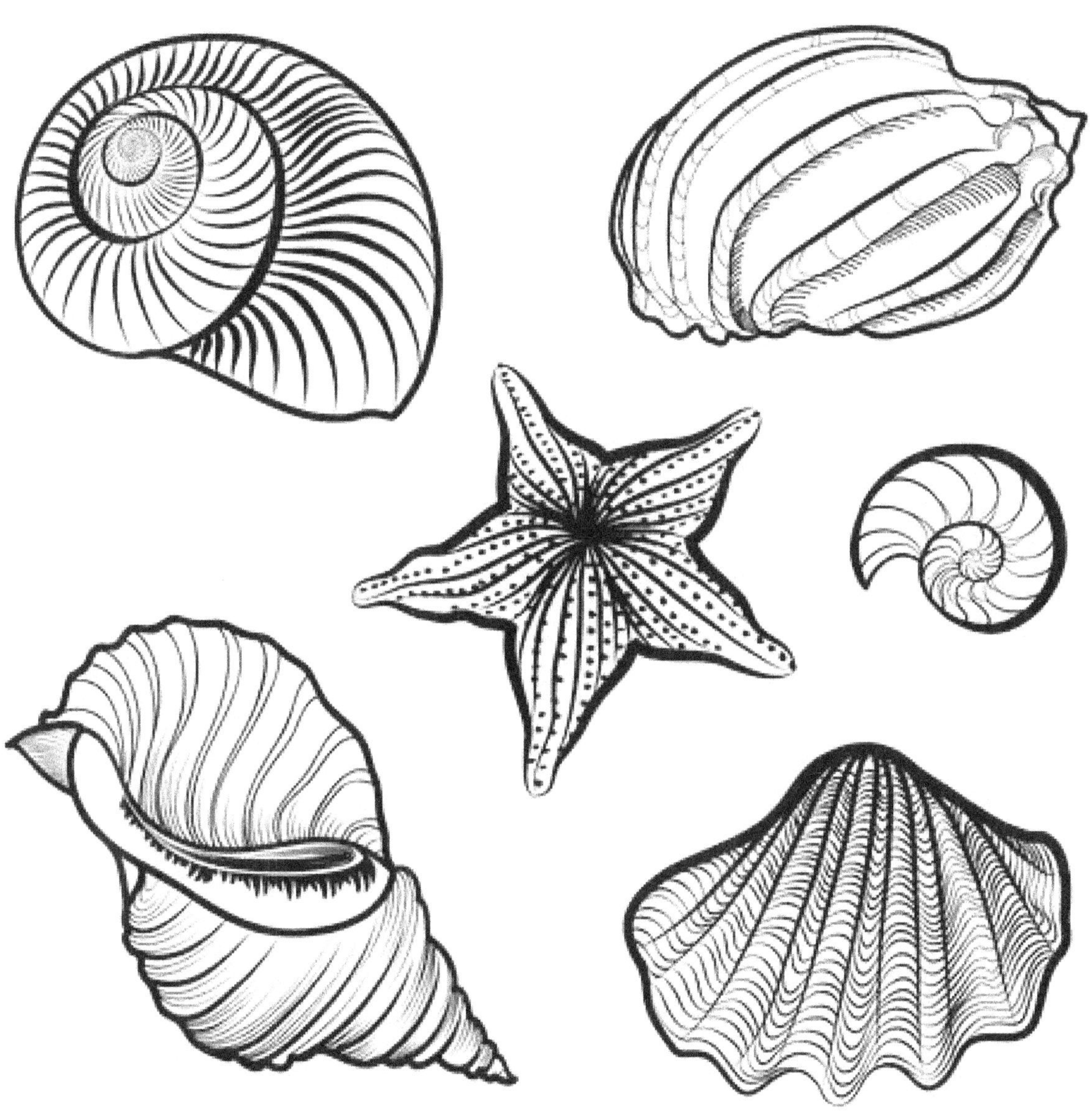

DRAW/SKETCH

SEA SHELL

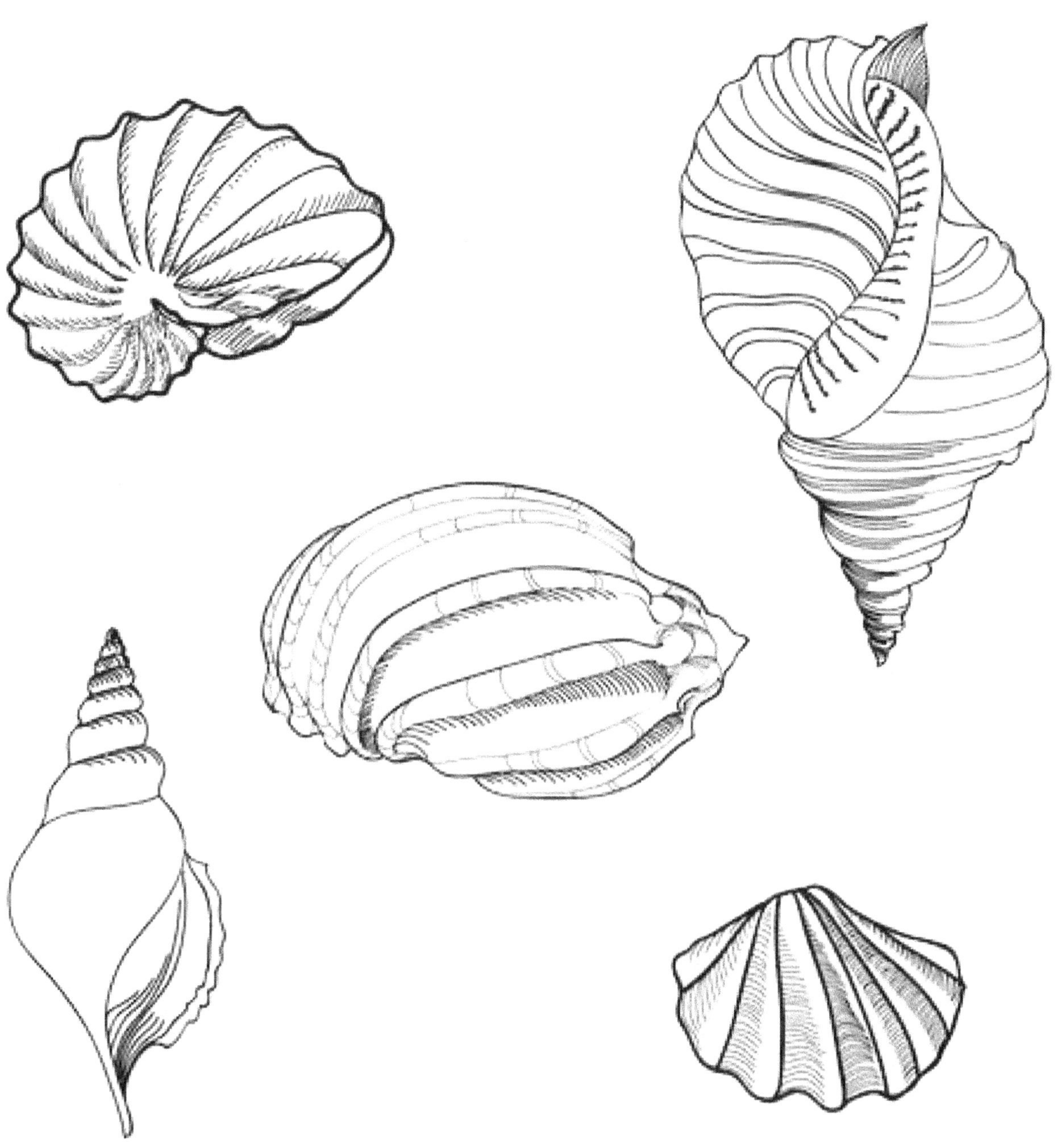

DRAW/SKETCH

ANIMALS

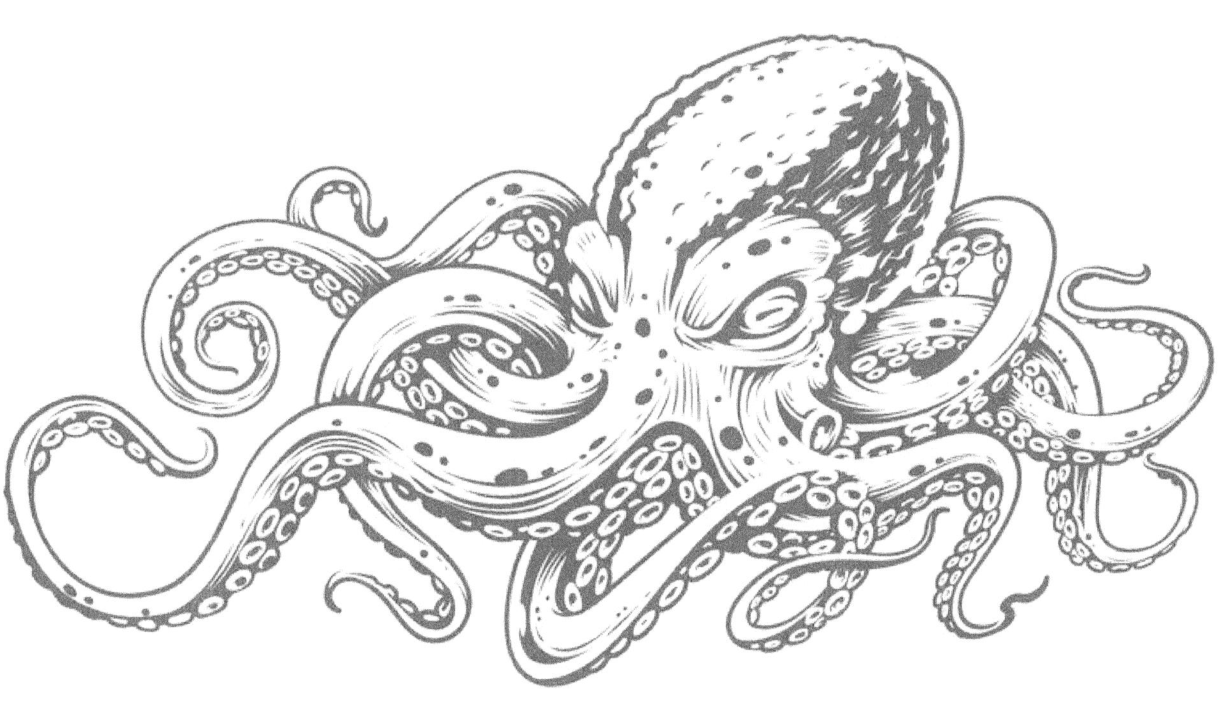

DRAW/SKETCH

ANIMALS

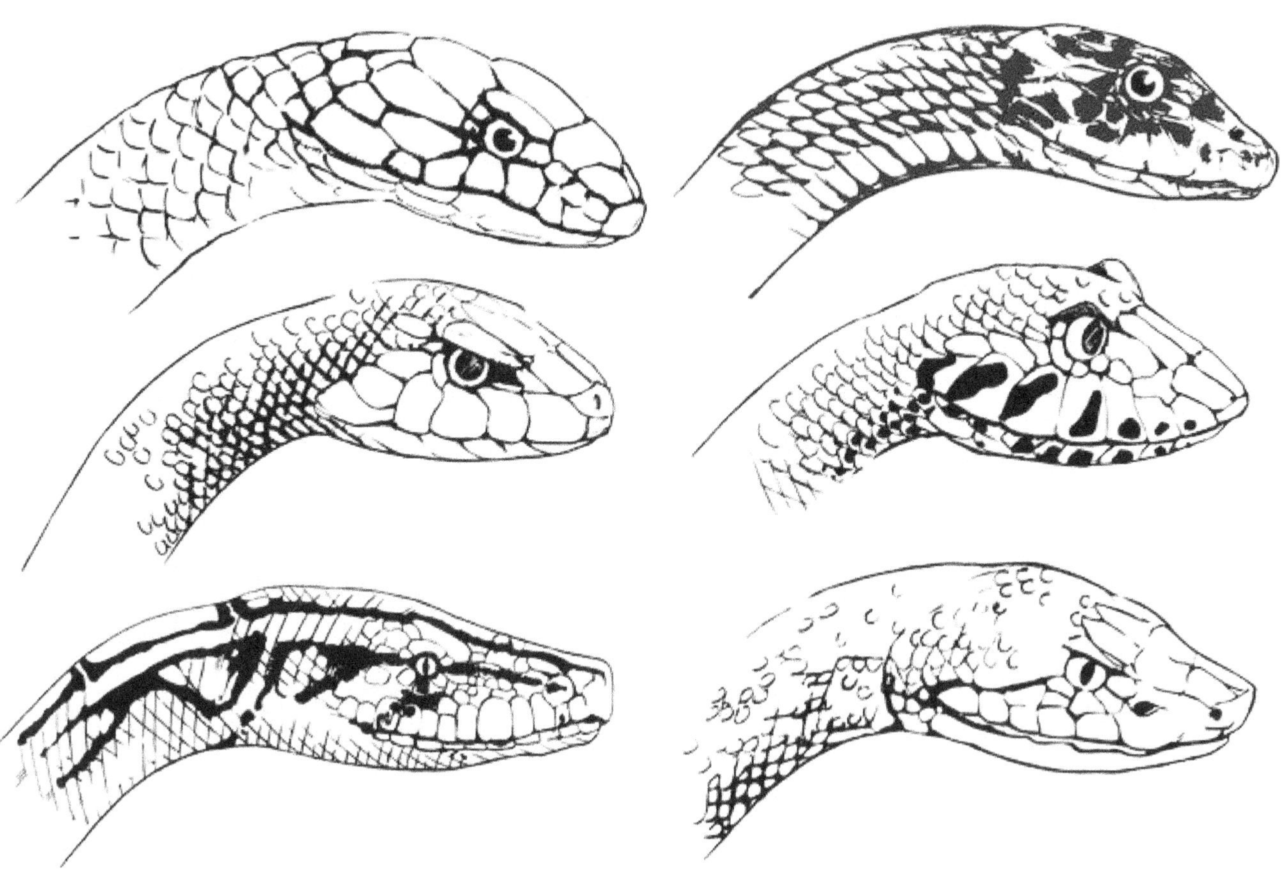

DRAW/SKETCH

ANIMALS

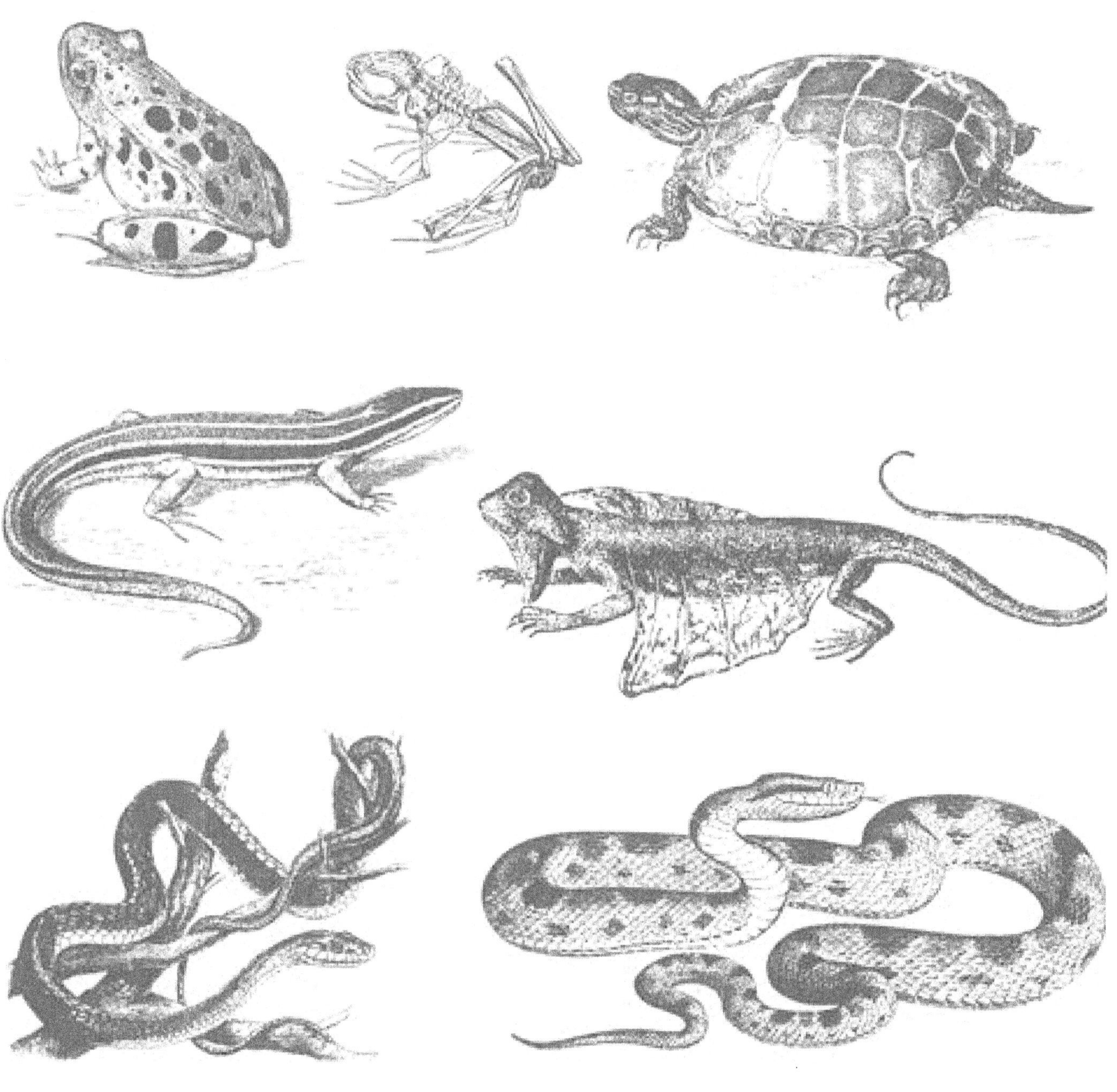

DRAW/SKETCH

MUSHROOM

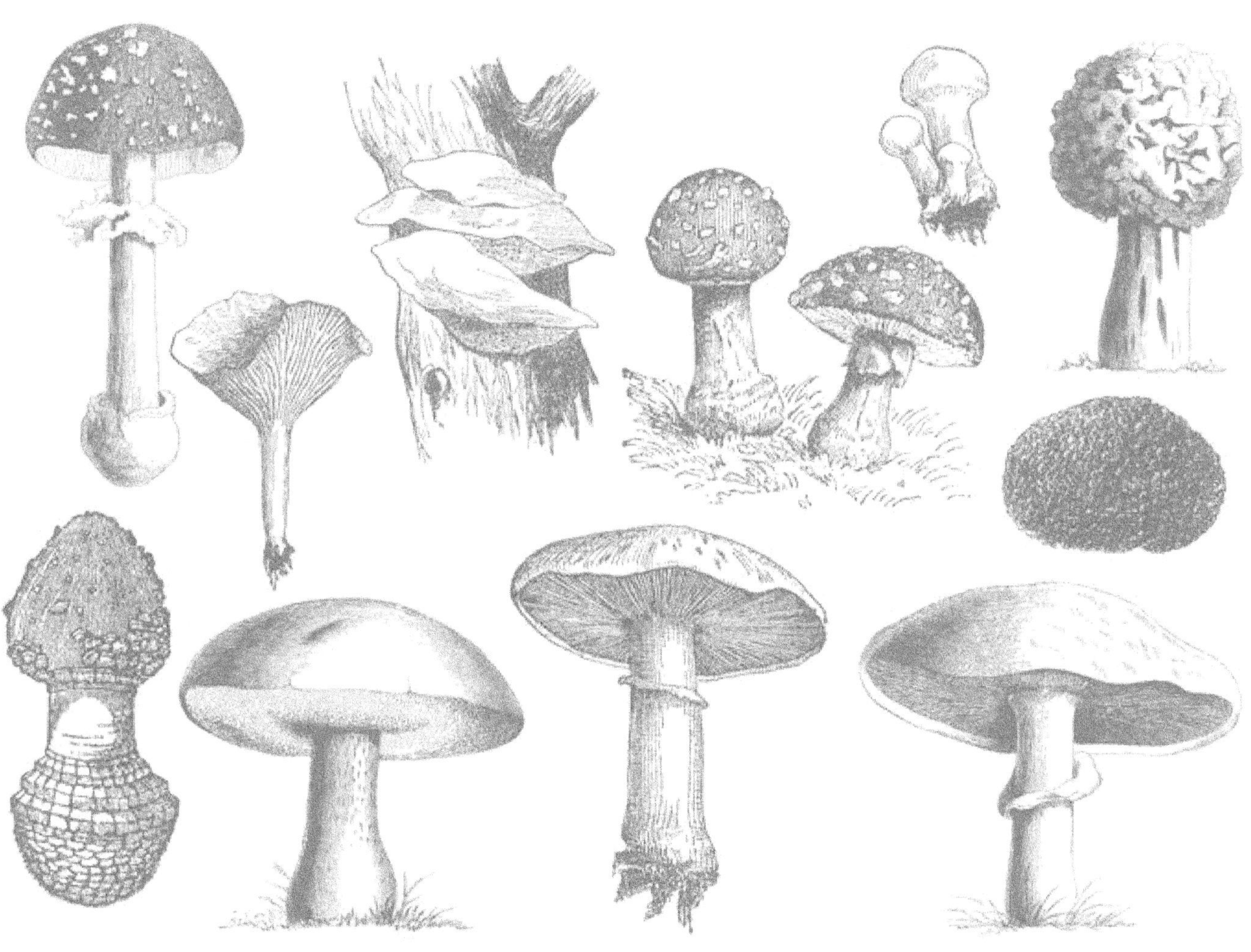

DRAW/SKETCH

FOOD

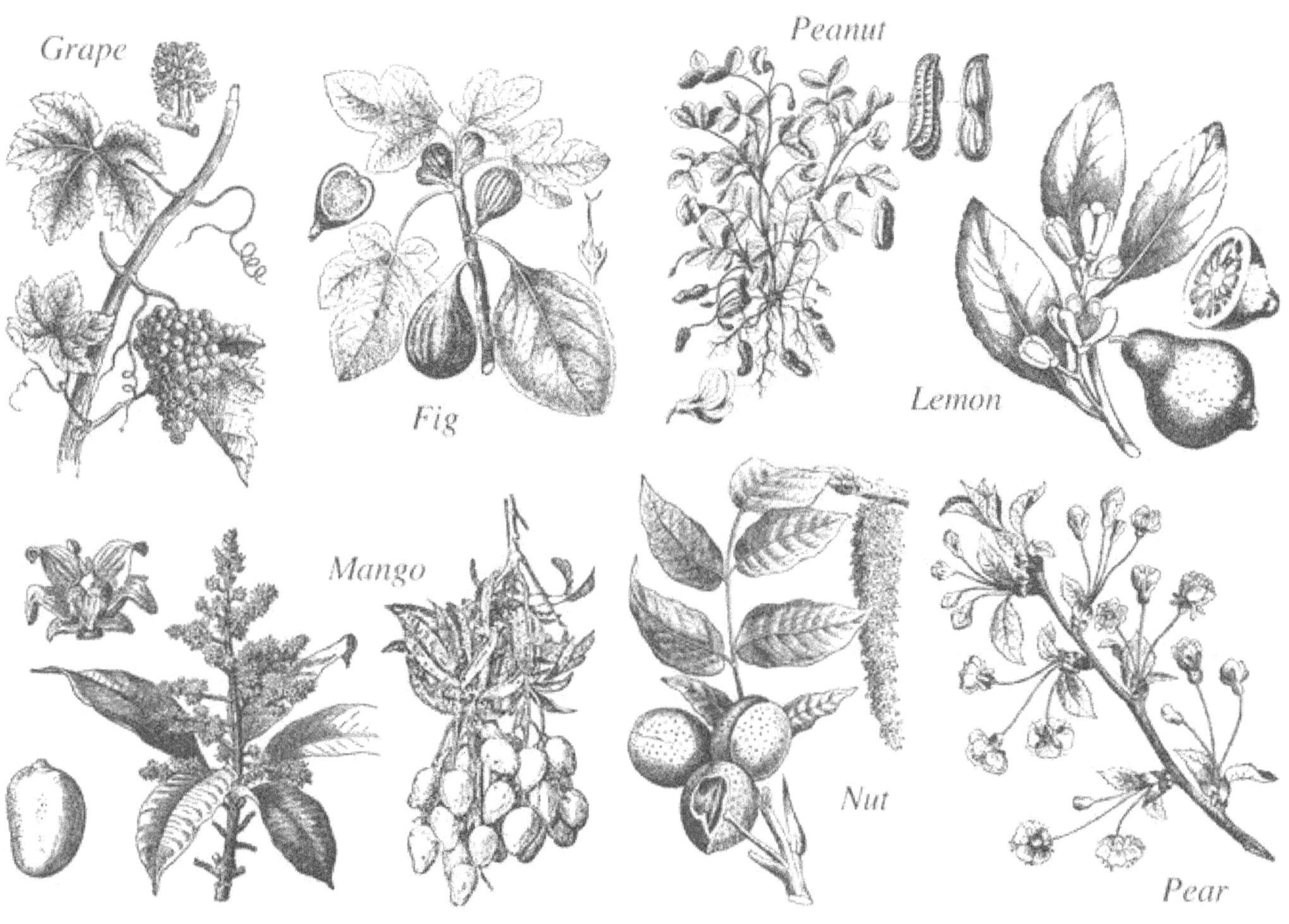

DRAW/SKETCH

FOOD

grapes
raisins
cloudberry
blackberry
strawberry
dewberry
cranberry
raspberry
huckleberry

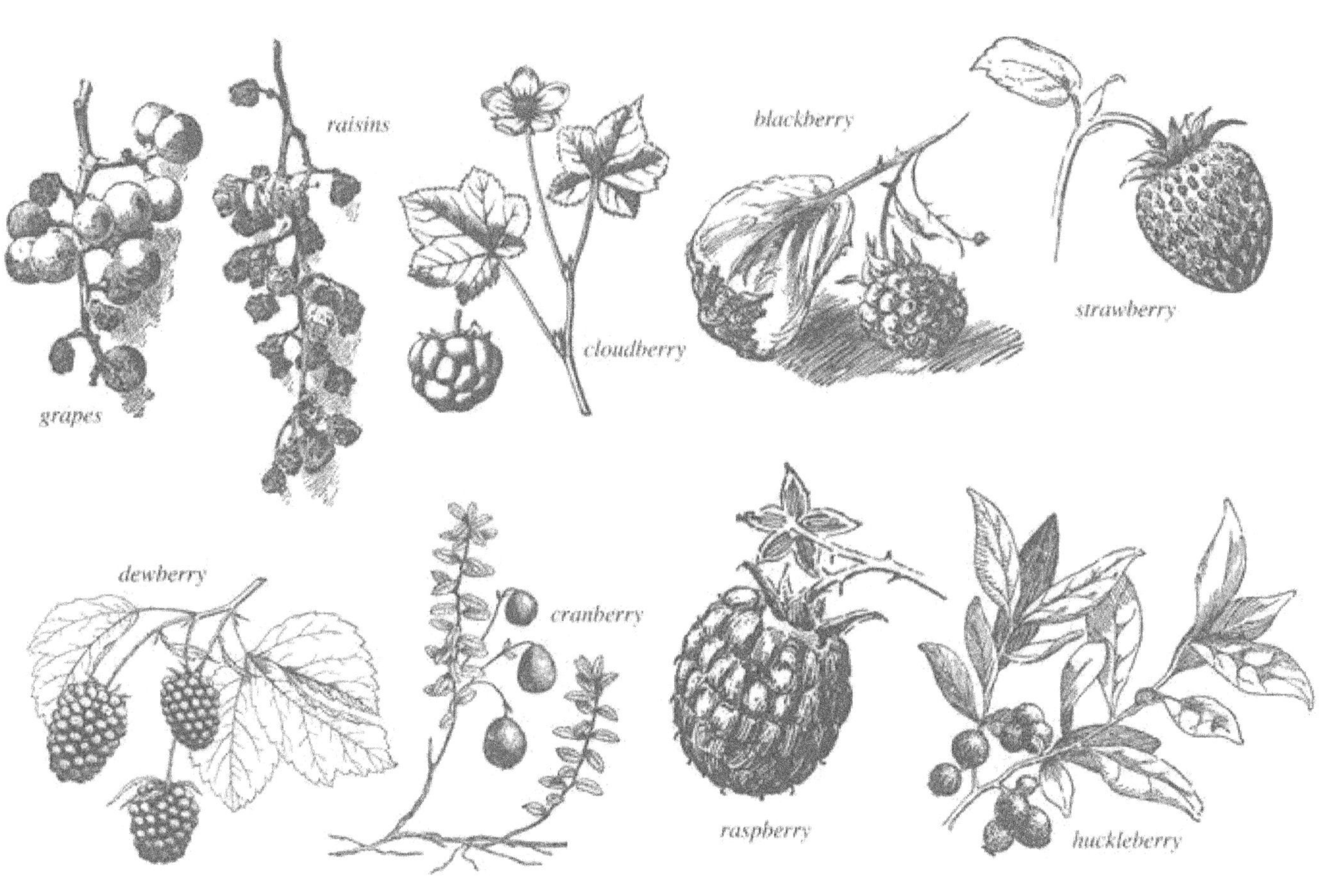

DRAW/SKETCH

ITEMS

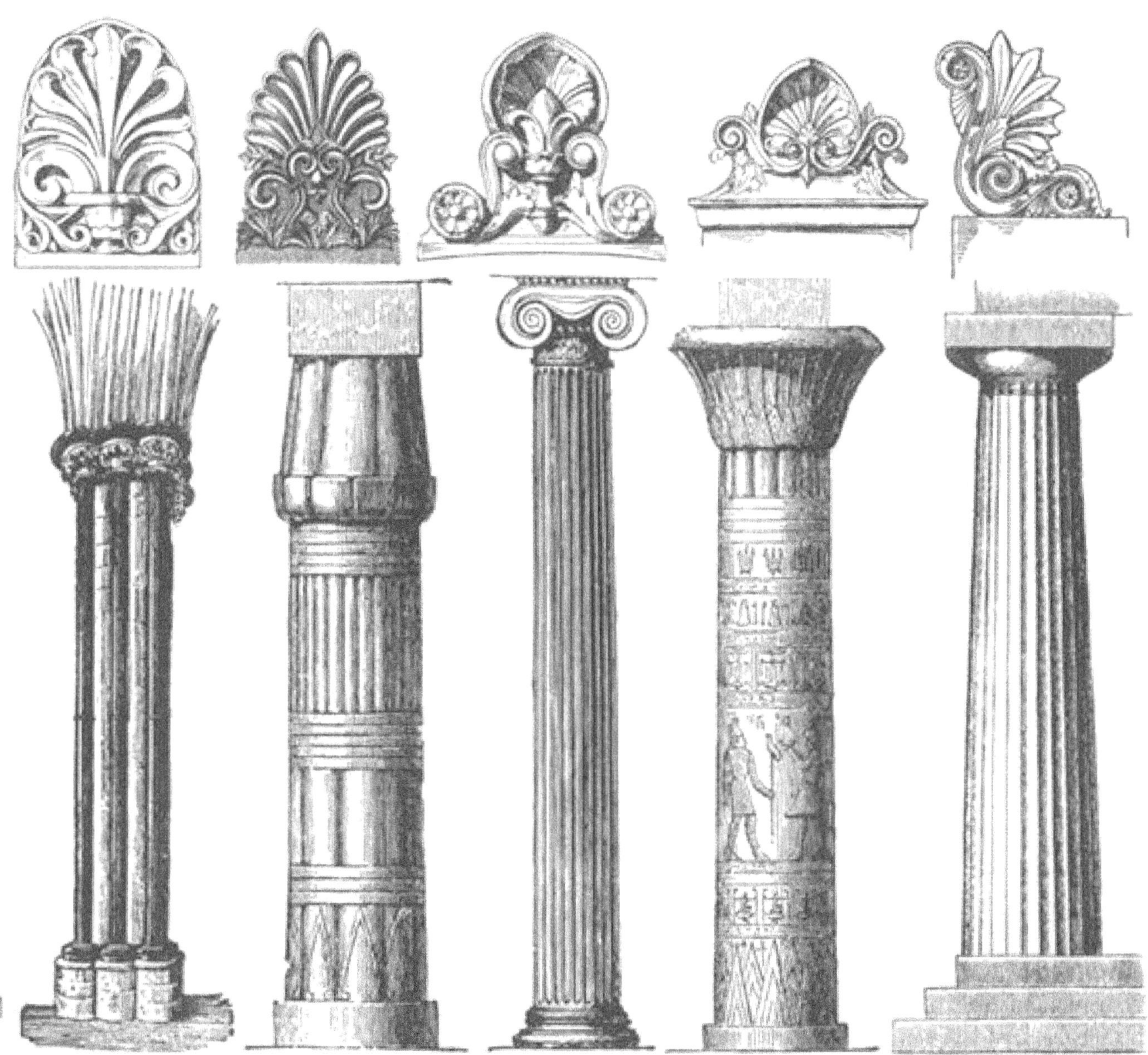

DRAW/SKETCH

JUDGEMENT

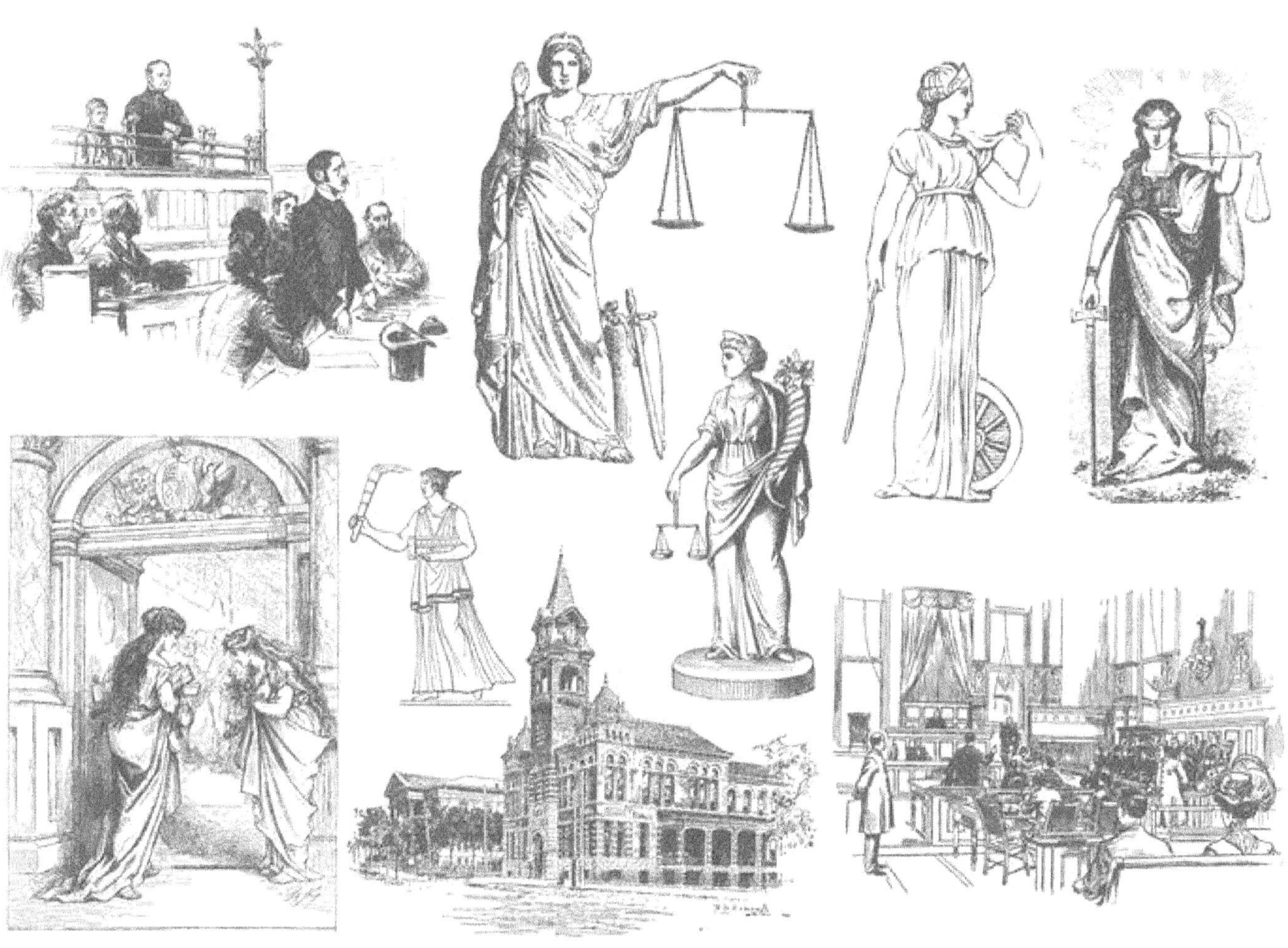

DRAW/SKETCH

PEOPLE

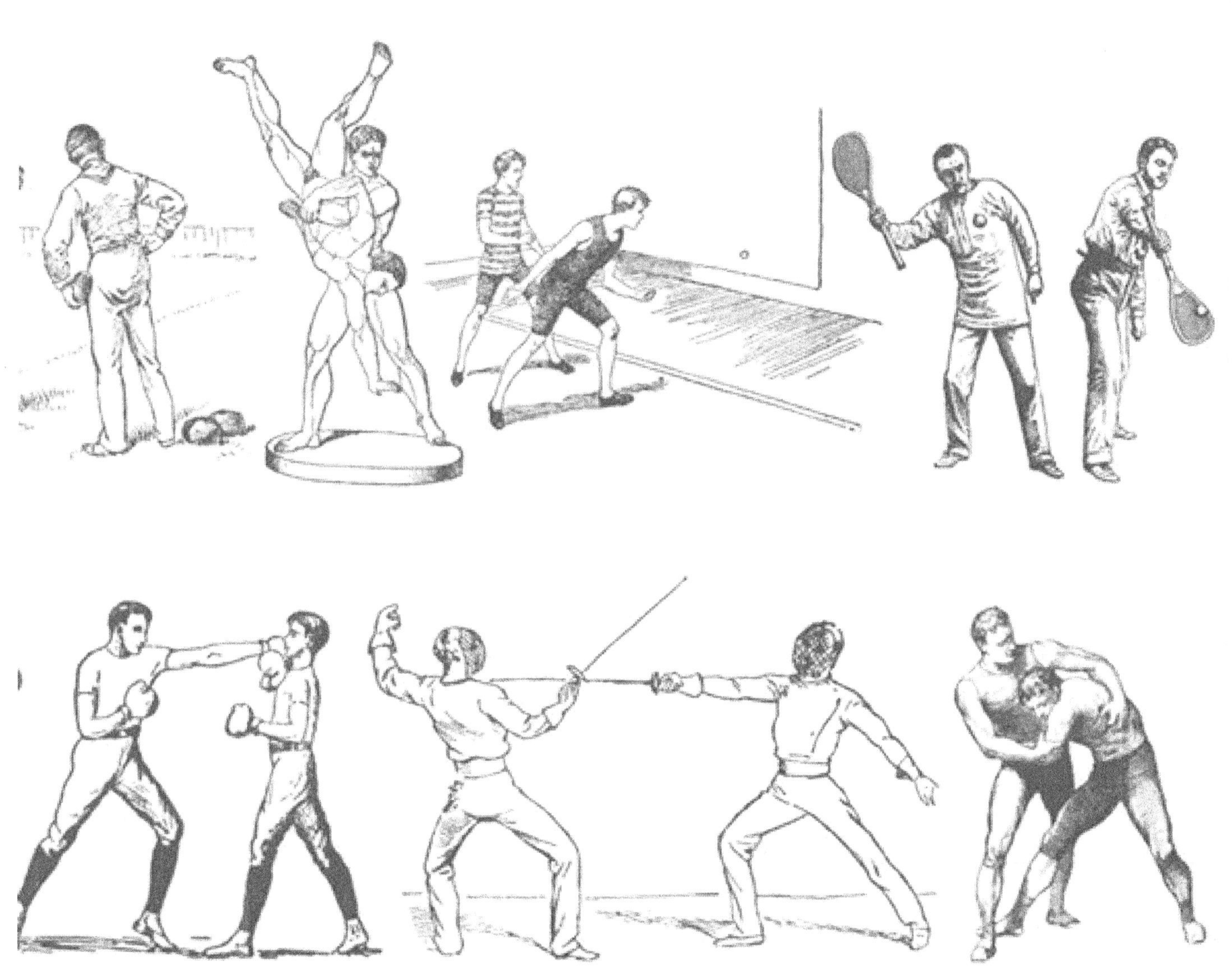

DRAW/SKETCH

ITEMS

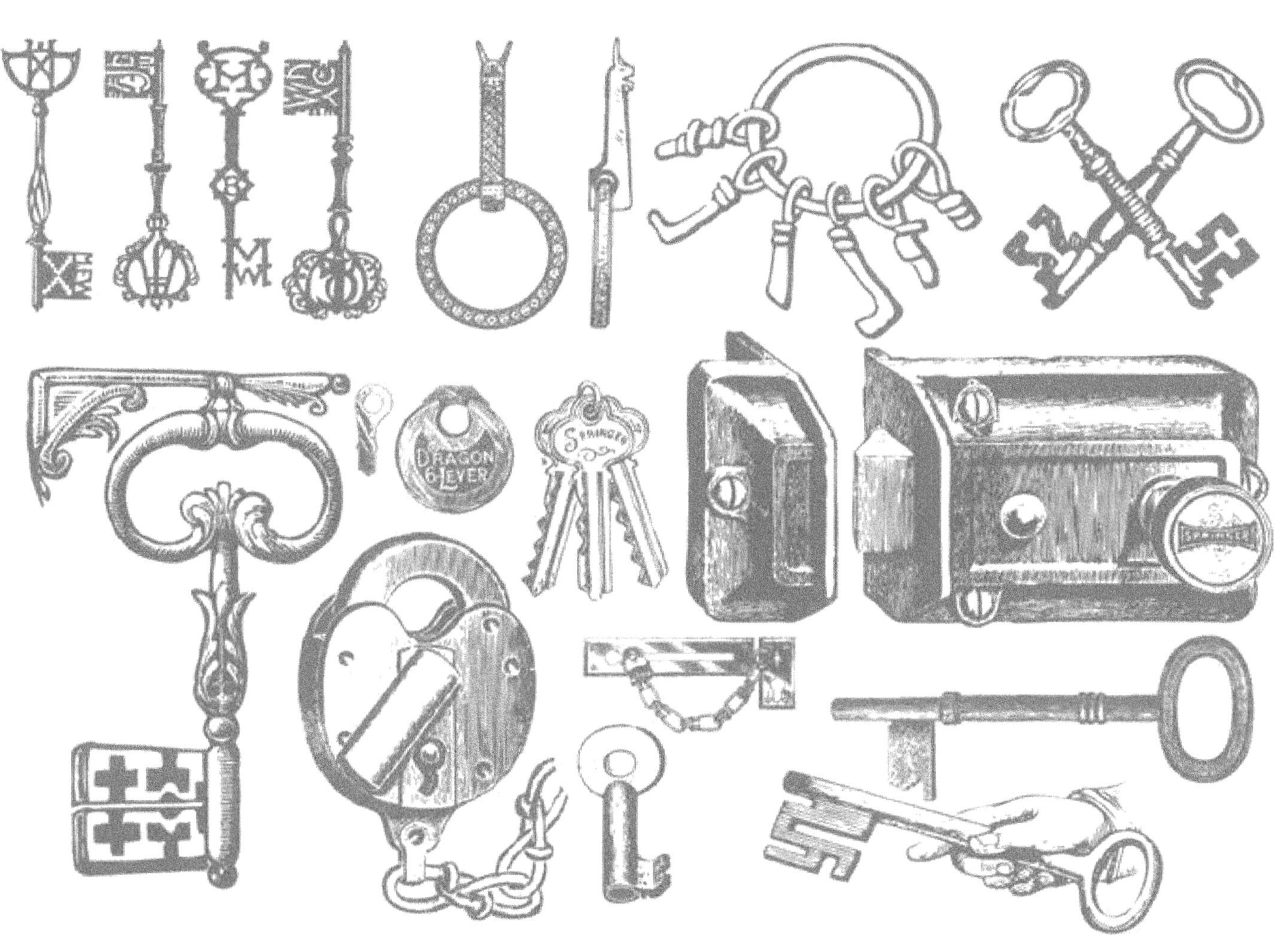

DRAW/SKETCH

PEOPLE

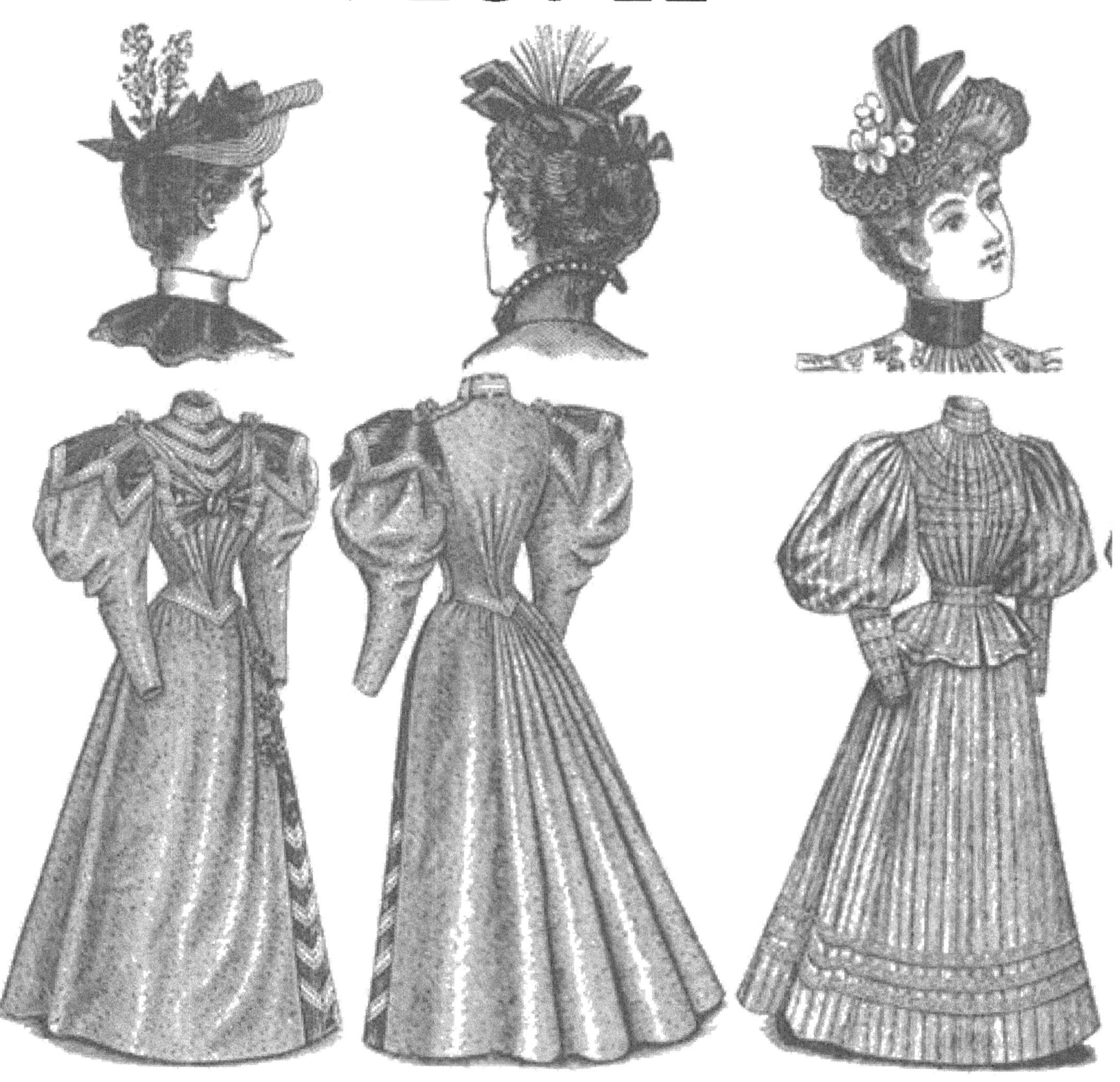

DRAW/SKETCH

HATS/PEOPLE

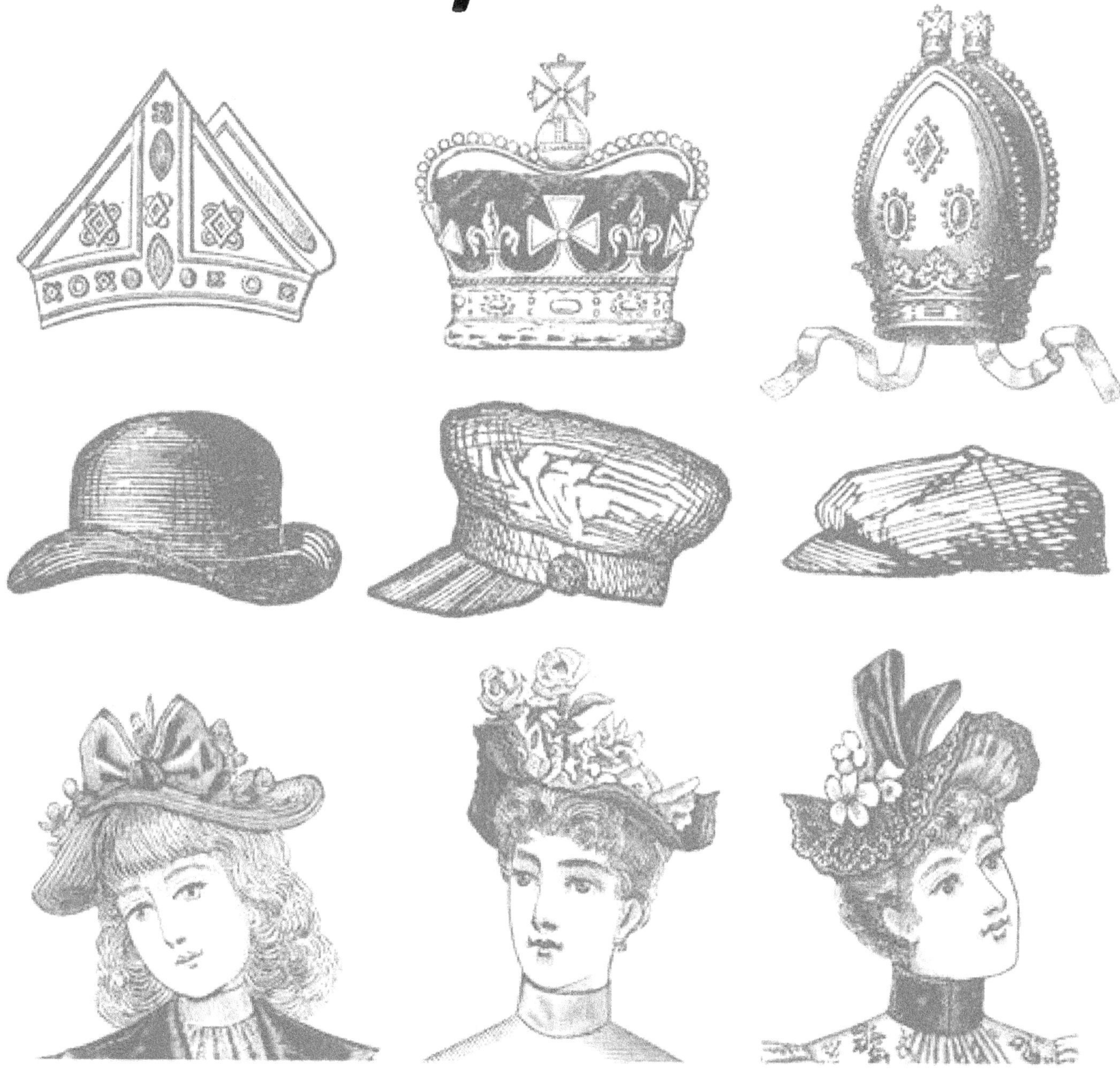

DRAW/SKETCH

CAMERA

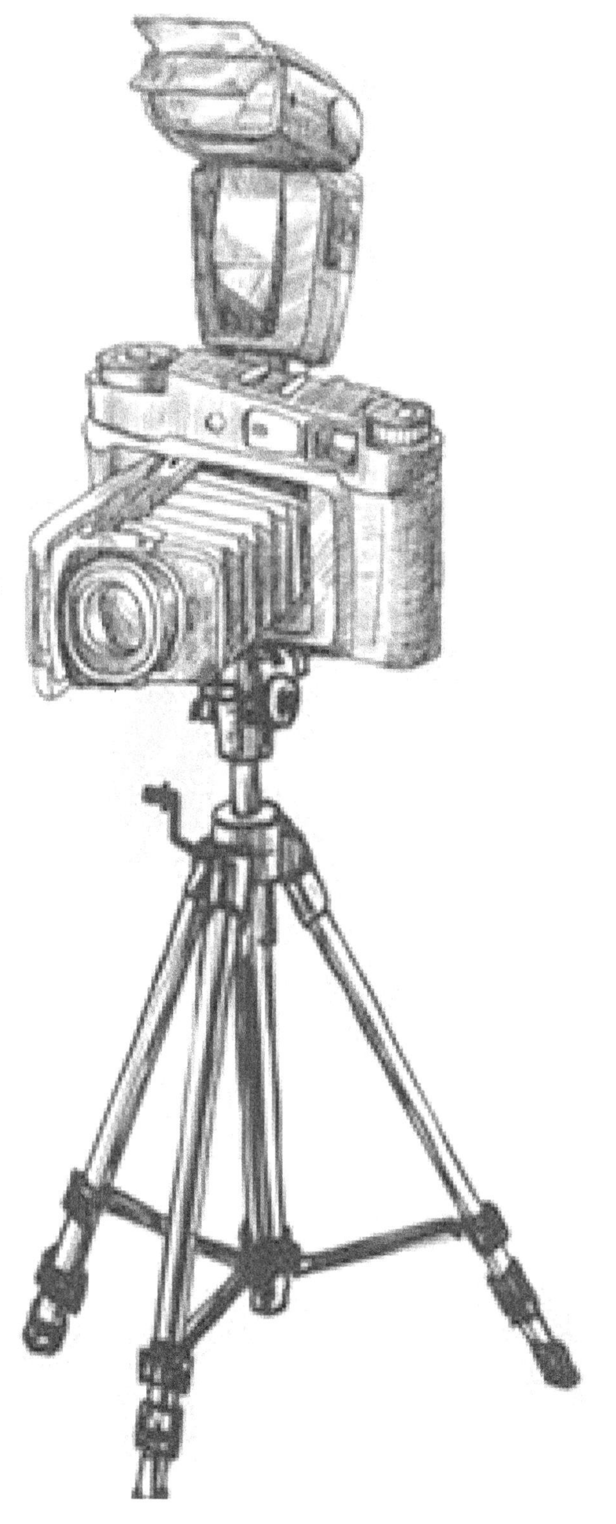

DRAW/SKETCH

COMPASS

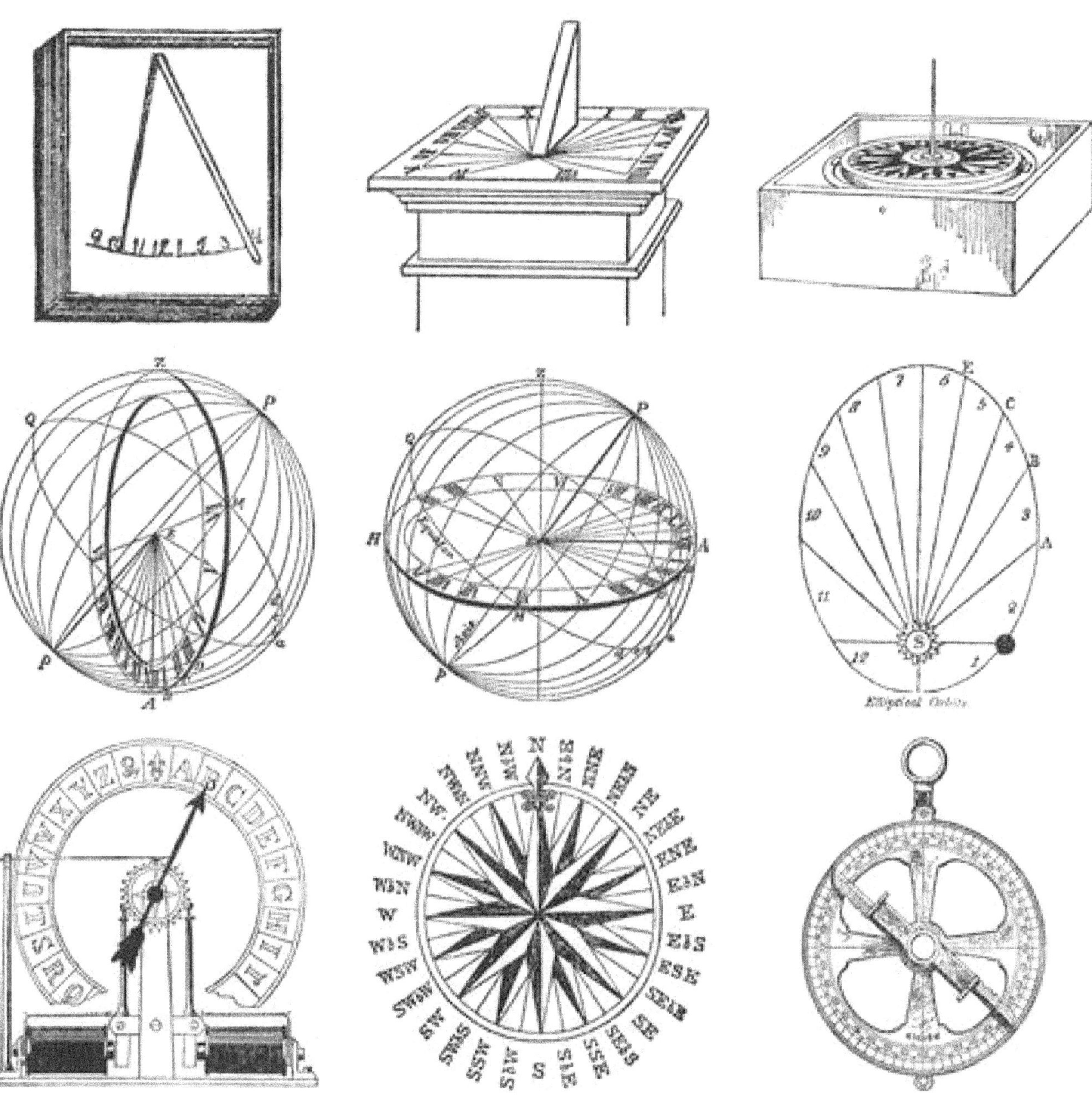

DRAW/SKETCH

TREE

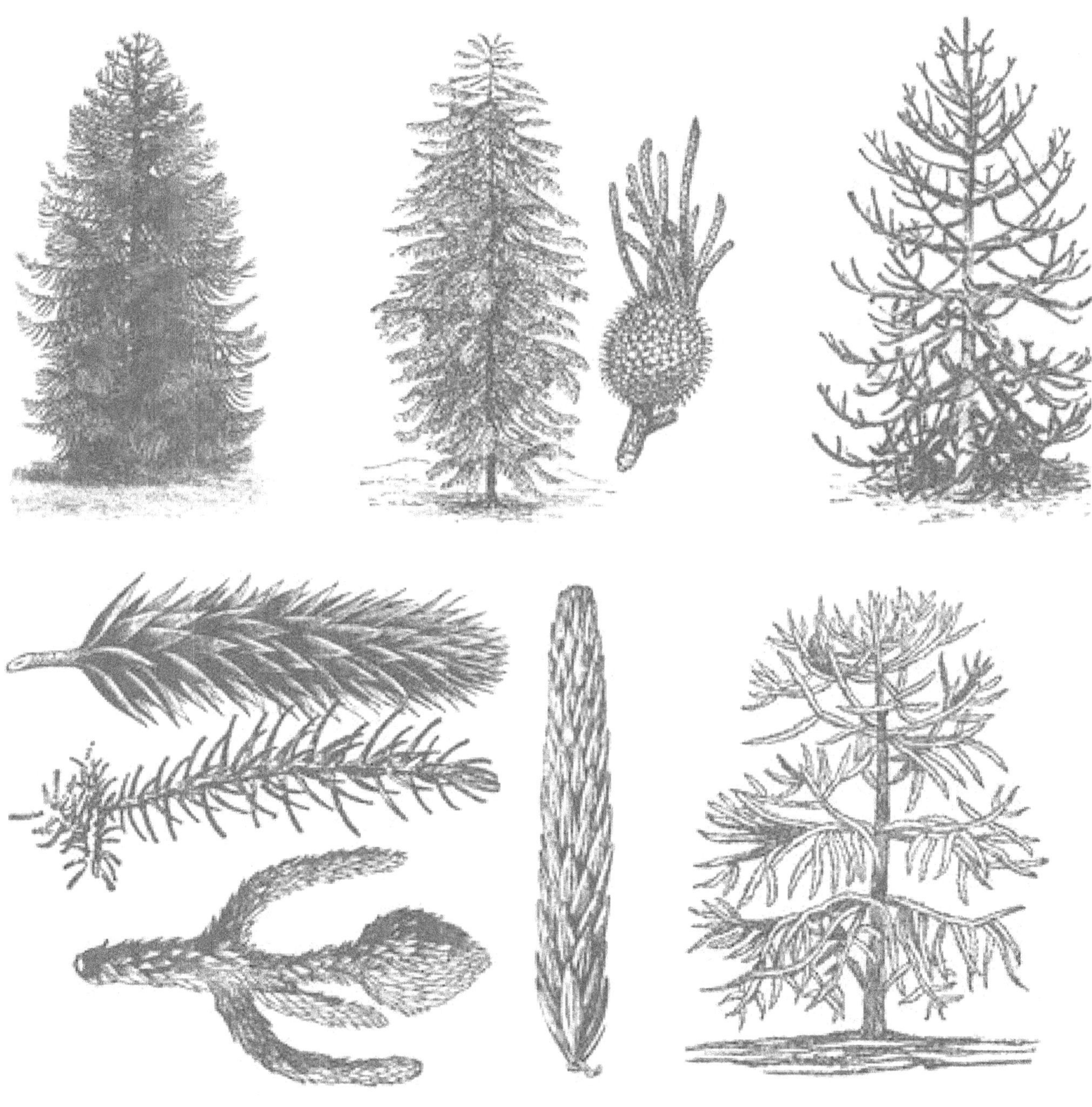

DRAW/SKETCH

ITEMS

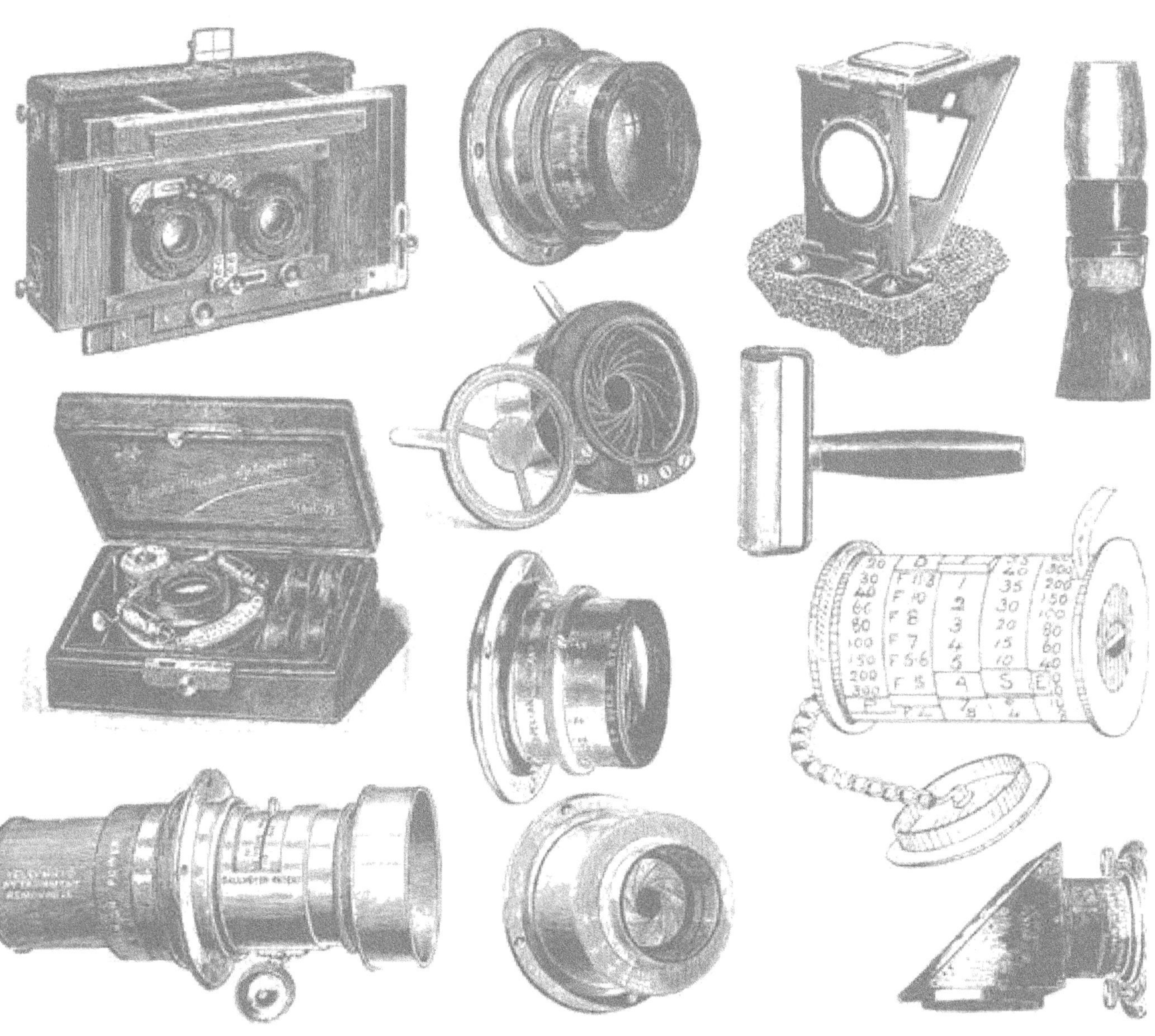

DRAW/SKETCH

FOOD

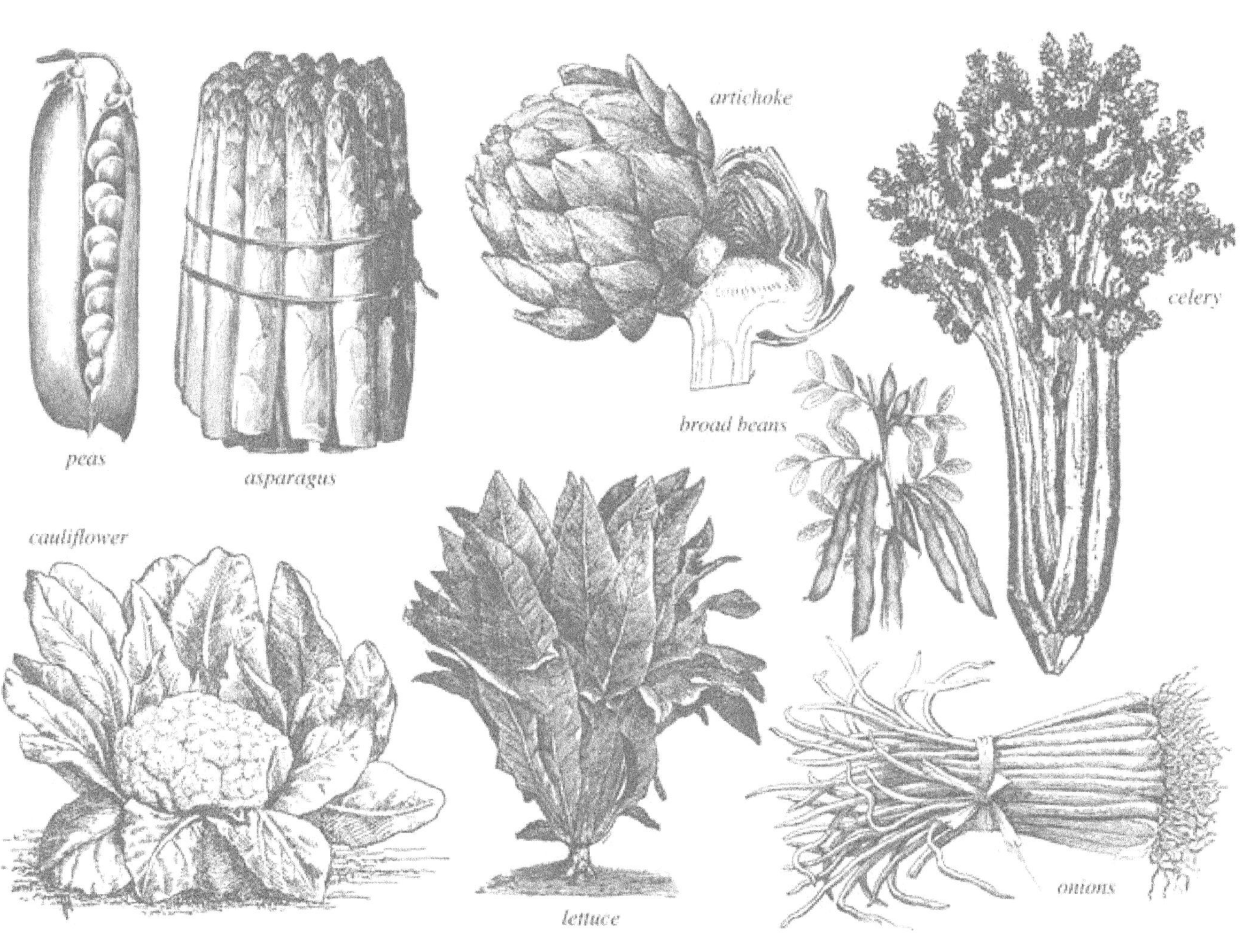

peas

asparagus

artichoke

celery

broad beans

cauliflower

lettuce

onions

DRAW/SKETCH

ANIMALS

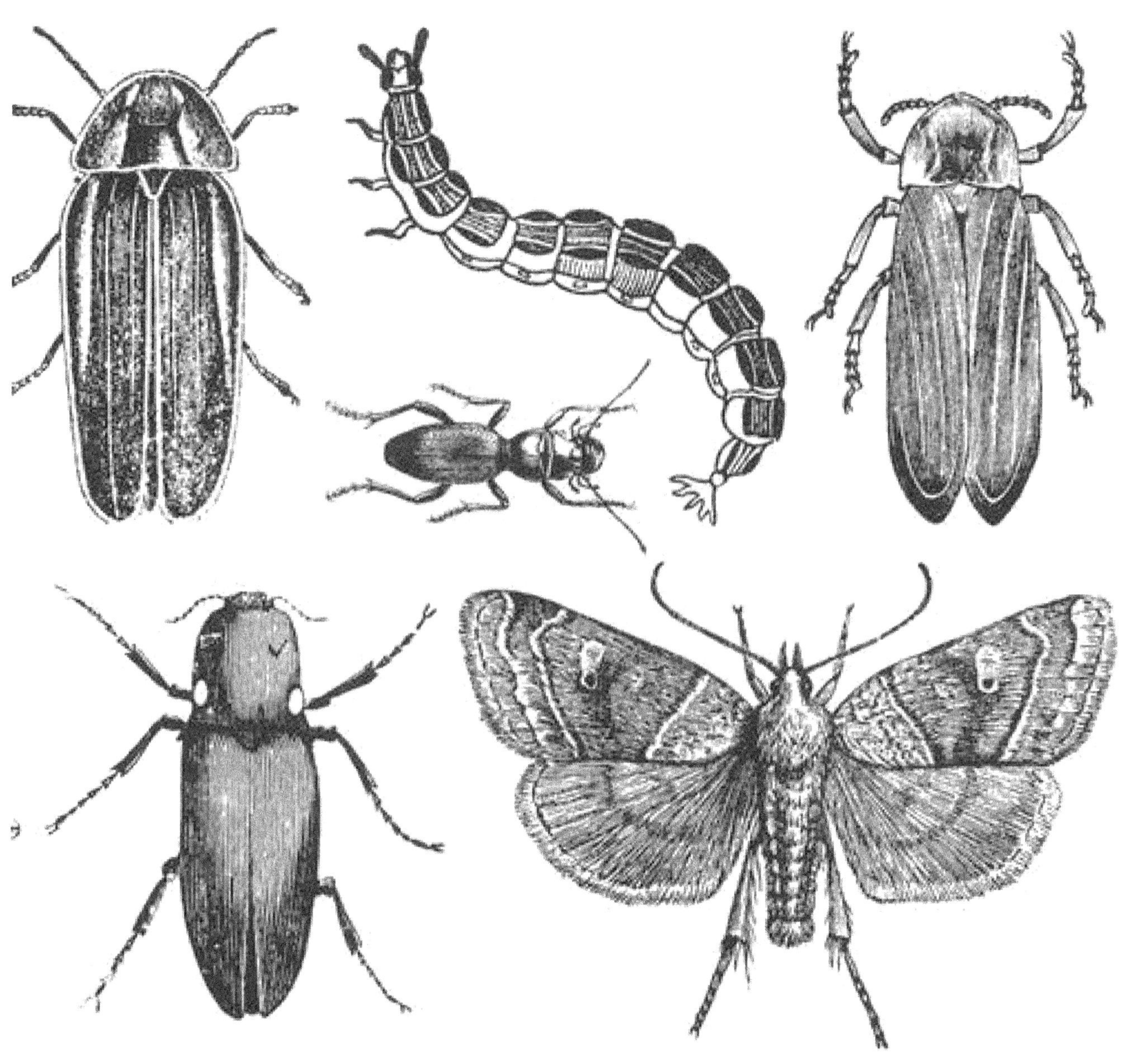

DRAW/SKETCH

FOOD

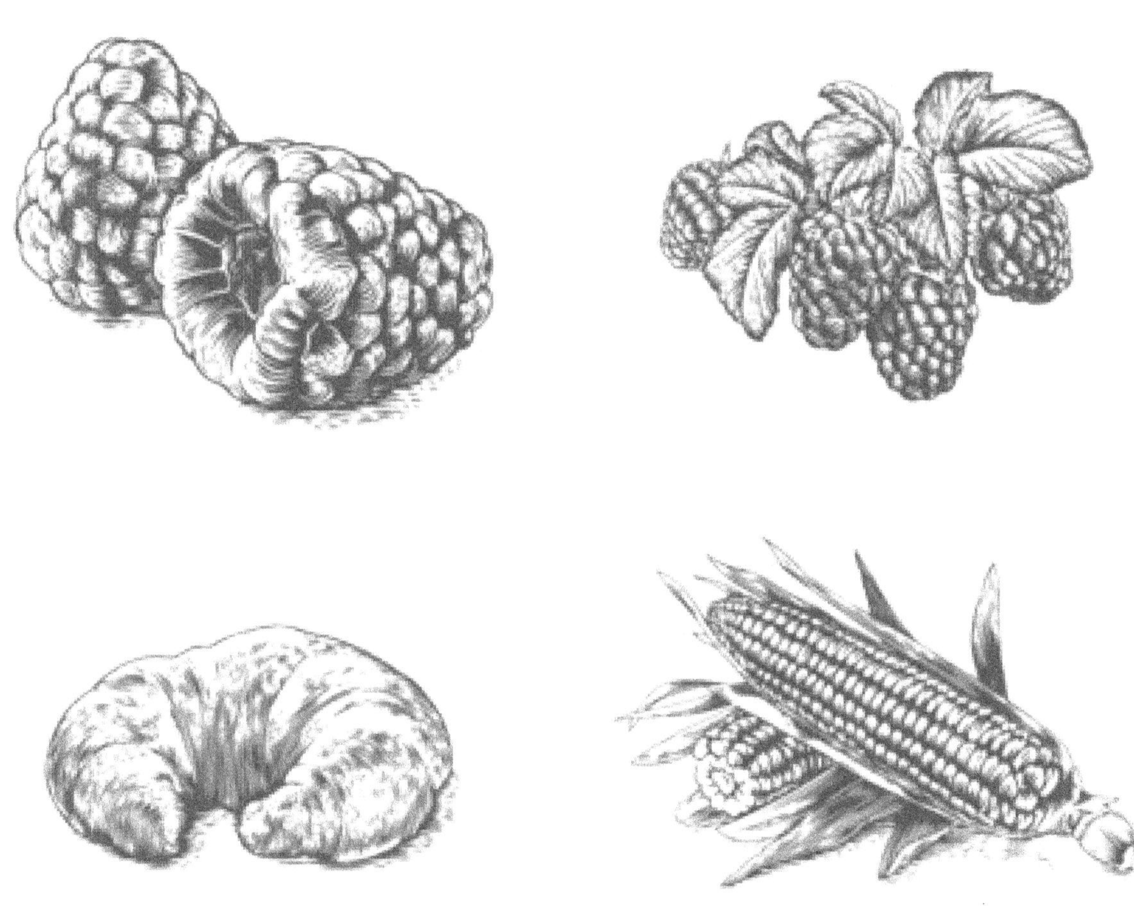

DRAW/SKETCH

ITEMS

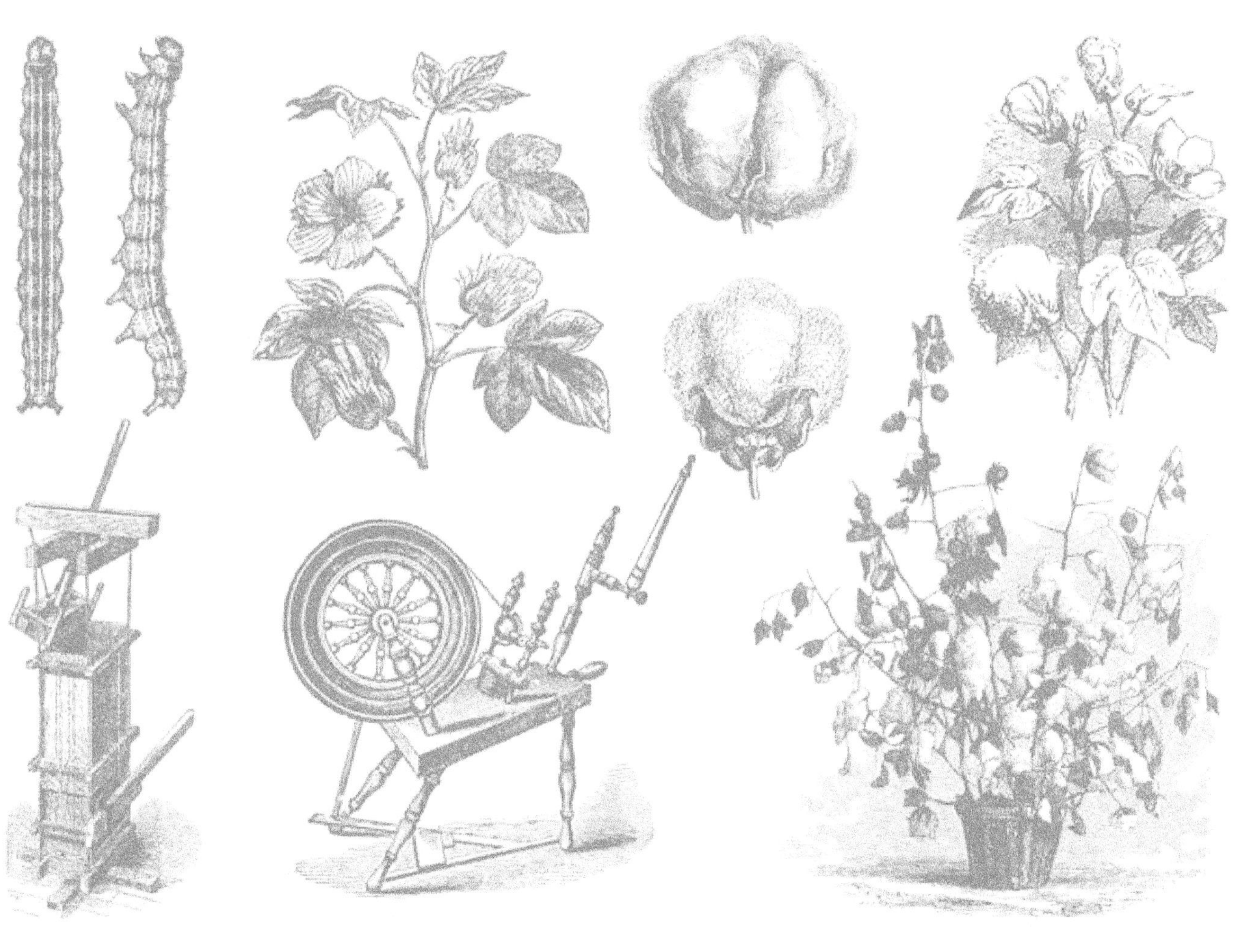

DRAW/SKETCH

MUSIC

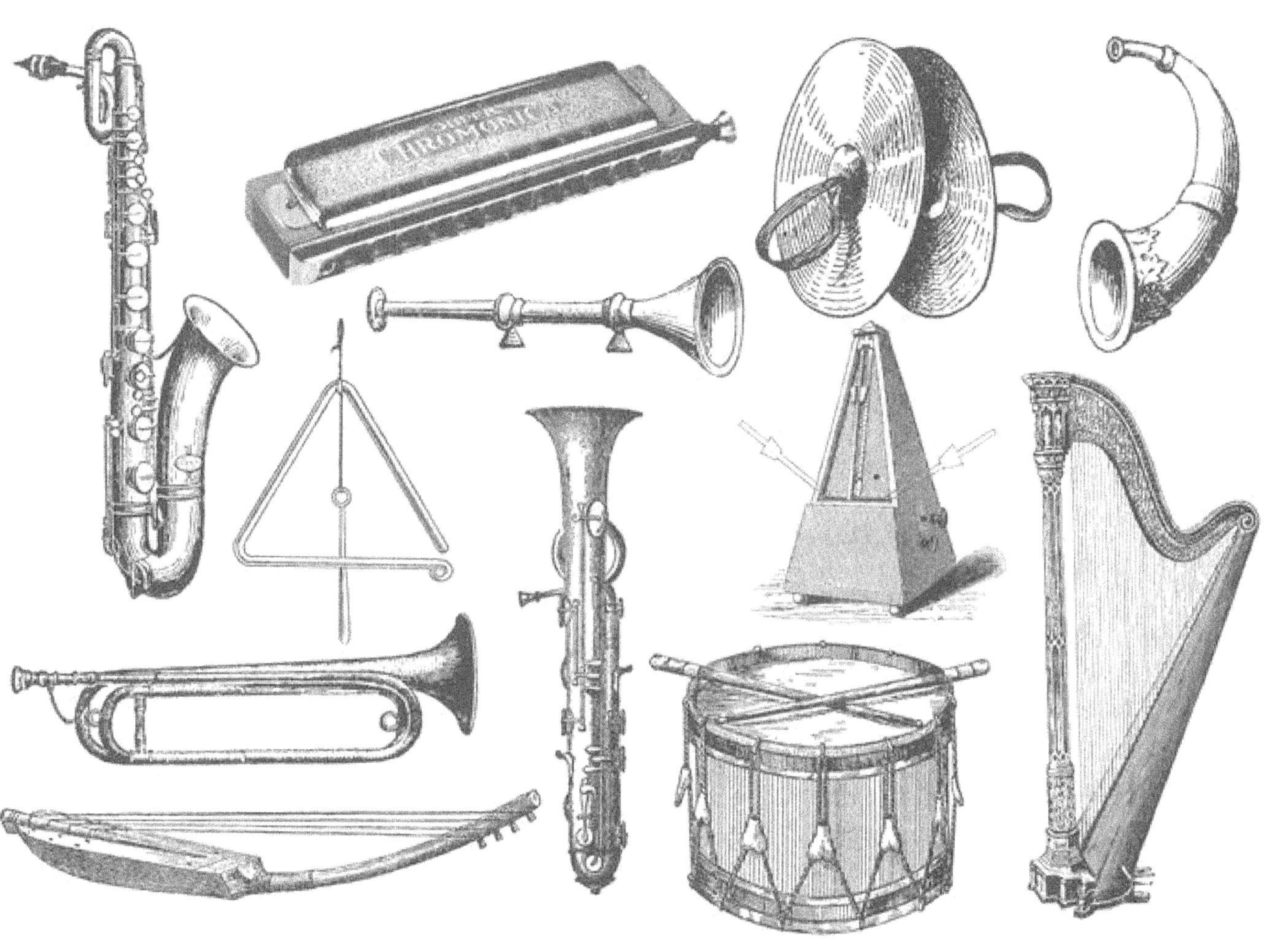

DRAW/SKETCH

PEN

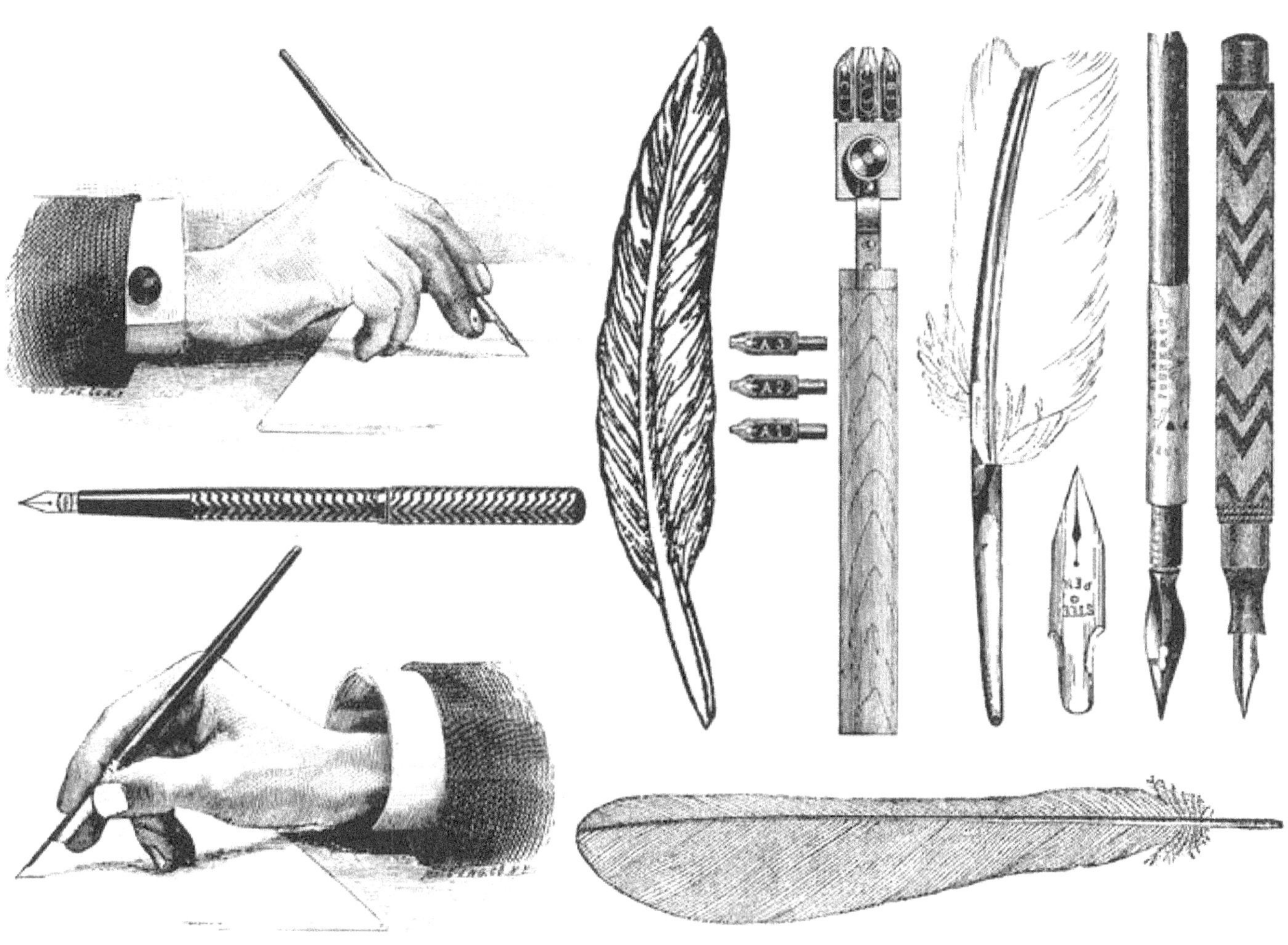

DRAW/SKETCH

ANIMALS

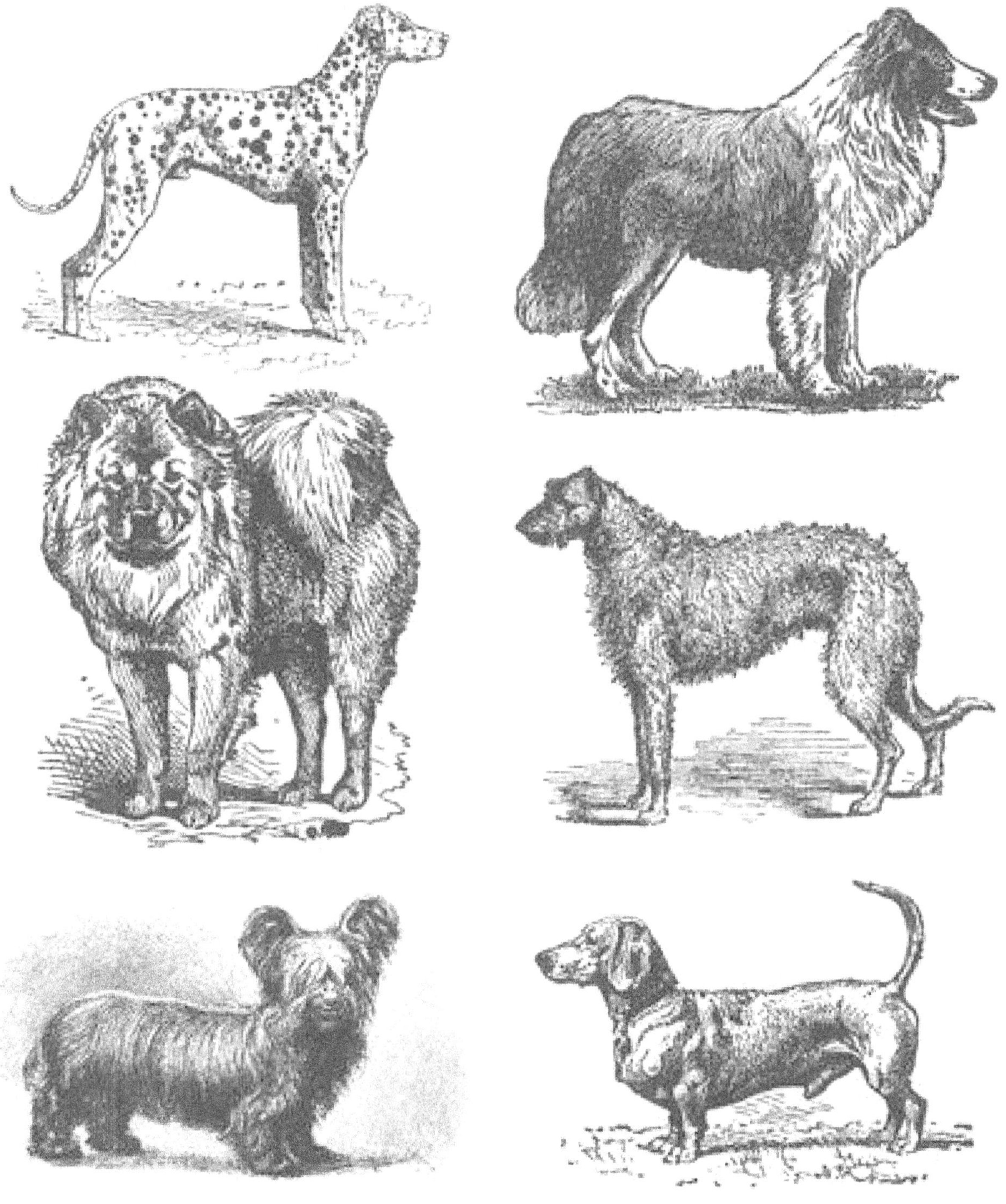

DRAW/SKETCH

SEW

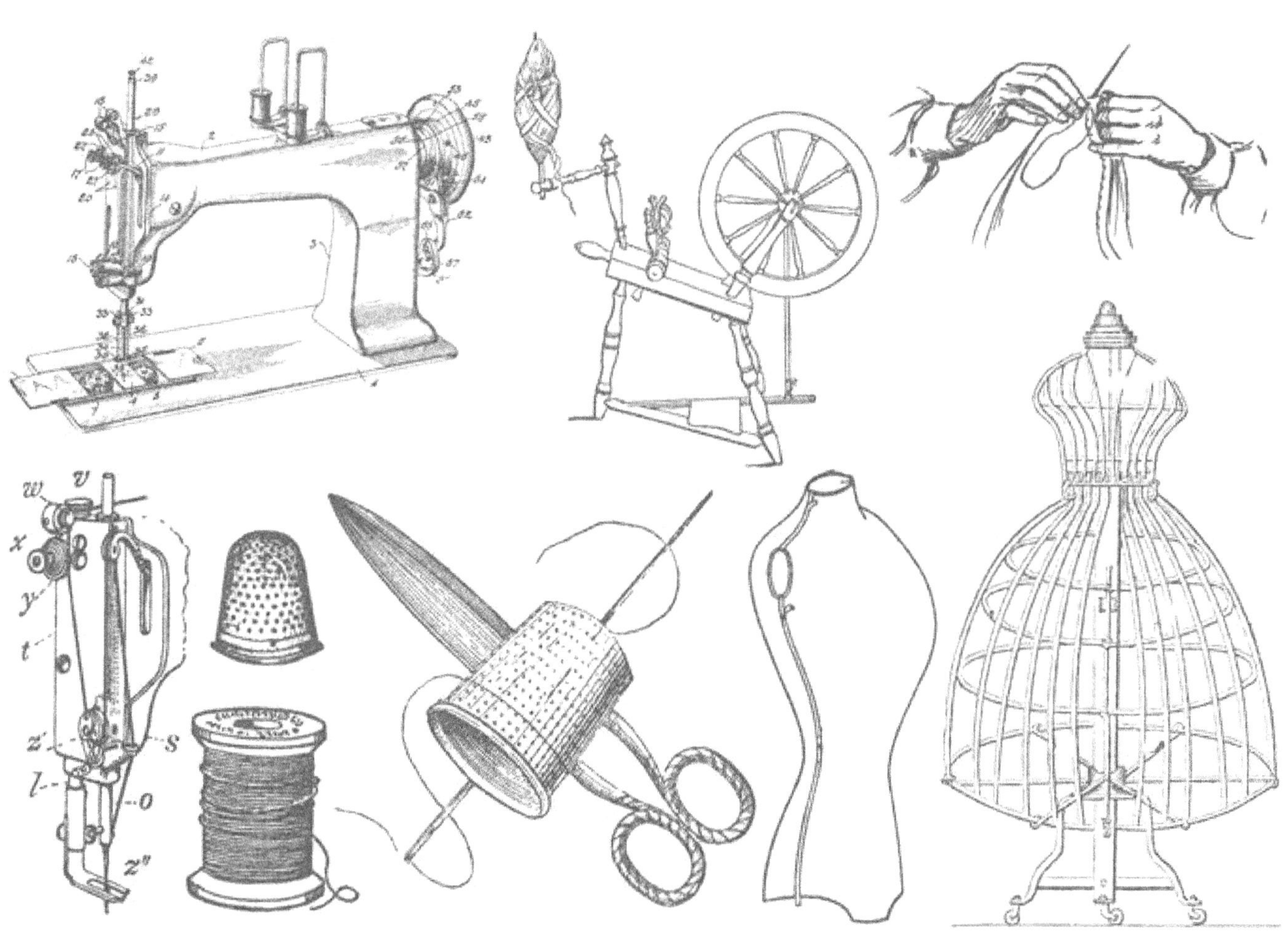

DRAW/SKETCH

ANIMALS

White Throated
Sapajou
Colobus Monkey
Sloth
Lemur
Aye Aye
Capuchin Monkey
Red
Ape

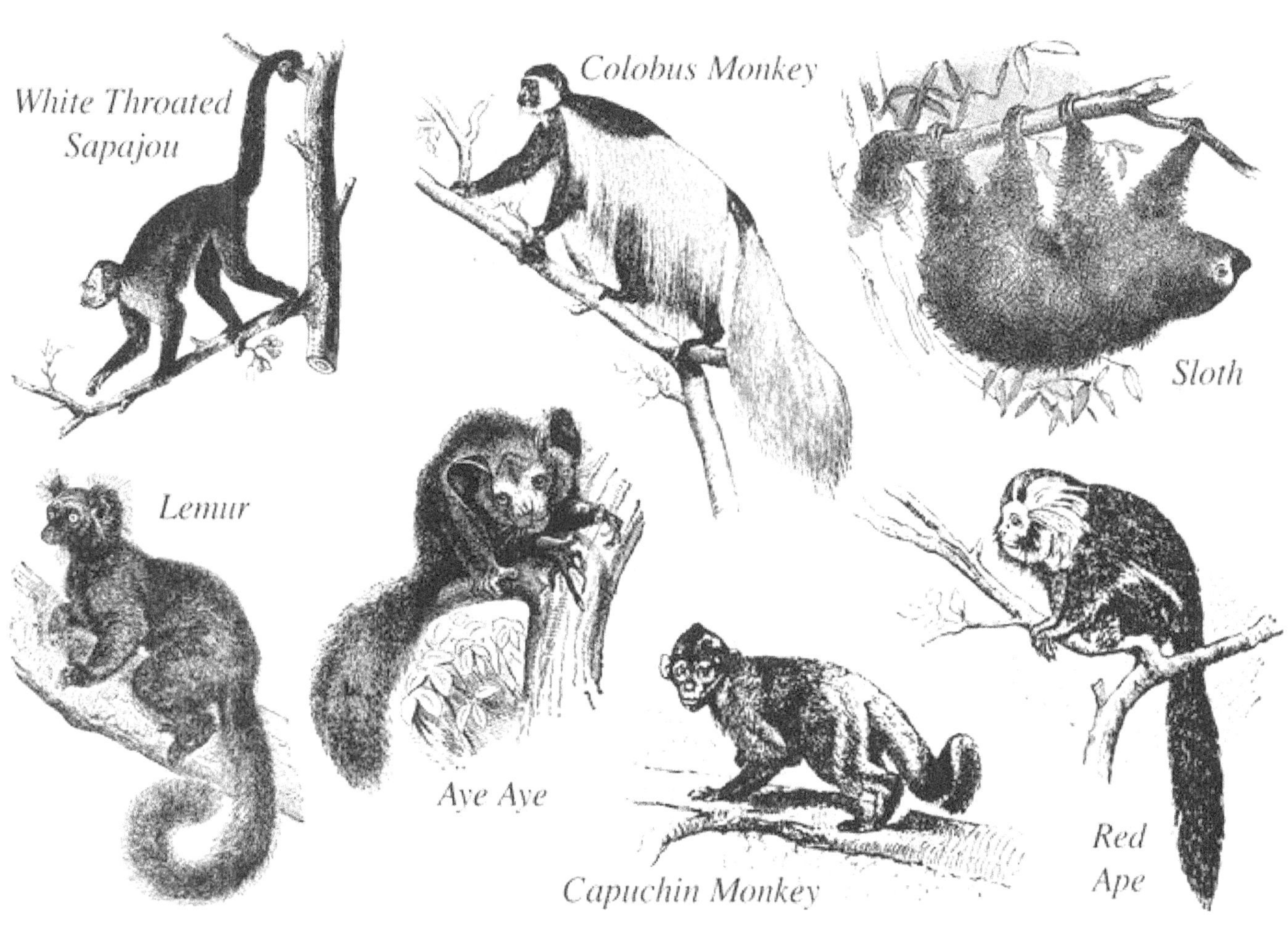

DRAW/SKETCH

ANIMALS

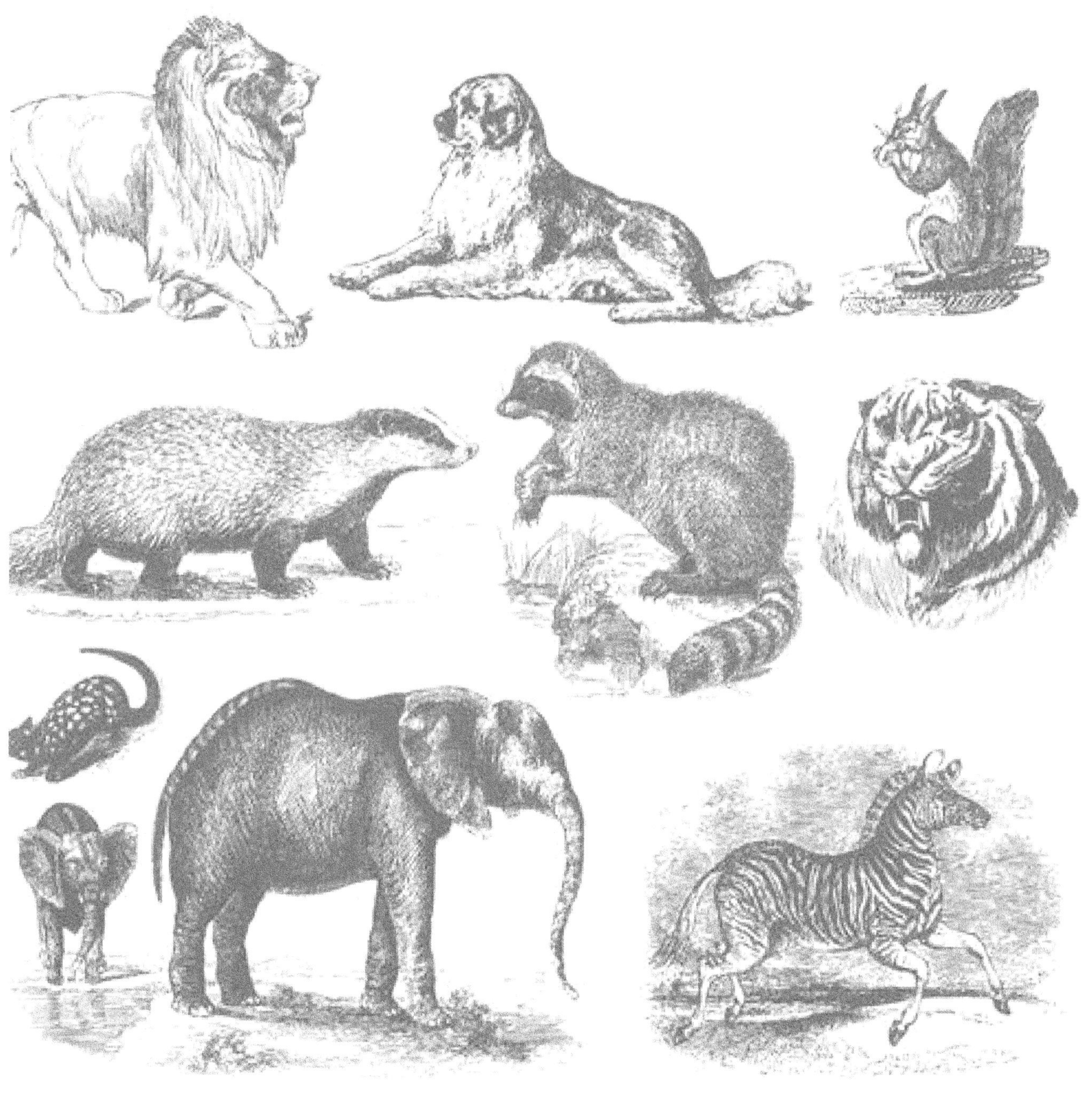

DRAW/SKETCH

HAND

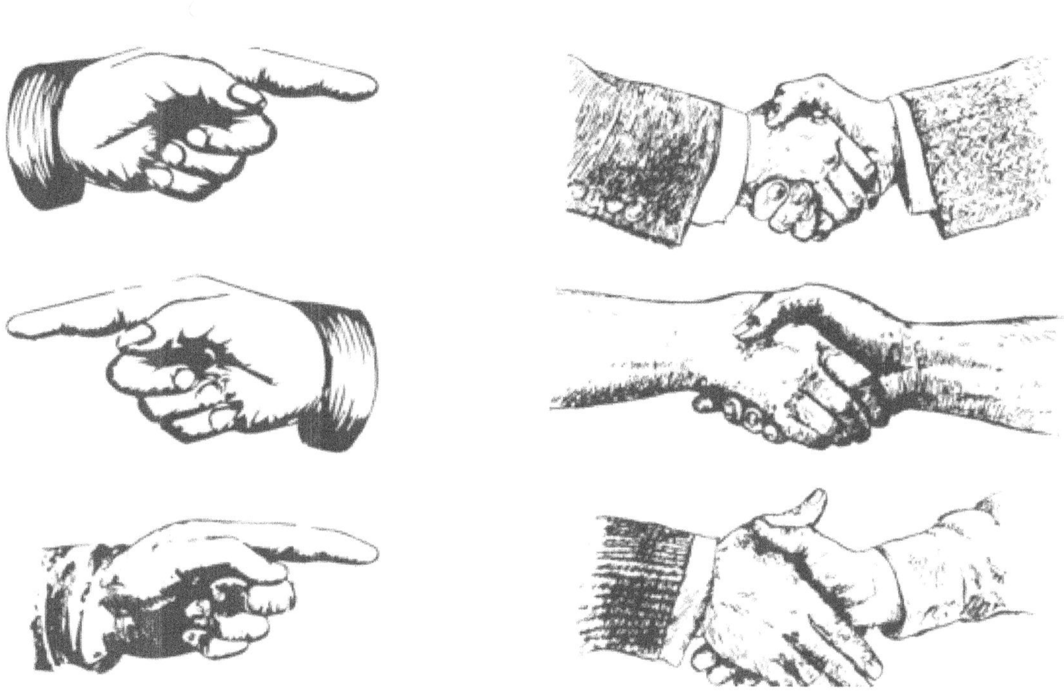

DRAW/SKETCH

HAND

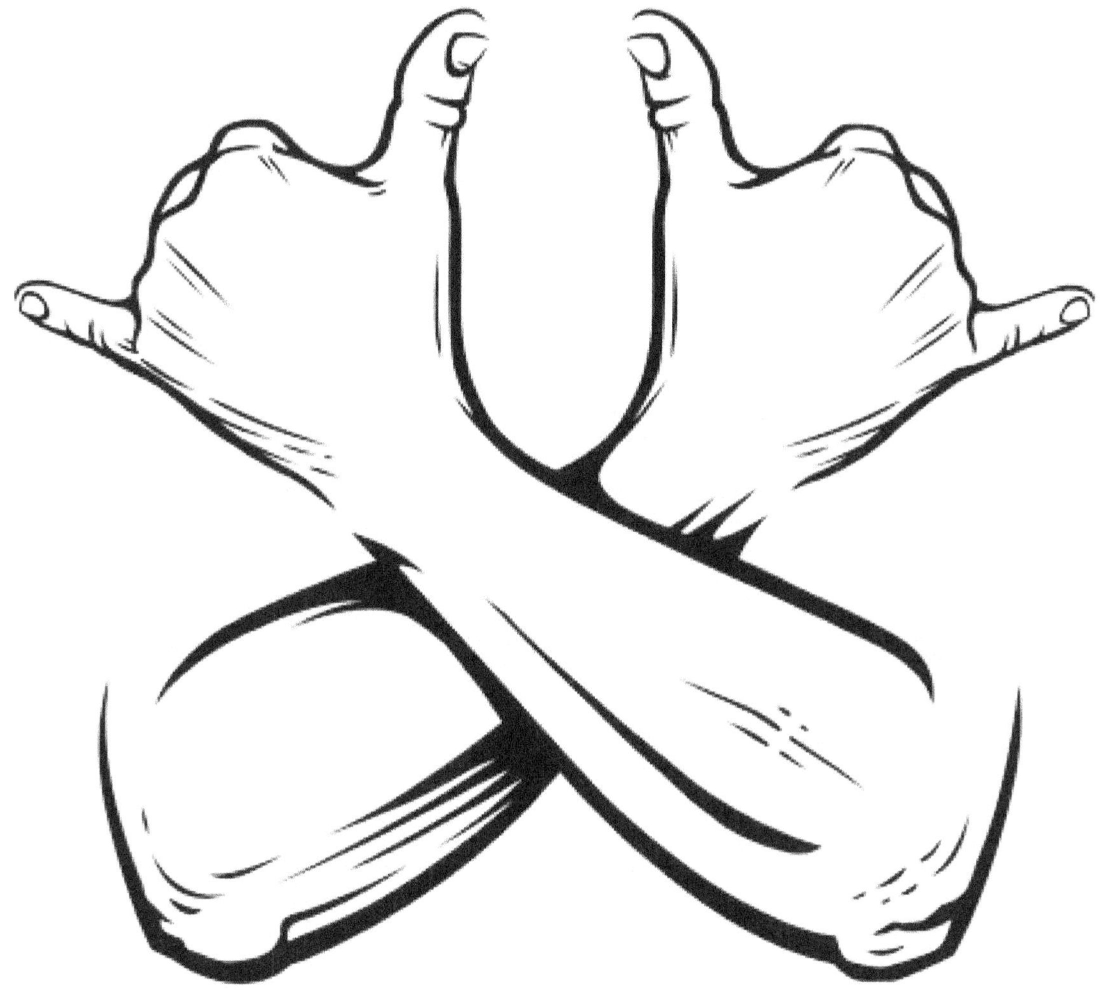

DRAW/SKETCH

FINGER

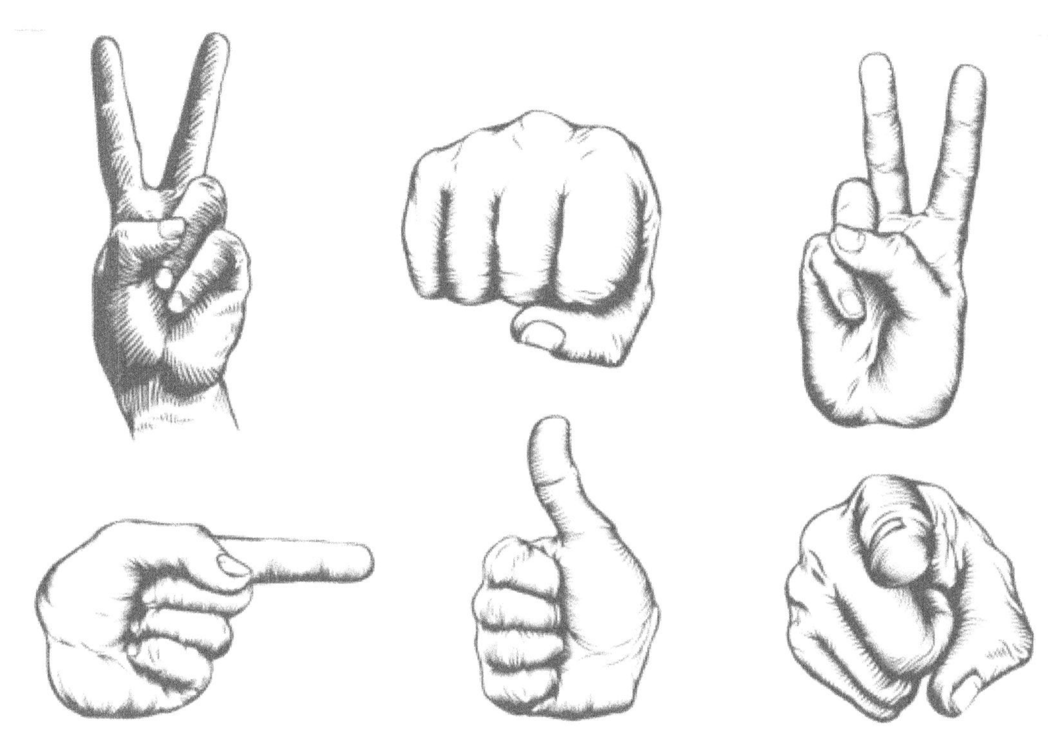

DRAW/SKETCH

HAND

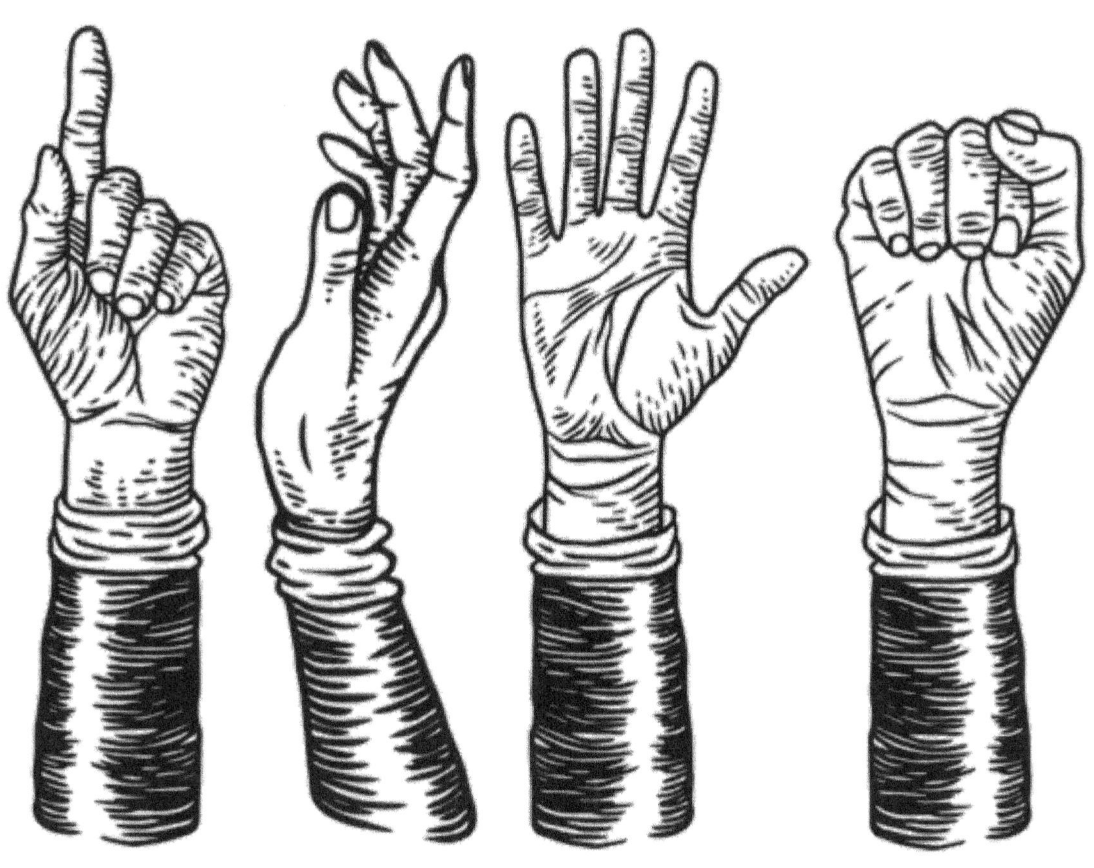

DRAW/SKETCH

BUILDING

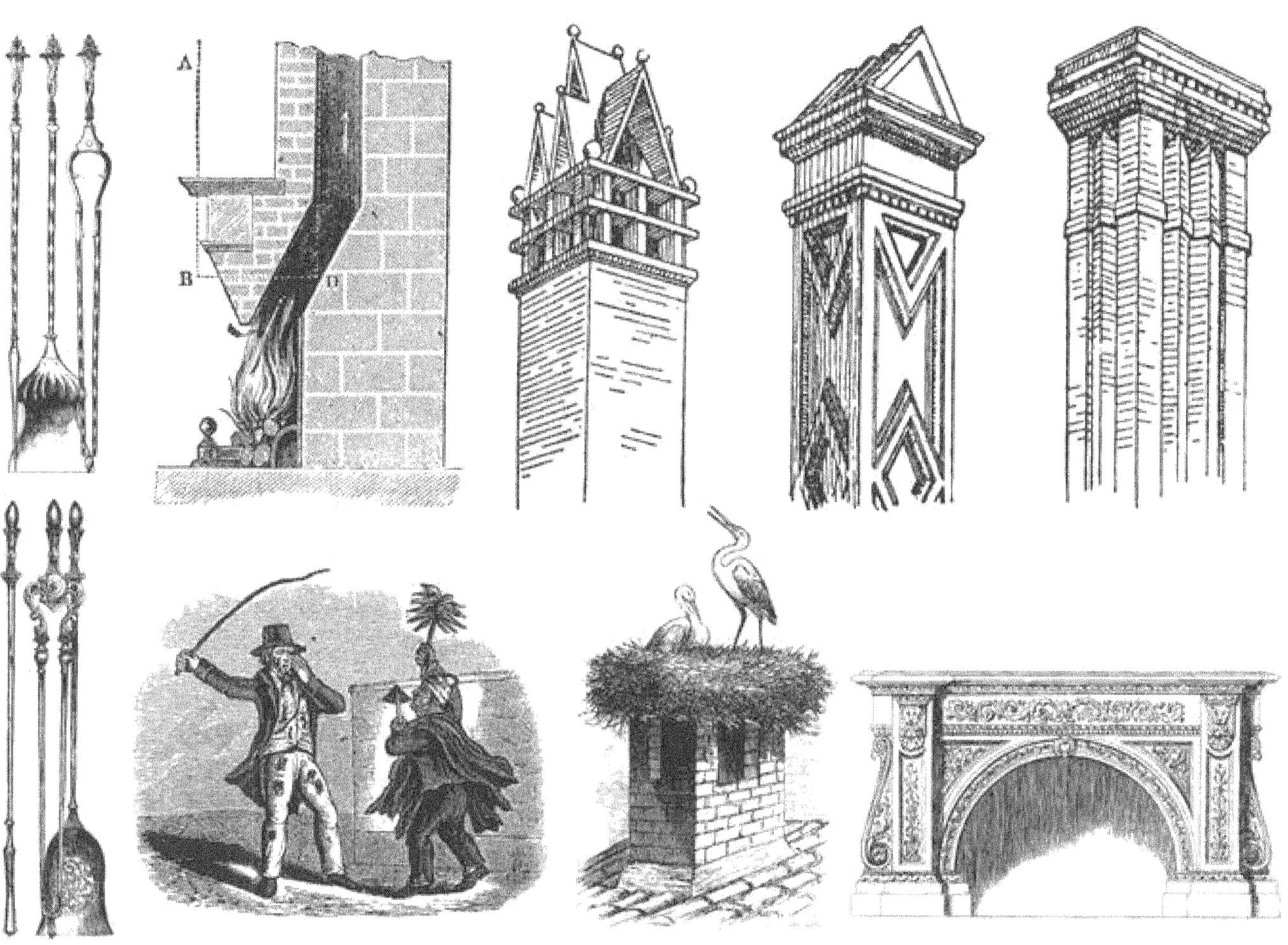

DRAW/SKETCH

ANIMALS

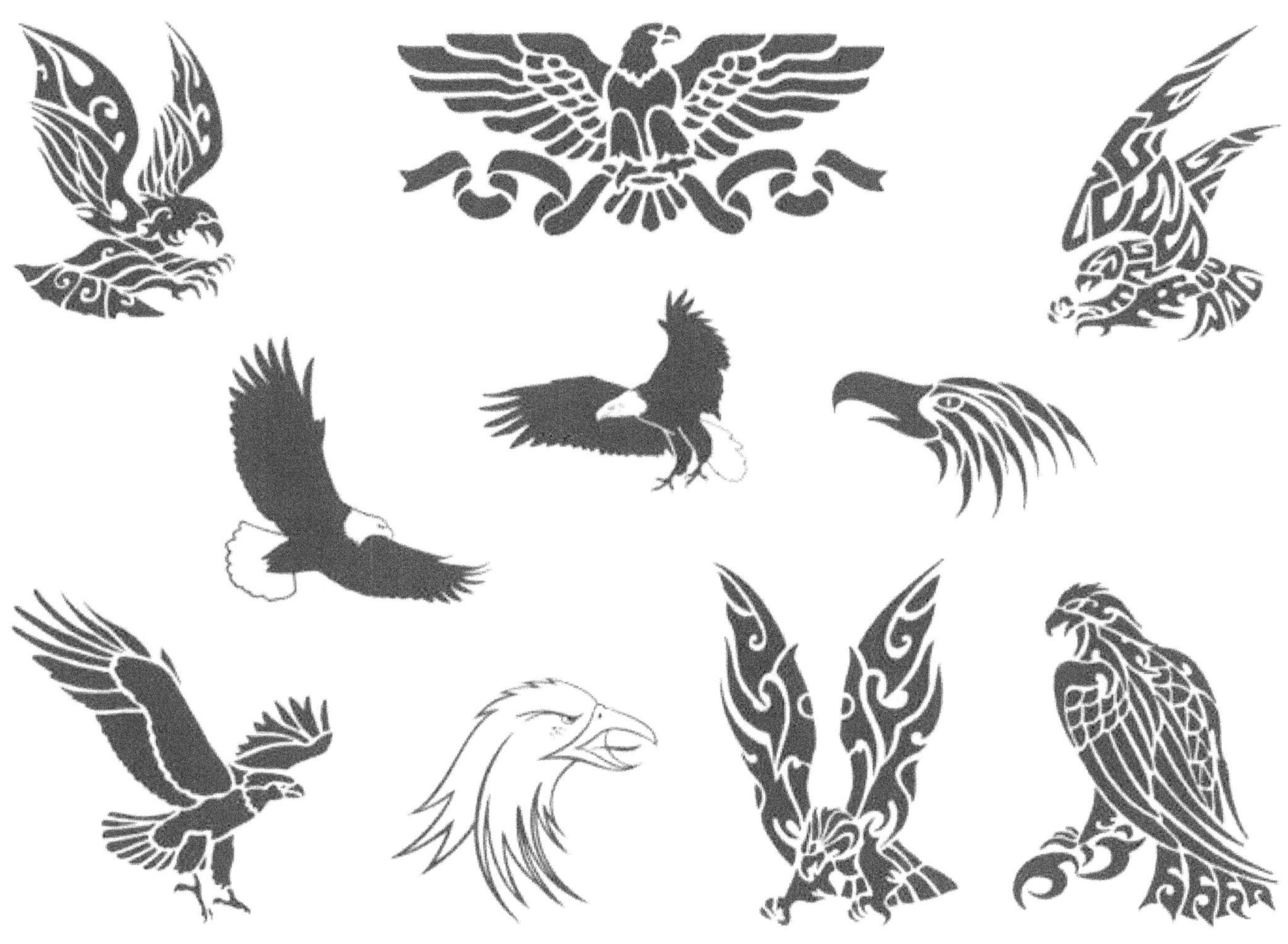

DRAW/SKETCH

AIR PLANE

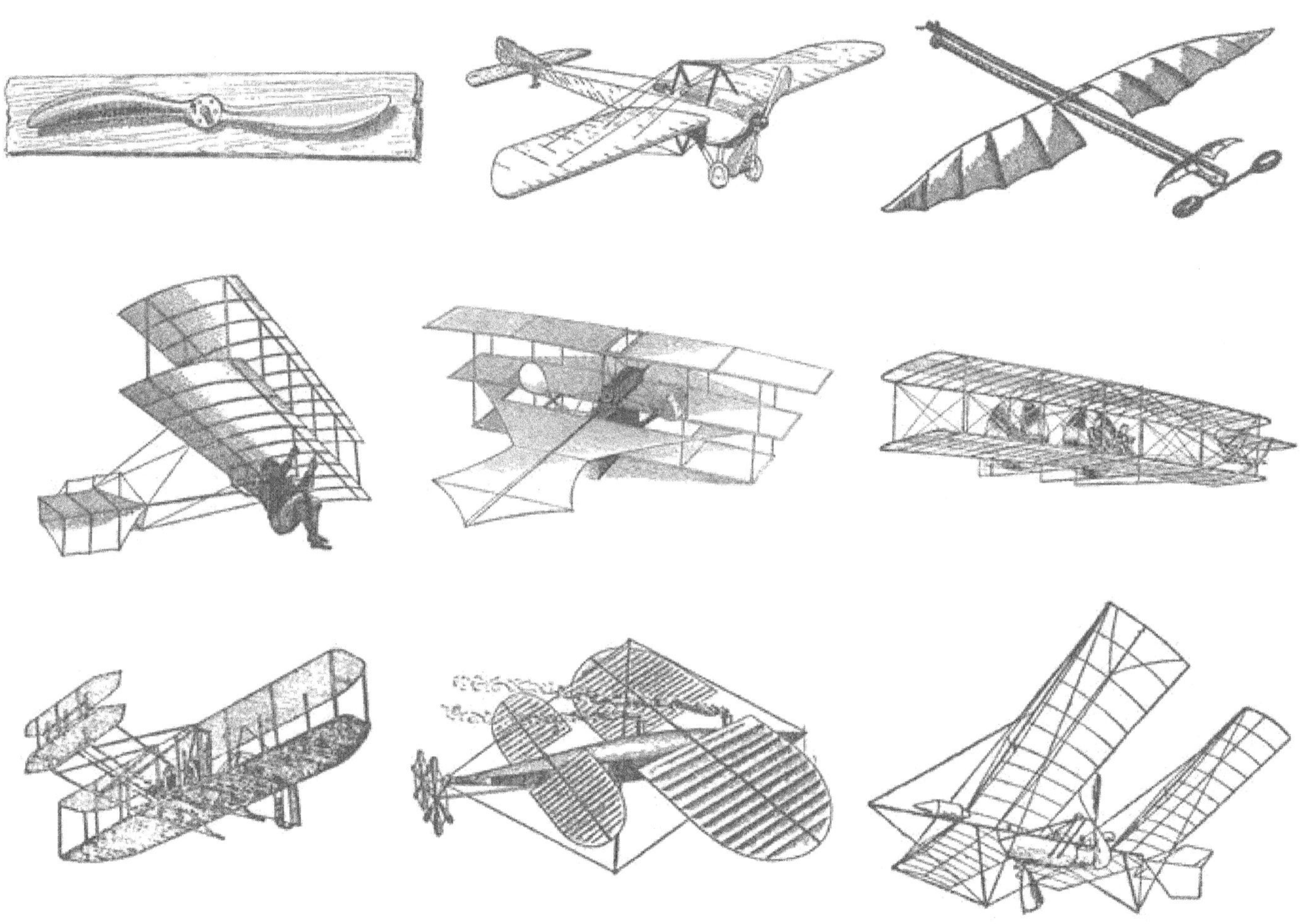

DRAW/SKETCH

WATCH

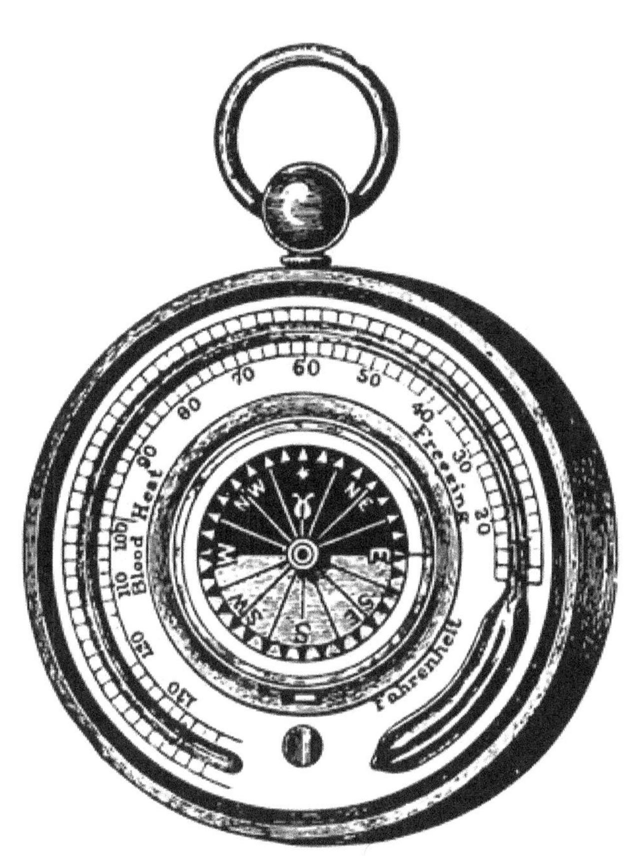

DRAW/SKETCH

ANIMALS

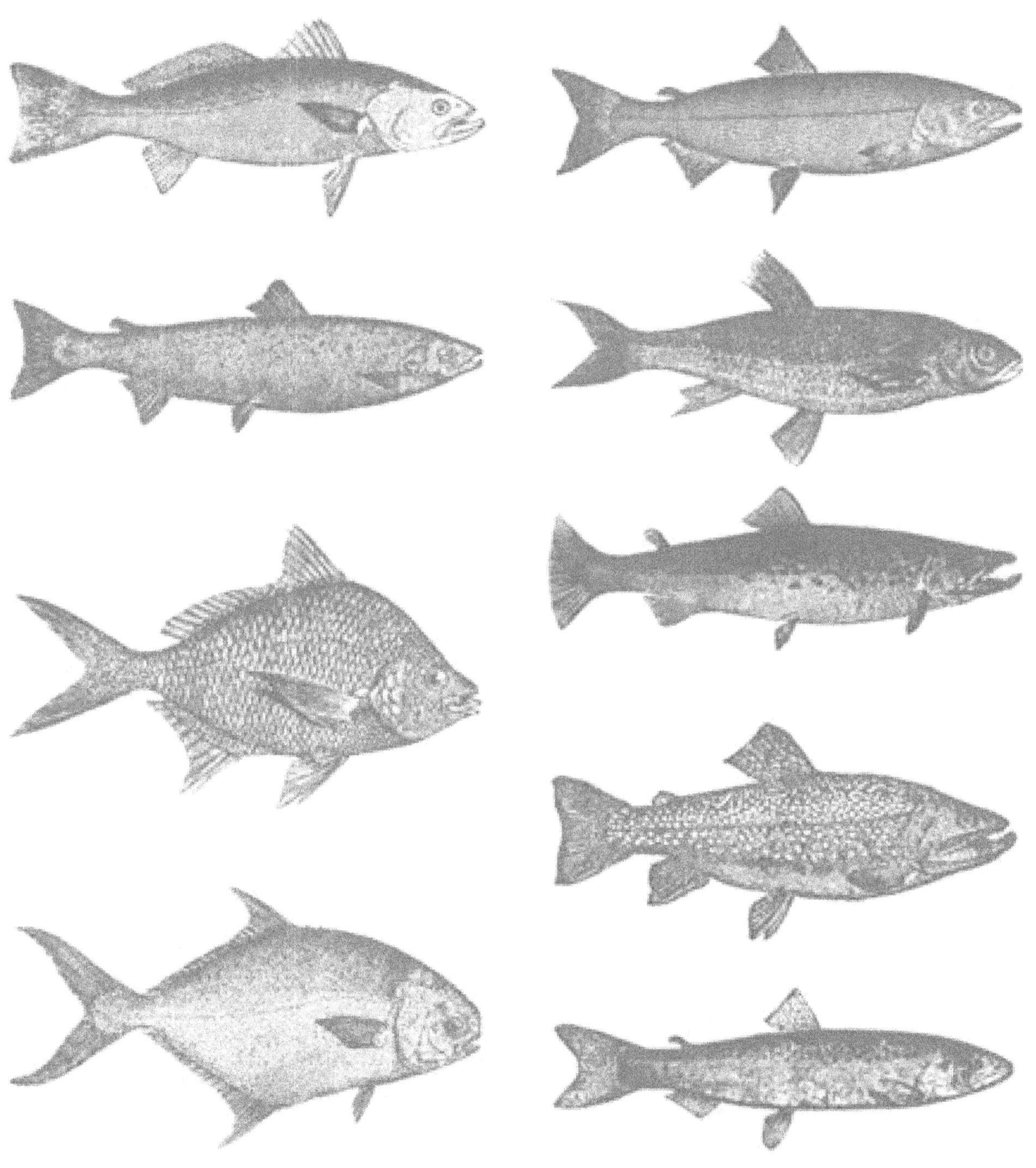

DRAW/SKETCH

BIKE

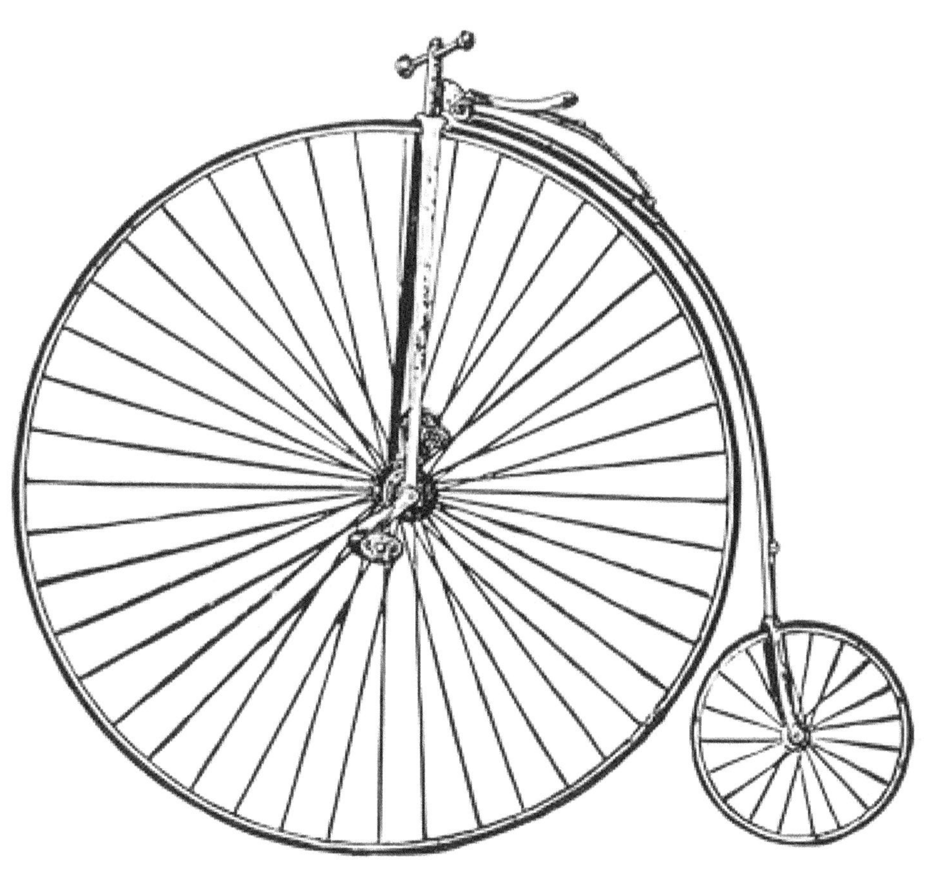

DRAW/SKETCH

FISHING

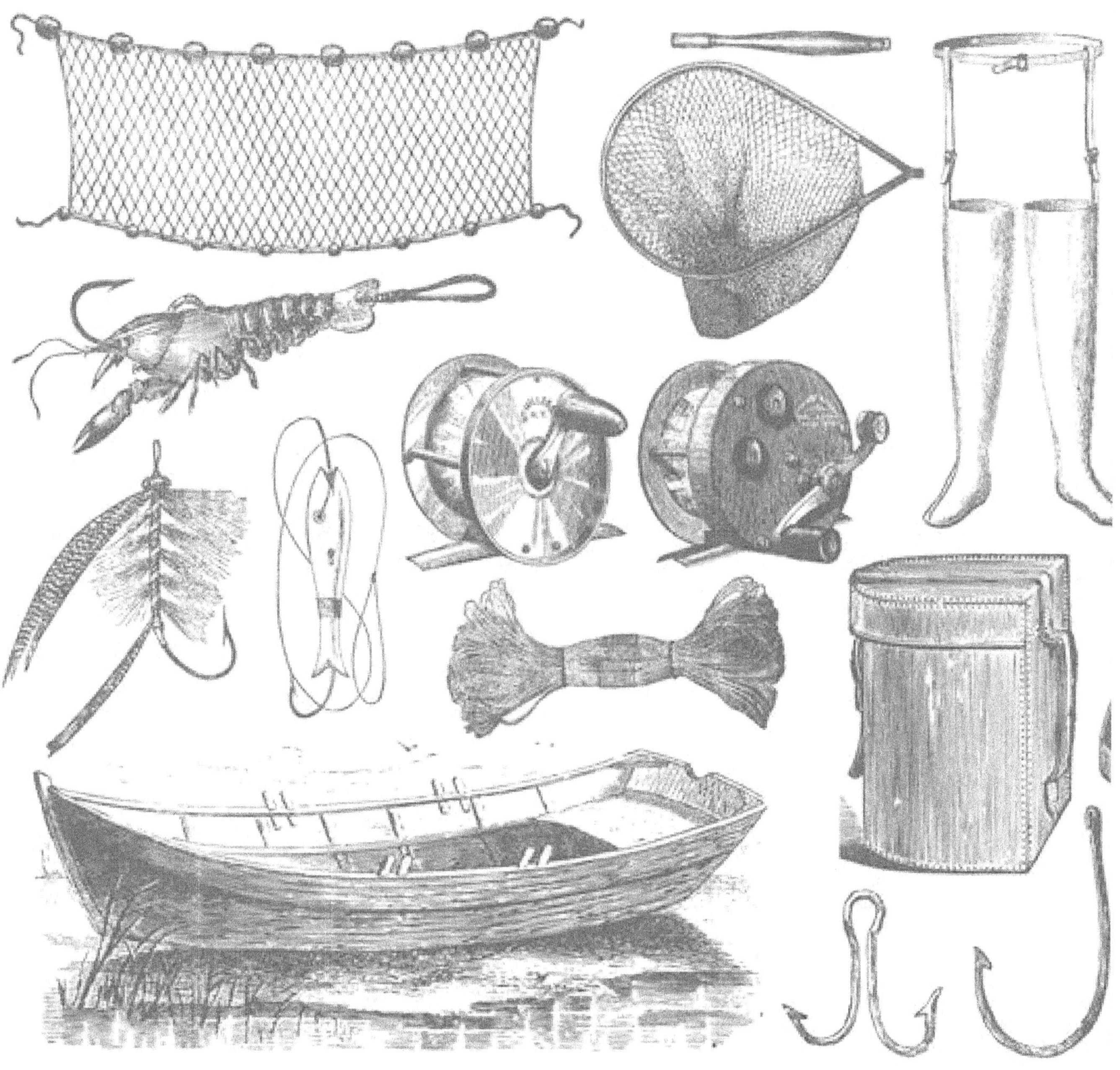

DRAW/SKETCH

SPORTS

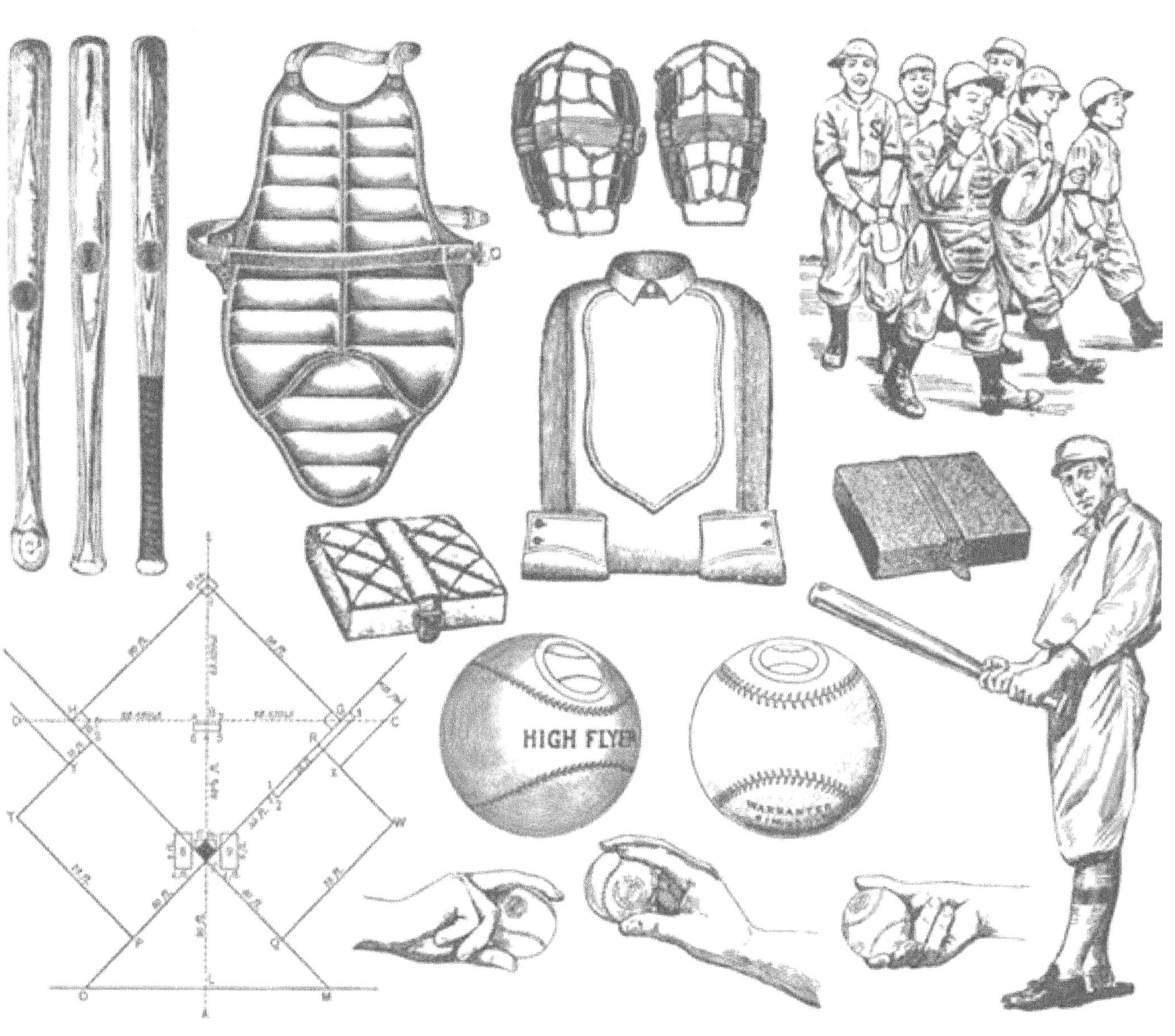

DRAW/SKETCH

SPORTS

2ND BASE.
90 FEET
90 FEET
3RD BASE.
4 FT.
6 FT.
PITCHER.
60 FT.
HOME PLATE.
BATSMAN.
CATCHER

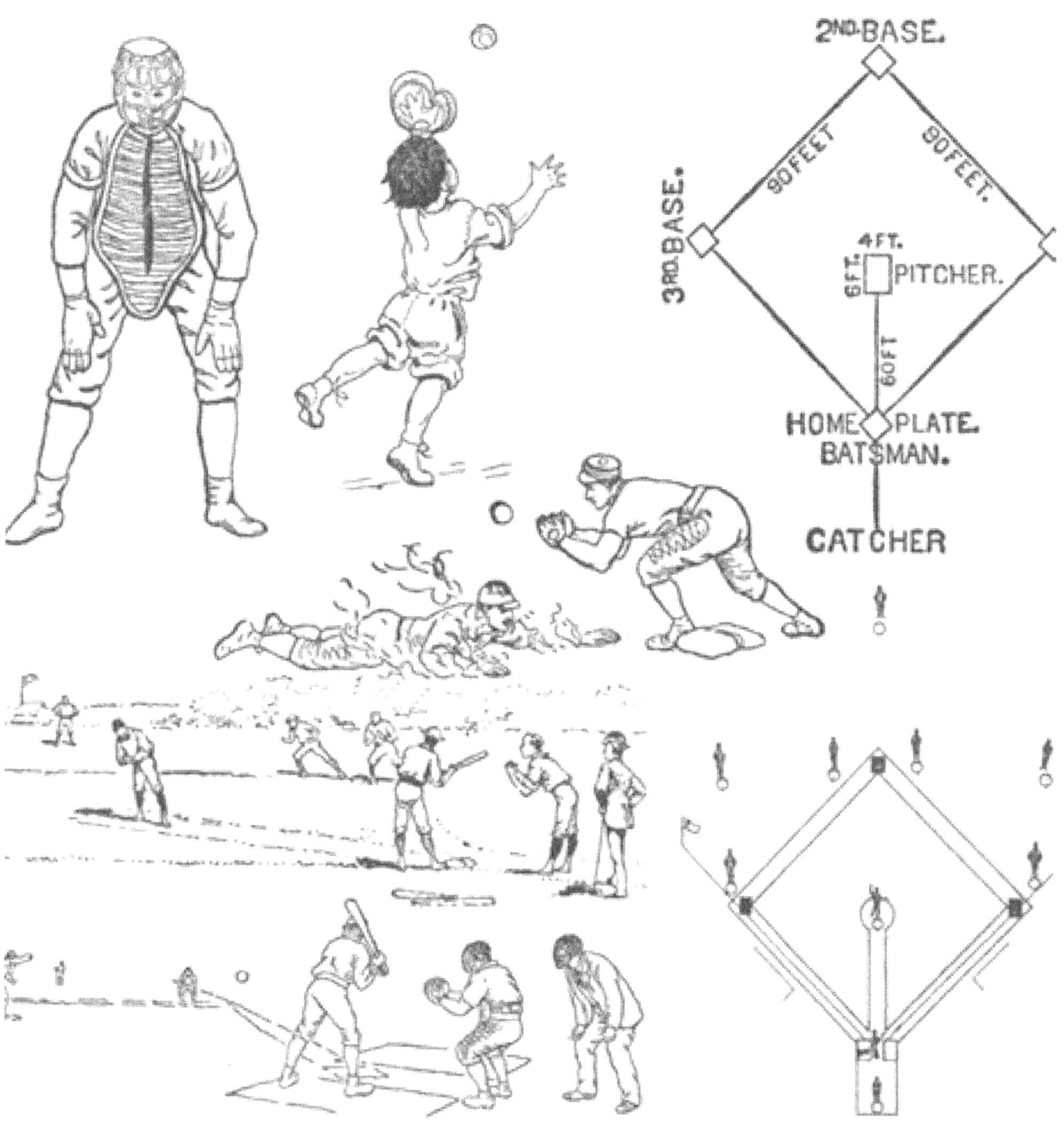

DRAW/SKETCH

SMOKING

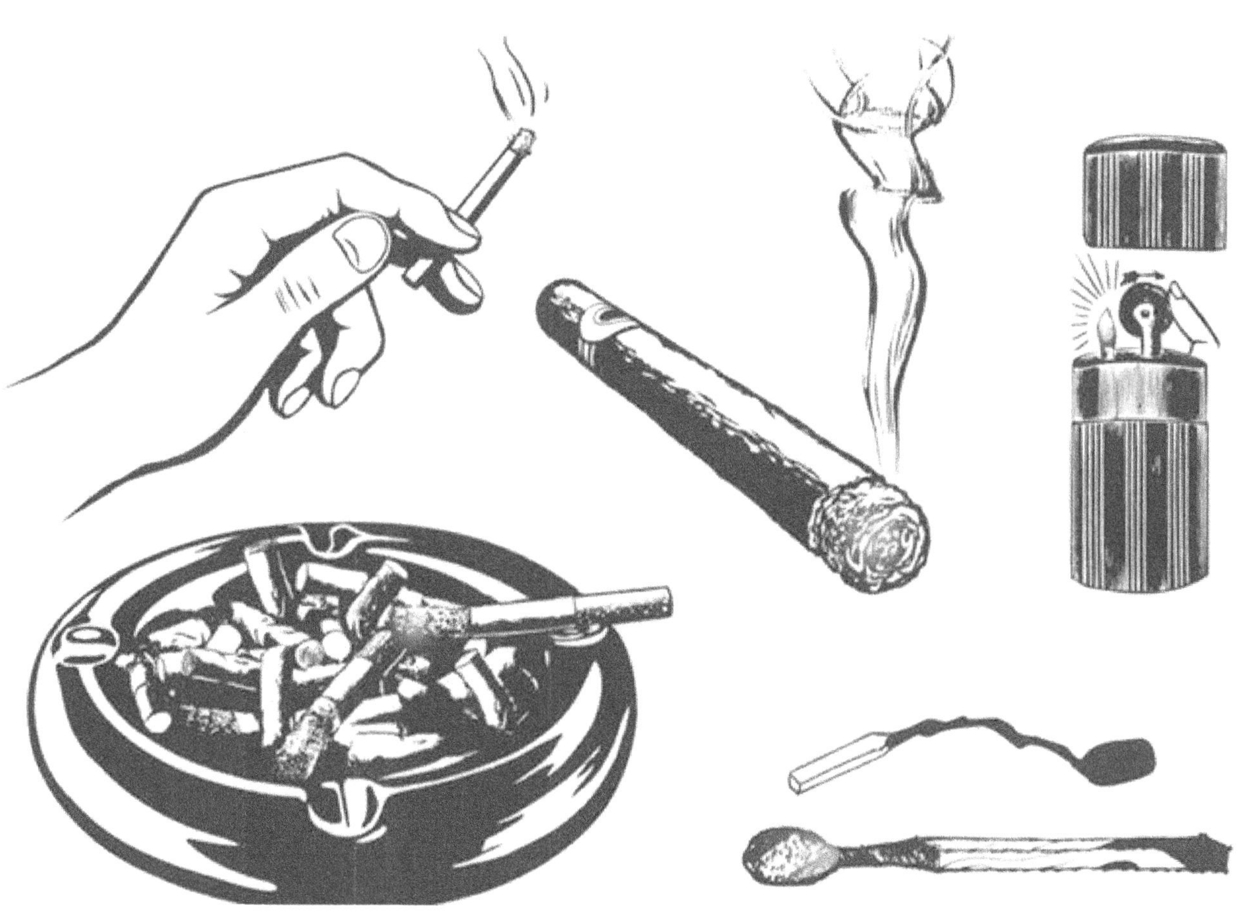

DRAW/SKETCH

ITEM

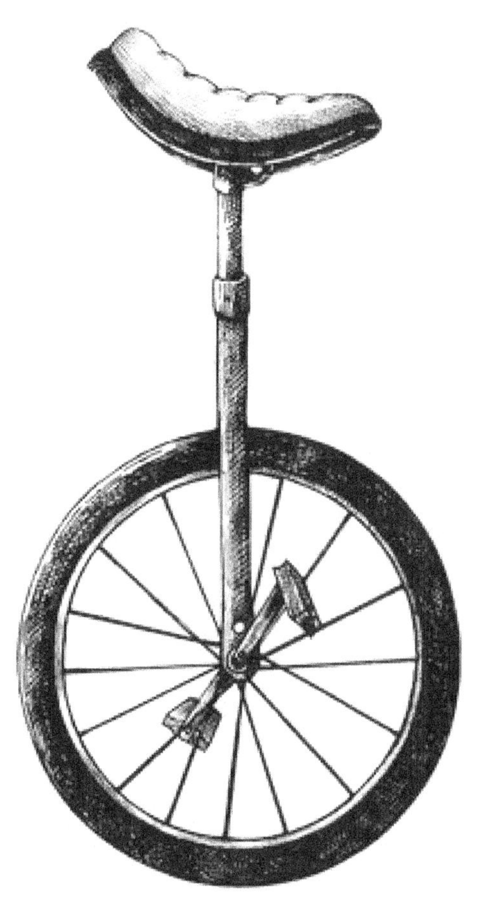

DRAW/SKETCH

ITEM

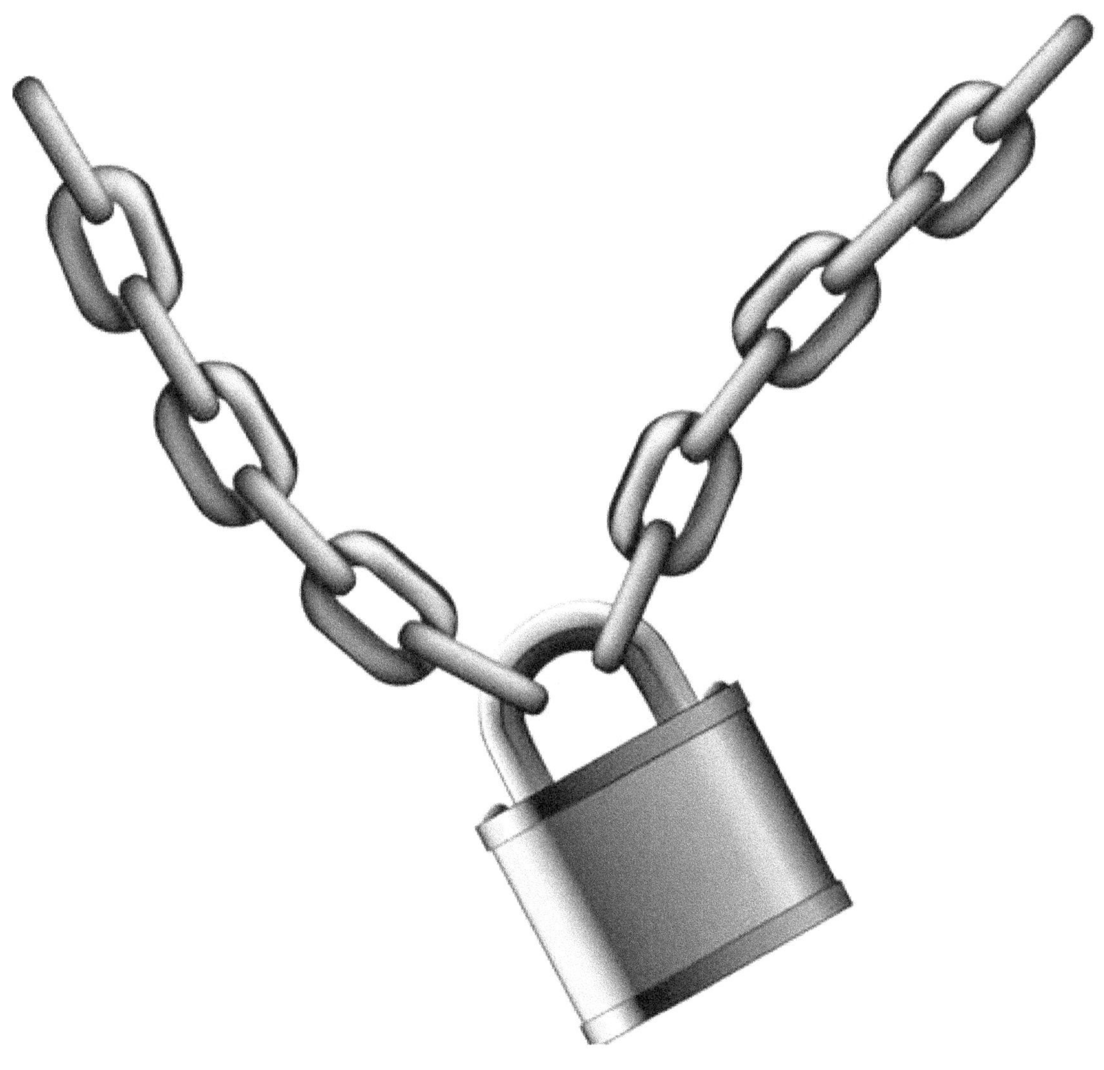

DRAW/SKETCH

DRAW/SKETCH

DRAW/SKETCH

DRAW/SKETCH

DRAW/SKETCH